What Becomes You

American Lives

Series editor: Tobias Wolff

What Becomes You

AARON RAZ LINK & HILDA RAZ

University of Nebraska Press

Lincoln and London

Publication of this volume was assisted by
The Virginia Faulkner Fund, established
in memory of Virginia Faulkner, editor in
chief of the University of Nebraska Press.

"Looking at Aaron" originally appeared in
Creative Nonfiction 26 (Fall 2005): 66–74.

"Scars" originally appeared in *GENDER-
qUEER: Voices from beyond the Sexual
Binary*, edited by Joan Nestle, Clare How-
ell, and Riki Wilchins (Los Angeles: Alyson
Press, 2002).

"Stock" originally appeared in *Fourth Genre*
6, no. 2 (Fall 2004): 104–14, published by
Michigan State University Press.

*Library of Congress
Cataloging-in-Publication Data*
Link, Aaron Raz , 1965–
    What becomes you / Aaron Raz Link
and Hilda Raz.
        p.   cm.   — (American lives)
        ISBN-13: 978-0-8032-1081-3 (cloth :
        alkaline paper)
        ISBN-10: 0-8032-1081-7 (cloth :
        alkaline paper)
    1. Link, Aaron Raz , 1965– 2. Female-
        to-male transsexuals—United States.
    3. Jewish transsexuals—United States.
    4. Transsexualism—United States.
    5. Gender identity—United States.
    6. Raz, Hilda. 7. Parents of transsexuals
        —United States. I. Raz, Hilda. II. Title.
        HQ77.8.L58A3 2007
        306.76'80973—dc22   2006035800

Set in Minion by Kim Essman.
Designed by A. Shahan.

I say, beware of all enterprises that require new clothes,
and not rather a new wearer of clothes. If there is not
a new man, how can the new clothes be made to fit?
| HENRY DAVID THOREAU, Walden

Contents

Preface

What Becomes You has taken us ten years to write.

One of the authors is a teacher, magazine editor, poet, and a participant in public conversations about women's lives and work. The other is a scientist, teacher, and historian as well as a performer, an investigator of our myths of difference—status, race, gender, sex. We have chosen to write this book not from a theoretical perspective but from a lifetime of family and professional collaboration. Part of our contribution is the reminder that life explodes all theories.

Our best teachers in living and writing this book have not been those who offer neatly bounded abstract explanations, regardless of intellectual discipline or radical/conservative flavor. The real experts were messily making a fuss—performing on stages, pages, and the streets, wearing clown noses, mastering the arts of illness, exploring the body's limits, dancing in wheelchairs, representing themselves in multiple colors, cultures, and tongues. This book represents a fragment of that work, a forty-year collaboration between the authors in the fine art of making a fuss—or, paraphrasing Emile Zola—living out loud.

What Becomes You is a work of nonfiction. *Nonfiction* is a funny word. It tells us in bold and definite terms what something isn't while leaving us completely in the dark about what it is. But, as they used to say on Mutual of Omaha's *Wild Kingdom,* all the events here, whether actual or created, depict authenticated facts.

Aaron Raz Link did indeed have a sex change, and Hilda Raz did indeed give birth to him, with original equipment, and we did indeed write this book. But this book is a work of creative nonfiction. While the events described actually happened (and if you buy this book you will indeed find a graphic and accurate description of his penis), the interpretations of events by the characters with our names are not always those of the authors. And sometimes we don't agree with them, or each other. The Big Truth we learned (okay, there are five more Big Truths hidden in the text, and we're not going to tell you where they are) is that reality is in the mind of the beholder.

Scientifically speaking, years have passed since most of the events described in this book happened, and most of our cells have been replaced by new ones. The authors have become whole new people. In fact, the people appearing in this book aren't even made of cells. They're made of paper and what we hope is nontoxic ink. Which brings us to another term for what this book is: *memoir*. In other words, it's a story—a story the authors believe is true because it happened to them. In *What Becomes You*, the story is about a man, a woman, and a sex change. The soundtrack is mostly without violins. We've included other stories—ones about men, women, family, and the roles we expected to play as men and women, straights and queers, majorities and minorities, subjects and authorities, and heroes and villains and clowns.

This book also is not autobiography. The full story of Aaron's life includes an episode where he is suspending prechilled butterflies from his boss's eyebrows for a segment of *Good Morning America*, hiking in the Grand Canyon with his family, and performing theatre in three countries on two continents and in drag on the high school lawn of the Hoopa Indian Reservation. These were good times. If this book were autobiography, they'd be included. Aaron's experience also includes an amazing family that has welcomed him through a sex change as well as several other equally interesting adventures, and allows him to boast that his relatives include several brilliant teachers, musicians, and writers, a painter, a photojournalist, a chef, a composer, a graphic artist, and a guy who does some juggling. For instance, when Aaron and his brother John were kids, their dad made them their very own submarine along with Star Trek communicators and pirate swords. This generosity was not only great, it was part of that rarest and most precious of experiences, a childhood safe and rich with both dreams and the resources necessary to believe they will come true. Trust us, if this were autobiography, you'd see these stories on every page.

But this book isn't Aaron's life or a picture of a world the authors know and love. It is a book about pieces that didn't fit the picture. As a result, the most confusing and difficult pieces play the largest roles. We think this story of pieces that don't fit is a little bit of the story of all our lives, but that's up to you to decide.

In the first years Aaron spent creating his life as a man in the world, he did not want anyone else to write or speak of him as a woman. This restriction made Hilda's job a little more difficult.

Aaron is a man, and his gender experience of springing full-blown into the world at thirty is an experience of the body, a man's body, and the roles men play. He stepped through that door and saw wonderful things. Somewhere along the line he realized other men also see and feel these things, but from the moment of their birth they are conditioned to silence. He was not. He got very interested in talking.

But left behind was a strange sense of something else important, something left out of that story. Aaron doesn't remember ever being a woman. Because he could not say anything about his experience of being a woman, he didn't want anyone else to talk about the same thing. About *their* experience of his being a woman. But Hilda remembers. It's a tricky business.

One of our friends has suffered profound brain damage, which changed his body, personality, and memory. We asked him once if he ever felt, as Aaron did, a sense of responsibility for this other person he can't remember—the person his loved ones remember he was.

"No," he said. "Not at all."

"Why not?" we asked.

He smiled. "Because I can't. That person doesn't belong to me."

In the end both Hilda and Aaron had to give up the person they thought belonged to them. What they gained is the people they are now and each other. And this book.

As far as the authors go, we continue to enjoy duking it out with our former selves on a regular basis, a kind of do-it-yourself Fight Club. Hilda has continued to write and publish, teach poetry to graduate and undergraduate university students, and edit a magazine. She still lives in the same house where Aaron grew up as Sarah.

Aaron has transitioned once again, this time from Professional Biology Educator and Historian and Philosopher of Science to guy who does some clowning and acting. This is not as big a leap as you might think, given that one of the grafts performed during the sex change was the addition of a sense of humor. Though this procedure can be extremely painful, especially when performed on a person's most sensitive areas, we highly recommend it to all our readers.

Acknowledgments

HILDA

Rabbi Nachman of Bratslav is reputed to have said, "Whoever can write a book and does not, it is as if he has lost a child." My part in this book is for John Link and Aaron Raz Link, my children.

Aaron's courage, brilliance, and patience set us a high standard in the living and the writing. John was our active advocate and exemplary and candid reader through difficult times.

My husband, Dale Nordyke, is an example of the artist who works steadily over a lifetime to express vision, a great ambition. John Link and Maria Schoenhammer and their children, Anna and Eva Maria Schoenhammer Link, are my physical connection to a future world. The performer and teacher Jeff Raz, psychologist Sherry Sherman, and their children, Micah and Joshua Sherman Raz, as well as Jennifer Lenway and Amelie and Abigail Raz are the living evidence of the lives of Barton James Raz and Jonathan Raz, my brother and nephew, whose lives ended too soon. Dolly Horwich Raz and Franklyn Emanuel Raz have nourished us. Their lives, gifts.

Many people have helped us. Thanks to Robin Becker, Charlotte Sheedy, Carole Houck Smith, Carole Simmons Oles, Mary Pipher, Ladette Randolph, Kate Flaherty, Kelly Grey Carlisle, Erin Flanigan, Barbara Di Bernard and Judith Gibson, Laura and Burke Casari, Jennifer and Vera Cohen, Carmen Grant, Floyd Skloot and Beverly Hallberg, and the Department of English at the University of Nebraska, my colleagues. Part of this book was written with the help of a faculty development leave from the University of Nebraska.

Thanks to the editors of *Fourth Genre*, who nominated one of these essays for Best American Essays 2006, where it was listed in "One Hundred Distinguished Essays."

The poem quoted in "Three-Minute Autobiography" is from "Sailing to Byzantium" by William Butler Yeats.

AARON

My family has risen to every unimaginable challenge. Dale Nordyke and Peggy Williamson Link saw us coming and joined us anyway, with their whole hearts. John Link and Jeff Raz hung on tight and still found the strength to lend a hand. They, along with Paul and Eric Gregory and Laura Casari (who could have claimed anytime that she wasn't related), have my thanks and love always.

Thanks to Robert Seutter, who taught me to dance when I could not walk, and to Elizabeth Pillaert and the staff of the University of Wisconsin Zoological Museum, who taught me to investigate the body as a scientist when I still could not find my own.

Over the past ten years, I have had amazing teachers. I am grateful for each lesson, to the people at Gorilla Theatre, the Men's Group, VOICES, the Identity Project, Outside In, the Outremer Project, 2Gyrlz Performative Arts, Liebe Wetzel's Lunatique Fantastique, and the Dell'Arte International School of Physical Theatre. Also to Jeff Raz, Betsy Richard, Daniel Nidzgorski, Mara Neimanis, Jesse Sutherland, Lauren Worsh, AXIS Dance, Sojourn Theatre, Augusto Boal and so many others doing Theatre of the Oppressed, and the theatre and movement communities of Portland, Oregon, and San Francisco, California.

Thanks to Bob Mathis-Friedman, John (alias Paul) Snead, Rebecca Newman, and E. Ann Hinds for being the daily difference between a lonely road and a grand adventure.

This book is for my mother, Hilda, because we both laughed when she told me I could write in my first book: I owe it all to my mother; and for my father, Frederick Martin Link, always before me; my partner, Daire Martin Elliott, always with me; Anna and Eva, Micah and Joshua; and the other kids who will be figuring this stuff out when we're gone.

What Becomes You

Aaron Raz Link

The Sea

When I was five years old I decided to become a scientist. My mother had bought me a book, the first of a mail-order library on biology topics; one would arrive every couple of months, and I'd wait for them like the Fourth of July. The first one was called *The Sea*. I thumbed raptly through it; the only thing wrong with this book was that a couple of pages in the middle seemed to be stuck together. Finally, more curious to know what was on these pages than in the whole rest of the book put together, I tried to pry them apart. What I had thought were two pages unfolded into one, falling open like Pandora's box, spilling its contents across the floor. The page was a glossy color portrait, cross-sectioned like a medical chart: the secret insides of the ocean. I grew up in Nebraska. I had never seen the ocean. I recognized only the fish, which seemed insignificant among the brightly colored objects of this world. Were they buildings? Decorations? Geologic features, internal organs of some huge oceanic body? At the bottom of the picture was a strip of yellow paper. On it, in a curious stagger suggestive of meaning, were printed the most incredible words: "Pink-Hearted Hydroids." "Dead Men's Fingers." In a sudden rush of understanding, I realized that the objects were *living creatures*, and these were their *names*. The pattern of the printing matched the place of each creature in the picture above. I spent hours working the words over, pointing to each portrait, naming all the animals. Everything made sense. It was like Helen Keller with her fingers in the water, feeling words form for the first time.

Everything makes sense now.

Taxonomy is the science of naming, of relationships. It makes order out of chaos, arranging the bewildering world of experience into understandable categories: *Hallucigenia sparsa, Felis catus, Homo sapiens, one, no, four, no, five, no, wait, only one subspecies . . .*

These names create and document an agreement about the nature of the world we live in. Underneath that knowledge is another, deeper understanding—that when we look at something, we make up what we see. Taxonomists are science's dictionary writers, the invisible magicians of the mind. We invent the categories. Then everyone believes in them. We do, too.

People have to believe in something.

I believed, more than anything, that I wanted to be a taxonomist. Taxonomists create two kinds of ordering systems, *natural* and *artificial*. Natural taxonomies arise out of differences within the bodies and lives of the creatures named; the creatures sort themselves out, in a way, and the investigator merely records the result. Artificial taxonomies are designed to create an arbitrary but useful order for outside investigators. You might say a natural taxonomy reflects the true order of the universe, and an artificial taxonomy is just somethin' somebody made up. In another light, an artificial taxonomy is one somebody knows they made up, and a natural taxonomy is one they don't know they made up.

To be a good taxonomist, all you have to do is figure out which kinds of order are natural and which are artificial.

The work of a taxonomist begins with paradox. Sometimes you discover conflicting records that are supposed to refer to the same creature, but these descriptions cannot be reconciled; they seem to refer to different types entirely. If you're a taxonomist, reconciliation is what, as they used to say, separates the men from the boys.

ABOUT THE AUTHOR

Aaron Raz Link creates theatrical shows and exhibits. His most recent exhibit, Other Visions, documented the art and culture of the extremely little-known Outremer people. Aaron has performed and toured internationally, taught and created with the object theatre company Lunatique Fantastique, the Clown Conservatory of the San Francisco School of Circus Arts, Hand2Mouth Theatre, Tabuki Theatre, 2Gyrlz Performative Arts, Sojourn Theatre, and enough festivals, conferences, schools, and LGBT community venues that the list won't fit in this space. He's been a maskmaker and street performer in Portland, Oregon, and is happy to say that drag queens sent him to clown school, making him a graduate of the Dell'Arte International School of Physical Theatre.

From the author's professional résumé, 2006

ABOUT THE AUTHOR

Sarah Link is a professional naturalist and historian of science (BA, Biological Sciences, Washington University, St. Louis MO, 1986; MA, History and Philosophy of Science, University of Wisconsin–Madison, Madison WI, 1989). Link attended college on a merit-based full scholarship in the humanities. In graduate school Link specialized in the history of representation, studying scientific justifications of social prejudices and writing a thesis on the work of Charles Le-Brun, a French court painter whose combined human-animal figures document the basis of our scientific and popular stereotypes of ethnicity, culture, age, and class. Link spent the next seven years as a professional naturalist and teacher, working in a number of major American museums and zoos.

From the author's professional résumé, 1990

ABOUT THE AUTHOR

She is EXQUISITE—one of the most beautiful faces I've ever seen. Enormous golden brown eyes, shaped like mine but lighter and luminous brown-gold. Their expression is alternately wise or coy or amused. She flirts and pouts without crying, for effect. Her hair is fine and flyaway with some curl and waving at the ends and beautiful in color: a light brown streaked with blond. Navy blue and black look best on her—unorthodox for a small girl but very becoming nonetheless. Her father *adores* her. She often tilts her chin down and looks up, always with the same effect: the observing adult is struck dumb by her—is it beauty? A Florida friend described it as an attention/intensity of expression. All is focused on her eyes. I've seen strange and nonsympathetic doctors, good friends, tradespeople react to her in the same way. Truly a fine asset for a woman!

From the journals of Hilda Raz, 18 January 1967

ABOUT THE AUTHOR

FEMALE TRANSSEXUALISM. **Clinical Features** Female transsexuals, though anatomically normal, are the most masculine of females. . . . these females are exclusively homosexual if measured by the anatomy of their sex objects, but are heterosexual if measured by identity. As with the males, they do not deny their anatomic sex, but they are, nonetheless, unendingly preoccupied with the sense of really being men. . . . Usually, as a child, this girl refuses to be a girl. . . . [from adolescence] she successfully appears as a male . . . without anyone suspecting her true sex. . . . At birth, this infant is seen by her parents as not being pretty or cuddly . . . her mother is unavailable for mothering. . . . This process is furthered from the start by the infant's unlovely appearance; had she been considered feminine, she would not have served as well for molding into masculinity. . . . From the start, female transsexualism is the product of trauma, frustration, conflict, and defensive resolution of the resulting pain. This [diagnosis] puts female transsexuals on a continuum with other very masculine women."

From Harold I. Kaplan, MD, and Benjamin J. Sadock, MD, eds., *Comprehensive Textbook of Psychiatry IV,* 4th ed. (1985)

Bias often appears in systems of classification. Irresponsible (or inexperienced) taxonomists do their classifying based on a small number of examples; their prejudices assume that all individuals will match the sample they're familiar with. *Exempli gratia:*
"Are you a boy or a girl?"
They're second graders; the ones who ask the question always are.
"What do you think I am?"
"Well," the small faces screw tight, thinking hard. "You don't have lipstick. You've got short hair. You're wearing pants, and, and, you don't have any makeup, and—" struggling to articulate the defining characteristics of the type here, "you go in the mud and stuff." They look up at me expectantly, confused. There's something else about me, though, something strange. They can't figure out what it is. Neither can I; my question puts off the moment when I have to give them an answer.

Once I asked a girl about six what she thought I was. She looked up shyly from her little velvet dress with its matching tights and patent-leather shoes. I was wearing my Victorian Explorer suit: spotless canvas drill pants and crisp blond photographer's vest. I was holding live tarantulas. I was a hundred feet tall. She leaned toward me and whispered, "I think you're a girl." Her eyes were bright with hope.

I bent down and lied for her, as if this were an act of mercy.

Good taxonomy depends on hard fieldwork. Responsible taxonomists gather as many specific examples as possible. One of my childhood heroes, the taxonomist Alfred Kinsey, gathered five million gall wasp specimens for one study and eighteen thousand surveys of human sexual practices for another. Good taxonomists know that *normal*, *average*, and *right* are words for three different concepts, the last of which is a moral judgment; it isn't taxonomy's job. They seek out individuals at every extreme of the type's range, to understand their variations.

Taxonomic classification is based on three factors: morphology, behavior, and genetics.

In spite of problematic areas—the frequent lack of correlation between variations in a single gene and complex features of morphology or behavior, historical connections between the theories of American and Nazi genetics—genetics remains the primary modern tool of division.

In basic science books I learned that human genes are arranged into twenty-three pairs of bundles called chromosomes. Twenty-two pairs are identical in men and women. The twenty-third pair comes in two forms: two similar chromosomes (XX) or two different ones (XY). People with two similar sex chromosomes are women. People with two different sex chromosomes are men. I quickly graduated to advanced textbooks, where I learned other interesting facts; in birds, for instance, the reverse is true. Also, some textbooks will give different information. For instance, the first researcher to publish a count of human chromosomes simply miscounted; the wrong number, often accompanied by a correct photograph, was republished in generations of textbooks.

In humans and other mammals, many other combinations occur in addition to XX and XY: XXY, single X (XO), and so on. In my textbooks such people were described as having stunted growth, mental retardation, and other disorders. There was, however, a description of a small Latin American village where XY children are often born with what appear to be normal female genitals. When they go through puberty, testosterone levels trigger the descent of their testicles into the lips of their vaginas, which become a scrotum. Their clitorises grow, becoming penises. They grow beards instead of breasts. The book concluded that they all became perfectly normal men; that is, they all stopped wearing dresses and got married to women. It did not mention that they also have smaller than usual penises, a rudimentary vaginal opening, and a split scrotum, as I do. A different syndrome in XX individuals creates male genitals of typical appearance; genetic sex is only visible at puberty, by menstruation through the penis.

Though genetics is the modern standard, genes are invisible. They are properties of cells, not individuals. Determining genetics directly requires killing the specimen, monitoring its breeding, or keeping its tissues in a restricted, sterile environment. As a result, most types are divided by other standards, which are assumed to be genetic. For instance, my genetic sex (XX, without intersex conditions) is not known directly but indicated by the fact that at twelve years of age, my body appeared and functioned like that of an average-looking, normal adult female. Morphology, the visible form of the body, is the oldest and most common standard by which individuals are classified.

The light is dim in the little antique store. My friend and I have just moved into our first home together. He's tall, skinny, delicate, unathletic. I'm eighteen, which means Victorian Explorer has been knocked out by a black T-shirt, cowboy boots, and a five-buck buzz cut. Our decorating budget is a penny jar.

A man emerges from the back room. I think he's going to kick us out, because you're supposed to have money in this part of town. We keep coming back because there's no place else in Missouri for us to go. I bend over a case of expensive old jewelry and try to look serious. The man slips up with a sliding walk. His voice is wispy and exuberant, punctuated by extravagant and graceful gestures. Without our saying anything, he seems to understand how it is with us: no money, the need for beauty like air, a refuge in the face of bigotry and isolation. I start relaxing; for the first time in a long time I feel at home. So I stand up to join the man with my friend, holding salvaged prisms to the light, spreading rainbows. He sees the tits then.

Suddenly he goes cold and formal. He says "Mister and Missus," talks football to my friend, says "your wife" and "the little woman," biting off the bitter words. He hates them as much as we do. The prism comes down out of the light. We buy it anyway, lose it for a few months, find it again, pretend it is new. In the cold of winter, we needed rainbows. Besides, by then I could wear my leather jacket all the time. I never took it off anymore.

Since wild animals are difficult to observe closely, morphological (or "traditional") taxonomists kill unusual-looking specimens to identify them or depend on easily observed surface features like color and plumage. Since these are often the same features that wild creatures use to identify each other, morphological taxonomy is effective. But only as long as in the wild, each type is clearly and separately marked.

Other taxonomics accept that creatures may appear in many different dresses in different parts of their range while belonging to the same fundamental type. What remains in these cases is behavior. Certain creatures, for instance, are indistinguishable in appearance but are considered separate species because they will not breed with each other. Different habits or dissimilar songs isolate them.

I'm eighteen. I'm standing in front of the college library when a young woman races up to me, shouting, apparently overwhelmed with joy. I'm still looking for the friend she's greeting when she seizes my arm. "Hey," she says, "wanna join a lesbian group?" I stare at her. Her face falls. She is young and energetic and earnest and it's like I've kicked a puppy. "You are a lesbian, aren't you?" she stammers. "Oh, God . . ."

Her friends are making large disapproving gestures at her from a safe distance. They piss me off. I awkwardly admit some affinity with homosexuals. Her face lights back up. "Sure you are. Well, I mean even if you aren't sure, come anyway. We'll have a wonderful time. There's food," she adds hopefully.

I spend an afternoon at what seems to be a Girl Scout meeting. Instead of cookies, sewing, and leadership, we have revolution, patriarchy, and leadership. Actually, there are cookies. The women sing a song. They talk about their breasts. I do not talk about their breasts; that would be rude. They mention casually but repeatedly how the problem with everything is men. I seem to be out of the bonding loop.

One of the women once shared her supper with me, on a night I was hungry and cold and didn't have a dime. At the time it seemed an incomprehensible, perfect act of generosity. Now I realize she did it because she thought I was a lesbian.

I quietly avoid future meetings. But early one morning she shows up at my home. She seems concerned about my friend, who has answered the door in his bathrobe, deeply embarrassed, trying to hide his hairy legs from view. She's afraid he's furious she's here. She thinks something bad might happen. She asks me if I am okay in this situation. I don't tell her about the scar on his knee where the knife I threw at the wall rebounded, how he's decided being hit is better than being alone, the nights I spend crying in my beer and listening to Joe Jackson wonder who the real men are. She tells me she no longer sees any point in trying to read anything from other than a lesbian-feminist perspective.

In practice, most taxonomists use a combination of all three approaches in order to classify the living world. The struggle of all taxonomists is to find a way of naming that makes sense to them, to the nature of the creature named, and to other investigators. Taxonomists also classify themselves as *lumpers* and *splitters*—those who tend to include unusual individuals within an established group and those who divide groups to ensure that each group contains only similar individuals.

He writes me a nice letter. He's heard I'm transsexual. He's afraid of offending me, he doesn't want to assume anything, but he'd like to talk. He tells me he has Klinefelter's syndrome (XXY), one of the defects described in my textbooks next to nude photos against grids of measurement, black bars over the eyes. Doctors gave him treatment while he was still a kid, he says; testicular implants, hormones that helped him grow tall, put on muscle, grow hair, lose hair (he laughs and pats his balding head), make his penis grow. He got everything I wanted, without question. His package deal came with a tour in Vietnam, then seventies big-city gay life, AIDS, and a lot of questions his VA doctors won't answer. He's a few years older than I am.

We talk shop for two hours, laughing in sheer relief—swapping dosage information, names of good doctors, pharmacies, research on hormones, liver damage, keeping things up: spirits and strength and fight and weight and dicks and syringes. People drive by. Their windows reflect a middle-aged boot fag and a baby dyke, talking together, or maybe a couple of queers, or people.

Every specimen needs a record. State: county, city or township, range, quarter, date collected. Specimens without records are useless; who knows what jurisdiction they may fall under, which categories must be enlarged to include them. God, as my mother would say, is in the details.

ABOUT THE AUTHOR

Snout-vent length 87.5 cm, right hind foot 21 cm, weight 70 kg. Tail absent. Oregon: Multnomah County, City of Portland, southeast quarter, 2005. Significant deviations from type.

ABC

I became a transsexual in the spring of 1994, when I was twenty-nine years old, on the day I saw a postoperative transsexual body for the first time. Transsexuals, after all, are only people who change the male or female forms of their bodies, in whatever way possible. Without the knowledge that the body's form can be changed (not *mutilated*, but *changed*), it's impossible to be a transsexual. Change happens only when one ceases to know it is impossible.

Why it was that I—a scientist, a historian of science studying the social uses of biological "facts," the son of a feminist activist, someone who had spent years researching the history of culture and prejudice through the human image—had gone twenty-nine years without ever having seen an image of a transsexual male body is another question entirely. It's a question that interests me very much. But it isn't the first question people ask.

When I explain that I couldn't really be a *transsexual* until I knew what one was, people often rephrase—when did I first realize I was a man trapped in a woman's body? The only answer I have is that I have no such memory. The only body I've ever had is this one (invisible in print, and subject to interpretation). I don't remember much about what my body looked or felt like for most of my life. It isn't a woman's body now, and while I know it's very different from how it was, I'm sure I would have remembered buying a new one.

This body has changed since I was born. It will change more before I leave it, in ways I can't anticipate. How do any of us recognize ourselves, given the changes we go through between birth and death? Depending on your point of view, trapped within this question are answers about auto-immune disease, calls from God, cancer, pregnancy, schizophrenia, samsara, transsexualism. Like everyone else, I have had the same body since the day I was born. Approximately every seven years, most of my cells, like yours, have been replaced by new cells. I am trapped within my body only as little and as much as every other human being. To believe otherwise is to deny a miracle; I have changed and there is only one of me.

So, how am I different from normal people?

My personal theory, based on my training and experience, is that I have a subtle biological variation, a weak spot in the sensory/cognitive system that allows the body to recognize itself. I believe this is true of some (but not all) transsexuals as well as some (but not all) people who experience lasting effects from severe physical trauma in infancy, some people vulnerable to certain neurological and autoimmune disorders, amputees who never experience phantom limbs, and so on. Sensory experience and nerve structure constantly modify each other in these systems. People blinded early in life whose eyes are later repaired must learn to see over a period of years; their eyesight improves as their brains rewire and they re-create "seeing," but sight often remains confusing and limited through their perfectly normal eyes. Whether this is a mental or a physical process is a nonsense question. Recent research has noticed humans learn by experiencing other humans' actions as if they were happening within their own bodies, and found that autism involves a failure of this system's ability to recognize itself in other people. I seem to have a similar, milder trouble recognizing myself in myself. That the primary difficulty was with sex and gender seems reasonable in a species whose bodies change most quickly and radically at puberty, and in a culture where gender is the earliest and most important connection made between self and body.

However, I live in a culture that also denies the brain is both the mind's playground and an organ of the body. So little investigation has been done in Western medicine about these systems. The only abnormality (disease, defect, or deformity) I ever had that biology or medicine can currently identify was poor eyesight. So this discussion turns back to what people usually seem to mean when they first ask about my transsexuality—how long have I been different from other people? All my life, of course.

Which brings the question of what makes each person different to a simpler, more confusing place.

The first memory I have is of falling across an enormous shining surface. Its patterns and colors shift in a constant, dazzling, impossible play, too complex for me to grasp. Somehow, though I try very hard, I can't touch what I can see. The world is full of an incredible beauty that I will never be able to hold still in my hand. This is the first mystery. And that's all I remember.

For years this fragment haunted me. It would have been a closed book for the rest of my life, except my mother was there when it happened and was still there twenty years later, sitting with me at her kitchen table, drinking coffee and talking about memory. I told her mine.

She looked confused. Suddenly she looked up and laughed, then told me this story:

"I took you to Miller's Department Store with me one day; you were maybe six months old and I was absolutely desperate to get out of the house. I put your red fleece suit on and your little knit cap with the tassel, and when we got there I just plunked you in your stroller and off we went. It must have been one of your first days out; you were excited, you kept reaching your little hands out for everything. I only turned my back for a moment, only a moment really. It couldn't actually have been more than thirty seconds. I still don't know how you managed to get out. I'd just turned around to find a salesclerk; there was this huge crash, and there you were on the floor on top of a pile of magazines. You were fine. Somehow you'd managed to push over an entire rack of glossy magazines, one of those wire floor racks, they're enormous, and you were just pushing and plowing them everywhere. So there I was with three salesclerks trying to pick everything up, and you, and magazines everywhere. You looked like Fafnir on your hoard. It's funny. I'd completely forgotten the whole thing until just this minute."

For years I didn't know what had happened to me, which is only saying that no story I could have told would have made sense to anyone. Only at the point where another person's memory intersects with mine do we have a story.

If I am indeed different, who am I different from?

I have an astonishingly good memory for details. When I take a fossil shell into my hand, its touch releases a name onto my tongue, neat as a gumball machine. Frequently, these words—*Mucrospirifer mucronatus, Exogyra ponderosa*—have lain unspoken in my memory for decades. On the other hand, I can't remember what I had for lunch yesterday. For years I tracked the smells of insects and flowers, the details of limb bones, the patterns of artificial flavor dispensed by Good Humor trucks in August, and let observers define for themselves what they saw. I was too busy to listen. There's another factor as well. How often do any of us sit down to tell our own stories? Do we require fame? Children? The approach of death? What are we waiting for? I waited until my mandatory psychiatric evaluation.

These memories may have nothing to do with why, decades later, I chose to take testosterone injections and have my genitals rebuilt. We may assume I am indeed different. We can decide the person I am different from is my mother. And we may believe my mother is most importantly a woman. Or not. We may believe that as a transsexual man, the person I am most different from is a nontranssexual man. Or not.

Why do we turn out the way we do? For myself, I began very early with the habit of puzzling over details, the little, terribly significant differences between one thing and another. In the heart of the matter was somehow the need to value all things equally. This ability made me a tremendously astute observer, and utterly unable to choose. The ability to discriminate somehow rests at the heart of the ability to reason.

By the age of six or seven I had a certain fascination with small objects, particularly the acorns of *Quercus palustris*, pin oak. These nuts fell in masses from the trees lining the streets between my mother's house and my grade school. The acorns of pin oak are round, very uniform, and extravagantly pinstriped in all the colors of honey—ambers, blacks, and browns. I collected them obsessively. What fascinated me was both their extraordinary, precise beauty and their lack of a consistent pattern. Each was different from every other. No one could be picked out as the most representative, the most unusual, or the most beautiful. Each was therefore equally precious; I had to save them all.

This freight of seed eventually wore holes in all my pockets. My mother used to go through my clothes surreptitiously tossing hordes of acorns out or we would have drowned in them.

One other thing about the acorns; when I was in grade school older kids used to throw them at the most despised kids, one of whom was me. In the winter, when acorns were unavailable, they used pieces of ice, in the spring, rocks. In spite of the current fashion for imagining childhood as a state of grace, I think these kinds of childhood memories are pretty typical. Of course, most kids don't grow up to have gender-reassignment surgery. However, I think the rocks must have had something to do with one choice I must have made very early. If you don't listen to what anyone says about you, you're free—as free as you can make yourself, in your room, alone.

I remember being fascinated by animals at an early age, particularly insects and spiders, and stymied by the difficulty of telling the difference between beetles, which I loved, and cockroaches, which terrified me. I finally settled in my mind that the difference was not in their appearance but in their habits—the impression they gave to an observer as they moved. This distinction allowed me to become fond of the common black ground beetles that trundled about everywhere, almost precisely the same size, shape, and color as Oriental cockroaches.

I remember reading a great deal. The books I loved were generally about animals or people living alone in faraway places full of animals. Very early on I encountered the fantasies of C. S. Lewis, which converted me not to Anglicanism, as the good man might have hoped, but to love of animals. I am still grateful for this gift and for the open view of Christianity it later provided me—though I grew up in the seventies, on the home ground of the Posse Comitatus, in the town housing the national headquarters of the American Nazi Party. I enjoyed Jack London's books but tended to skip over the parts about human beings. I was offered plenty of noble-horse books as well but liked only the first book in the Black Stallion series, which involved a large horse and a small boy living together on a small island, alone.

The one exception to my no-humans rule of reading was the Sherlock Holmes stories, which I loved beyond all reason. I remember spending the whole of a joyous autumn afternoon curled in a dry storm drain, reading them over and over. I did not think to stagger home until it had become too dark to read, at which time I discovered much of town was out looking for me.

I tended to linger between school and home, not being particularly fond of either place. In the middle were any number of iridescent wasps, deeply satisfying leaf shapes, variously striped acorns, and the elaborate patterns of melting ice. The world was a glorious place to be. I was generally several hours late to school. My stepfather, a small but loud man who was the main trouble with home, followed me to school once to find out why. He rode home on his BMW 750 to conclude with a mixture of rage and bafflement that I spent all this time doing nothing.

My parents divorced when I was four. Though I'm told I took it very hard, I have no memory of any sorrow. In fact, I have few memories of anything until I was about five. I am told this is normal, the brains of most children under five being more or less incapable of long-term memory. A year or so after the divorce my mother married again, an old family friend. My parents were friendly with each other; I spent every Sunday with my dad, whose office was one door down from my mother's, two doors down from my stepfather's, at the state university.

My dad taught me to love junk stores, wilderness, and classical music and, much later, to face what life brings with humor and dignity and to live with the choices you make with honesty, insight, and grace. He also married again; my stepmother taught me to love the extraordinary beauty of bats, fungi, and pomegranates and, much later, that a powerful spirit and a valuable life are not the same things as a nontraditional lifestyle and a sharp-looking résumé. These were lessons I needed.

My stepfather and I never got along; we mixed, like oil and water, measures of baffled love and equally baffled rage. Never abusive, he was consistently intolerable. I remember best two things about him. One was that he raged endlessly at me for being unable to tell time but was the one who finally figured out I could not read the clock because I could not see it. Figuring this out took some doing since I'd been memorizing eye charts for years (they were a test, after all, and one was supposed to do well). The other was that he was short, obese, and almost blind, and in the horrible years after puberty he communicated to me with silent and almost certainly unconscious sympathy the idea that a man could make up for any physical shortcoming, no matter how great, with enough intelligence, creativity, wit, and dedicated Ernest Hemingway imitation. All his gifts had this same quality. They were enormously generous, and the maintenance they required could ruin you. Whenever he got angry with me he used to step close, like a drill sergeant in the mirror, and roar, "What makes you think you're so special?"

Ten years later, long after the divorce, he decided a man should be able to fix his own house without help from a woman, fell off an unsupported ladder, and shattered his legs. He goes heroically on.

I liked school a great deal except for the people. In fact, I liked most things except for the people. I remember learning to count with colored sticks, carefully labeling jars of seeds A, B, C, putting jar A in a sunny window, jar B on a shelf, shutting jar C in a closet, and comparing results. Kindergarten infuriated me; I was asked nicely to nap and play with the other children every single afternoon, rather than being allowed to read. I remember telling my third-grade teachers that I wanted to be a microbiologist when I grew up, not because it was true but because it was a long word that I knew would impress them. But I also remember the real joy I felt that year when I understood the mechanism of sickle-cell anemia and my real confusion as to why adults would think reading the same books they read was so very special. We can just say that I didn't get along with kids my own age. It never occurred to me there might be good reasons why I was asked to play with them. I remember being outraged that the other kids hated me for getting an Exacto knife when they all got scissors. I was the only one who was left-handed, after all, and everybody knows those little scissors stamped "LEFTY" might as well be stamped "USELESS." The other kids thought I could have used right-handed scissors just like they did, which in its own way was perfectly true.

This kind of pattern, once you get caught up in it, is very hard to break. I don't really know what made everyone think I was so special. But I remember very clearly the moment I realized you can defeat the game of Red Rover. This is one of many games adults invent for children, the great advantage of this system being that the people who make up the game will never have to play it. In Red Rover, children are forced to hurl their little bodies across a large field into a line of other small children holding hands. Whoever survives the impact is declared the winner. I think. I was never too clear on the rules. I do remember being told we had to play these games because they were good preparation for adult life, which in its own way was perfectly true. What I realized early on was it doesn't hurt if you just let go of everybody else's hands before anyone hits you.

On the other hand, my teachers loved me. They were always impressed by my test scores. Adults were easy to impress. In addition to the satisfaction of doing something I was good at, the tests had another advantage. They made the adults treat me like another adult. I could spend time with them instead of kids my own age, use Exacto knives instead of blunt scissors, read instead of playing games, and never have to justify walking away from the line at Red Rover, much less hiding under desks and snarling wolflike at any kid who bothered me, actions that I understood could send nonadults to a vague flaming netherworld populated by child psychiatrists. Doing really well on tests also made adults smile at me. I didn't understand how important those smiles were to me until much later.

Mrs. Cox was not impressed by my IQ scores. A southern lady who refused to dye her hair, she used to take kids on her lap and tell them stories. This practice was universally disapproved of. I loved her beyond all reason. She was one of the few people other than my mother I remember being happy to allow me to touch her; I used to lean against her ample bosom and feel the rolling vibrations of her Carolina accent. I remember that she used to let me touch her cheek, a mystery that fascinated me. Under the dusting of scented powder it was as soft as the velvet ears of rabbits, the face of a very old woman. Mrs. Cox lived past her eightieth birthday. Though she asked especially to see me, I did not attend her birthday party. An adult myself by then, I was obscurely ashamed of the difference between what I had become and what I felt that I should be. At the time I thought this had something to do with not winning the Nobel Prize, and maybe something about my haircut.

I remember as a child I was desperate to be touched, but I do not remember knowing this.

I labeled jars of seeds A, B, C: A for sunlight, B for shelf, C for closet. I remember a young black teaching assistant in the fourth grade who would actually walk out on the playground with me to speculate on the curiously indented berries of a yew bush, the differences between red and black ants. He would take any question from me seriously, even ones about the curious behavior of humans, which I could not seem to understand. I loved him beyond all reason. He used to hold my hand.

One day he awkwardly explained that we couldn't hold hands any longer, though he could not seem to explain why. I was paralyzed with rage and confusion. It must have something to do, I thought, with someone being insufficiently impressed by my test scores.

Years later I had to give precisely the same explanation to a third grader who used to cling to my hand when I was a tour guide. What I did not say was that, by state law, any physical contact between an adult and an unrelated minor may constitute abuse. Mrs. Cox had told them all to go to hell. Being a Daughter of the American Revolution, she could get away with it.

I remember when I was very young imagining myself grown up. I would be tall. I would have a small den in a large city, with a fireplace and a roaring fire. I would be better than anyone else at something that involved looking at things very closely. What I did would matter. I would finally understand. And always, very nearby, would be Watson—steadfast, loyal, ready to turn to me with a smile and say, "How smart you are."

Adults—Advantages:
Tall.
Able to do whatever they want.
Can run criminal empires, win the Nobel Prize.

Disadvantages:
Fall through crust on top of snow; therefore, easily caught by wolves.
Clumsy.
Too much hair.

Most adults also didn't seem to realize they could do whatever they wanted; they would give elaborate explanations they didn't really understand themselves as to why this freedom was actually an illusion. Since I didn't share their illusions on the inescapable need for property values and vinyl shoes, I understood puberty was also elective. Increased weight was an unfortunate consequence of increasing height, but one I was willing to accept given that statistics from Isle Royale showed moose habitually fend off wolves as long as they fight rather than flee. I had been told, of course, that I would one day have the breasts and hormone cycles described in suspiciously pastel-colored advertising materials, but I had also been told left-handed scissors would cut paper and someone my age could not use an Exacto knife. The human world was full of lies. Other animals showed none of these features.

Puberty was an unpleasant surprise. I suppose it is for everyone. In my case it was obvious someone had made a terrible mistake. Whoever it was, it wasn't me.

By the time I was twelve, in addition to everything else I had stopped getting taller. My little stepbrother, like everyone else in Nebraska, quickly advanced to six foot one. People told me I was growing up, another sense-less statement given the fact that I'd been excruciatingly grown-up for years. I'd also understood that adults were a different species, and it had never occurred to me I would turn into one of them.

I can't say I reconciled myself to joining the adult species. I also can't say that I would have done so happily if my penis and beard had started to sprout when I was eleven; I can't say because that isn't what happened. I do remember games that divided us into boys and girls irritated me even as a small child. The idea that I was now supposed to be a *woman* was so transparently, overwhelming wrong that I was too stunned to even throw a tantrum. By the time I recovered myself, the absolutist language of popular science had made it clear to me that no tantrum I could ever throw would make the slightest difference. There was nothing I could say that would have made any sense to anyone else, except that something was terribly wrong with the way I was supposed to be.

By the time I was twelve, I was vividly aware that women had made this same statement many times. Given the way women have often been treated, I was aware they had every right to be outraged about the way they were supposed to be, and their outrage was expanding women's pos-sibilities and transforming their lives. This knowledge had no connection at all with what was wrong for me. Something had gone terribly wrong with my body, and I was unable to recognize its new forms and habits as my own.

But I still would not have said that I was a man. Even now much of my happiness with my body is that it is a man's body, but part is that it resembles much more than it used to the adult body I imagined I would have when I was a child. Was that body a girl's imagination or a boy's? The question would have offended me as a child—as if there were re-ally any difference between the two. I never imagined having a beard any more than I imagined having breasts, but the beard seems a minor varia-tion, something I have gotten used to: men of Middle Eastern descent usually have them, I'm a man of Middle Eastern descent, oh well, okay. The bone-crushing fangs haven't come in, either, but I'm adjusting well. Whether little girls have to reconfigure themselves more than little boys do, or whether they see themselves as having breasts and curving hips when they grow up, is more than I can imagine.

As a kid I thought girls and boys were essentially the same. I knew anatomy. I also knew the fabric people insisted I wear across my chest covered precisely the same anatomy as my brother's. Well, he had a big scar on his chest from his heart surgery and I didn't, but we both knew it didn't matter; he was my big brother, and if people stared at him and wanted me to cover my chest, well, people were stupid. Different clothes and colors and modes of play were invented for us by the same idiots who talked about our fellow eight-year-olds as boyfriends and girlfriends, the idiots who'd invented Red Rover. Everybody knew the important categories; they weren't *boy* and *girl*, they were *smart* and *stupid*, *popular* and *hated*, *kid* and *adult*, *alive* and *dead*. I couldn't be a kid forever, thank God. We were alive and we were going to grow up. But adults made for the American market come in two models: men and women.

My big brother grew up first, of course. Two and a half years older, he had been faithfully by my side all my life, guiding me through the dangerous shoals of childhood. When he began his transition from boy to man, all he could tell me was that, where he was going, I couldn't follow. I desperately didn't want him to go, of course, and I fought to keep him with me. Looking back at the transition out of boyhood from a man's perspective, I can see for the first time how little he must have wanted to go, either. Having had to let the doctors open up his chest at the age of five in order to live to adulthood, my brother knew decades before I did that sometimes you don't get things quite the way you want them.

Soon it was my turn. Now that I'd finally escaped naps and Red Rover, I wasn't eager to be a kid in anyone's eyes. I obviously wasn't a woman, a problem I seemed unable to explain to anyone. But if I wasn't a kid and I wasn't a woman, what the hell was I? My brother, for the first time in our lives, couldn't help me find the answers. He was fully occupied with male adolescence, colliding head-on with the colossal labor of being a man and staying alive at the same time.

Being a man, like being a woman, is something you have to learn. I spent my teenage years watching a lot of old movies. There were many suave, debonair, handsome men like Cary Grant and Boris Karloff. I knew any hope of resembling them was a lost cause. But there was also Peter

Lorre, with his peculiar soft face and lisping foreign accent, who I figured looked most like me. I think all men have to learn to see themselves this way, though maybe not as Peter Lorre. An underfed fifteen-year-old Norwegian with terminal acne who hopes to look like the Italian Stallion isn't any less unrealistic than I was. We both learn the first rule of American manhood; if you don't look like Cary Grant or Sylvester Stallone, you're going to be a loser. Given this rule, I can't answer why, when I looked for my own allies on the screen, even as a child I always looked at the men. The analysis that people identify with media images of men because they are more powerful than female images misses a man's perspective—that most of us are told from the start by these images that we're going to be powerless losers compared with either male or female stars. There's a good reason why so many queer men identify with movie queens; we know early in life that we're never going to pass as leading men. I hardly lacked for female role models—I loved my mother, Mrs. Cox, Marlene Dietrich, Mae West. Sal Mineo, Peter Lorre, and Elisha Cook Jr. hardly stack up to Mae West as power figures. But it was to the men I looked, and much of what I learned about manhood—including second-class status as a man—I learned from them.

It took me a long time to realize other people weren't satisfied with this solution. In some ways, I didn't realize how other people saw me until I was preparing for surgery.

In order to function—to use the "appropriate" bathroom, for instance—I had to know that other people didn't see me as a man. At the same time, I couldn't afford to understand how they did see me. I could see myself in Elisha Cook's determined, doomed little men, I could see myself in Harry Earles in *Freaks*, a dwarf with the face of a baby doll talking about how people never took him seriously as a man. I could even see myself in Johnny Eck, handsome, talented, "the boy with half a body." But I never saw myself as a woman. This is what can make any transformation difficult. No one can improve their situation much without seeing it clearly, and the more necessary the transformation, the more likely that seeing the current situation clearly will make it impossible to survive. Only linking the ability to see the situation with the power to transform it saves lives.

At the time, I had no power even to imagine my situation could be different. All I knew was that I wasn't really a woman or a child. If I knew anything else, it was that saying I was a man was sure to get me laughed at. The one thing I could never stand was to be laughed at. It would be thirty years before I joined the human race and went to clown school.

Scouting for answers to questions I did not know how to ask, I found creatures who were not men, women, or children, but who were not like other animals, either—these creatures looked more or less like human beings, though there was always something different about them. Though these creatures weren't really human, they weren't really anything else, either, so they had to live with people. They were called monsters. Monster stories usually featured a brilliant scientist. In my favorite monster stories, this scientist was the monster; these versions seemed most right. The one fact of my life untouched by puberty was that I was a monster.

Which was okay. Monsters were the good guys.

The only part of being a monster that was not okay was the books and movies all explained that humans hate you. If you start liking them, they may even kill you. In one way I'm glad I went through puberty when I was eleven; I can't imagine facing a lifetime as a tormented seventh grader with the casual ease I felt as a tormented seventh grader. Back then I didn't know you got anything better. So I was as free as I could make myself, in my own room. Unfortunately, I wasn't quite alone. I left even the body that no longer seemed mine in that world outside the door, but I brought with me the certainty that there was nothing outside but a mob of peasants, armed with torches of hate and laughter. This certainty locked the hate and laughter safely in with me, and made them mine. So my room became a closet, as such rooms always do. I did not know this small important truth, though I had seen the distorted, desperate seedlings that grow when a shut door excludes the light.

Love Gets Strange

There was just something about Martin Landau. When I was in high school *North by Northwest* played over and over in the one tiny art theatre in Lincoln, Nebraska. Perversion is wherever you find it.

In high school my best friend, Ivan, was a brilliant boy, smart, talented, beautiful. By the time we were fifteen he'd ranked just how much further each designer's sharpest suit would take a beautiful boy with a brittle laugh and a permanent tan out of Nebraska, and settled on Armani. By sixteen Ivan knew things I may never know. Where he wanted to go was not one of them. In the meantime, we settled on an even mix of art and explosives. He taught me a variety of useful tricks—how to make model rockets out of Air France barf bags and clay imaginary dragons with real potassium permanganate fire in them, how to con school officials into resting their hands on an electrostatic generator long enough to build up a really painful shock. Any kid could teach you how to do some damage, but Ivan taught me that when the damage actually occurs you can be long gone. We used to fill the payloads of model rockets with bright aluminum dust, creating UFOs on the radar at the nation's air defense headquarters in Omaha. Ivan's dad was a red-blooded God-fearing Air National Guardsman. At some point I realized Ivan cared less about activating our nation's nuclear arsenal than he did about pissing off his dad. I asked him once why he hated his father so much. He didn't mention beatings or Nazi sympathies or the Latvian Lutheran Church. What he said was, "My dad washes his hair with soap." I've never heard a purer hatred.

I didn't realize for years that Ivan was gay. He tried to teach me his easy, brilliant talent for caricature, his sure mocking humor, his fashion sense. How to smile. How to smile and take revenge. His quick eye took in my deficiencies at once, but I never twisted beneath his pen. For me alone, Ivan seemed to feel a fellowship, a kind of pity. He tried to help me. He said, "You know, you can walk into Tiffany's and insult the help. You can." I was a slow learner. He told me once all I really needed was an expensive watch—like the cowardly lion's medal for bravery, the tin man's heart.

I didn't know then what "gay" meant. I was a slow learner, too serious. When we went to see *North by Northwest* together, Ivan laughed and pointed out the thug in the pink suit who held his cigarette funny, but I didn't know what he was talking about. I had eyes only for Martin Landau. Maybe it was something in that tight black fifties suit that reminded me of the sleepwalker in *The Cabinet of Doctor Caligari*. Something in there . . . his skin, the black hair, the intense anatomical curve of his throat, his fiery pinpoint eyes, incandescent blue and hissing like a pilot light. That was it. The way he looked at the tall, square-chinned hero, the blond and cheerful heroine. The way he hated them. You'd never remember what James Mason looked like, but the voice that slipped between his lips was the same as the look in Landau's eyes, that alien thing. The alien thing made them beautiful. They were monsters, like me. Aha.

The shock of the moment when I recognized the actor: Martin Landau was in my childhood favorite TV show, *Mission Impossible*. He was my very favorite, because he was different. He was the man with the masks on. The disguise was always perfect—nobody but his friends would ever recognize him. The program never showed the part of the disguise that was impossible, how a mask could conceal a person so completely, but they'd always show him rip the mask off and return to himself at the last possible moment. I loved that part. In *North by Northwest*, there's a moment when James Mason's lovely alien voice says to Martin Landau, "You don't trust them. Is that your woman's intuition?"—full of mockery; I knew exactly what that voice meant. Martin Landau's guy is one like me. Aha. Landau looks up like he's been struck, which is how it feels when people say things like that, but what he says then turns out to be true. He doesn't trust the normal people, the square-chinned hero, the cheerful heroine. Since we were watching the movie, Ivan and I knew by then that the square-chinned hero and the cheerful heroine had fallen in love, and Mason and Landau were betrayed already.

Rule Number One: Do Not Trust Peasants with Torches. Never Never Never. Not Even If They Look Like Cary Grant and Eva Marie Saint. Not Even If They Say They Love You.

Like Martin Landau's character in *North by Northwest*, this was a rule

I already knew. In the seventh grade I ran into the Teenage Monster's Guide to Love, otherwise known as *The Phantom of the Opera*. This book explained the worst thing that could happen to a monster was some stupid human would fall in love with you. Romance was bad because normal people would only love you as long as they never saw your real face. Once they did, you were dead. It didn't matter if you could sing like an angel, build an entire underground city single-handed, and win the Nobel Prize. Dead is dead.

I took the advice to heart and avoided romantic entanglements. This decision was no hardship. Romance seemed to be the adult version of Red Rover. Without the elaboration provided by it and by sex, an interesting fact came clear; life offers a social animal two choices—you can be miserable, or you can be friends. This may be a general truth most adults don't notice until the first flush of youth has passed, which was when I first began to notice romance and sex. While the Age of the Village People pulsed around me, I spent the first flower of my youth in celibacy and straight leg jeans. It may seem like bitter medicine (the celibacy at least; I take some small satisfaction in the knowledge that I, like Ivan, made it through the seventies without ever adding fabric printed with beer cans into the cuffs of my pants.) But by and large I chose not to be miserable. There's a wonderful scene in James Whale's *Frankenstein* where everyone who sees the monster screams and runs away. Eventually, he stumbles into the house of a blind hermit. Instead of screaming and running, the old outcast engages him in a discussion of the values of companionship. He pours the monster a glass of wine ("Hmm. Drink good!"), lights him a cigar ("Smoke good!"), and settles them into a couple of easy chairs ("Mmm. Friend good!") This was, more or less, my experience of high school. These days I realize my own brand of bitter tonic kept me alive, sane, and reasonably supplied with friends through the years when terrible new fashions appeared in clothes and death.

Once day in the early seventies, a group of fashionable kids accosted me as I was on my way to school and began to shout, "Straight-leg jeans! Look at those straight-leg jeans!" I asked my brother what the phrase meant and learned they were making fun of me for *not* having fabric printed with beer cans sewn into the cuffs of my pants. It wasn't until after bell-bottoms went out of fashion and the same kids showed up wearing straight-leg jeans that I actually absorbed the lesson. By then I was fifteen and starting high school. For my birthday I asked my mother for a makeup kit. "Makeup?" she asked, as casually as possible under the circumstances. "Do you mean makeup to wear on the stage or makeup to wear every day?" At the time it didn't surprise me that she would think to ask this question. I said, "What's the difference?" She explained the different qualities of color and shade along with, quite possibly, some other distinctions I didn't process. I considered this mysterious question for some time. All the colors and shades sounded good. Finally I answered that I was not sure which kind I wanted; could I have both? She bought me three generous rounds of theatrical pancake and a lavish assortment from Maybelline. I fell loudly in love with a sparkling smoky eye shadow and disappeared into the bathroom, carrying everything. Unknown to me, my mother waited outside the door with bated breath to see which of the two kits I would choose.

In some Native American societies, the gender of a peculiar child is determined by setting out typical girls' and boys' toys, the local equivalents of Barbie and G.I. Joe, and seeing which they play with. I emerged half an hour later as Dracula. Sparkly gray eye shadow makes a great bloodless cadaver look.

Lesson Number Two: Following Fashion Is Not the Same Thing as Having Style (courtesy of Quentin Crisp). I figured this lesson out surprisingly early in life, in relation to questions of clothes and makeup. What I didn't learn for another ten or fifteen years was that Lesson Number Two also applies to questions of sex and romance, the clothes and makeup of love.

I actually don't remember minding the lack of sex in my high school years, and I was far too angry at the notion of romance to notice if I minded the lack of it. Besides, the fashion in Nebraska was for blond cheerleaders with black mascara and bangs starched into elaborate rosettes resembling masses of detached antennae. Since I never found these women attractive, and they seemed to feel whatever was wrong with me might be contagious, I had good excuses for not spending time with them. The fashion for ruddy well-marbled All-American football boys helped fuel a studious avoidance of too-close looks at men. Humans were just basically unattractive. I remember one mild high school interest in a local track star. I never bothered to try speaking with her, but I used to admire the way her hair stood straight back as if, even standing still, she was always running. There was something unadorned and necessary about the stilled rage of that face, those muscles rising hard and tight, the deltoids, biceps, structure visible beneath a plum-black skin. Something of the furiously beautiful economies of dragonflies, the feet of wolves, the flanks of deer. Something Nebraska didn't seem to have a place for outside of the stadium. Something . . . Oh, and Martin Landau was really, really good. I told myself I wanted to look just like that.

The problem with being a young monster in Nebraska is that, eventually, your friends will start dating. The problem isn't "the love that dares not speak its name," because love can't speak its name regardless in Nebraska. Love requires another word to soften the blow. If that word is "just," the love involved is friendship. If that word is "more," you're into dating. The practice of this theory is a withering crossfire. From one side, if a friend is dating someone else, they and their date will be joined at the hip, and you will never see them again. From the other, a friend who loves you enough to want to actually spend time with you will assume this love means you should be dating. What determines the direction from which the fire will come? Gender is a matching problem: same gender = "just friends," different gender = "more than friends." I'm afraid I failed the remedial mathematics of love.

As we moved through our teen years, my friends began to act very peculiar. They seemed to have a matching problem. Though we had formed an integrated group of friendly outcasts, they suddenly began to segregate themselves. The women went first.

In the days of my acorn-riddled youth, Diane was invariably the one standing beside me under the hail of seasonally variable small projectiles. On my tenth birthday she had ceremoniously presented me with a plastic box of handmade doll furniture—the Slime Mutant Temple Playset ("Contents: 5 (five) assorted mutants, 2 (two) charcoal braziers, 1 (one) Altar of Unholy Sacrifices.") Once, before the hail of acorns, we imitated one another. She wore the sober wool caped coat I imagined made me resemble Sherlock Holmes, while I took her Day-Glo yellow parka and scarlet fake-fur mittens. She strode into the fray, head down, ignoring everything. I flew frantically past on her metal flake Schwinn, a manic blur of attempted escape. The other kids hated us both equally; they used to yell, "Di's a dyke," knowing this taunt bothered her when nothing else would. They never noticed that neither of us was who we pretended to be that day. We rubbed our equal bruises and were enormously amused.

At fourteen Devi was both beautiful and brilliant, seemingly already grown into an adult world the rest of us only aspired to. She was tall, with elegantly tapered fingers and hair that fell to her waist in great open waves. I came slowly to realize her maturity had been paid for by the expectation that the children of Asian immigrants would be delinquents or geniuses and by her mother's constant fear that she was falling into the former category. We stood in awe of Devi's mother, a physicist never seen without her gilt-edged saris and forehead mark. One night Devi finally explained that her mother's imposition of an early curfew was the result of a traditional Indian belief that only sluts had curly hair.

Marianne was bluff and matter-of-fact, fresh-faced and calmly athletic. In later years she would spend her summers in the endless yellow heat of western Nebraska, sifting out tiny fragments of clay from prehistoric villages, then travel to Appalachian towns, teaching women the advantages of breast-feeding.

These three became such an unlikely clique that I was thrown into confusion. They'd begun to stand around together, whispering and glancing in a conspiratorial way. When my old friend Jennifer came to visit, she joined them. Jennifer and I, Di and I, had been friends since infancy, but they were strangers to each other. What had happened to friendship? Eventually, I gathered they were talking about some of our other friends. It seemed truly unsporting to talk about people behind their backs in such a fashion. Friend good, remember? And besides, their behavior was so strange, so unlike themselves—they seemed somehow to be *acting*. Something almost incestuous hung in the air around them. It took some time for the knowledge to penetrate my skull that they were *talking about boys*. Actually, I never figured it out. Devi eventually took pity on me, taking me aside to explain I was only excluded because "It's something you wouldn't understand."

Marianne had little patience for the game of romance and soon dropped out, finding a fiancé and settling down to be, for years, a reliable buddy and my only female friend. My mother began telling me more and more frequently that I should spend more time with women friends. I think the rest were a little embarrassed, not by me, but by themselves and their actions reflected in my eyes—as irrational and senseless as messages in a game of telephone. It was a women's thing. I didn't understand.

I hung out with the guys, who never talked about their friends that way. They were reliable buddies. Since dating is to love what fashion is to style, the only people you can count on to love you are the ones with whom dating is not an option. My reliable buddies were guys who liked women. I was young enough to think all guys felt that way. The disgust I felt each time one of them decided our bull sessions meant wedding bells mirrors the disgust I now see such men feel for men like me, who fall in love with them. Perhaps it is the same disgust I often see women show toward straight men, the purity of whose interest in them can never be counted on.

What I knew from growing up in Nebraska is that every fag is somebody's reliable buddy, gone forever. Ostensibly straight men fell for me like moths into a flame, reliable buddies gone, one after the other. Doug, Marianne's fiancé, once mentioned the special erotic charge he felt when seeing me from the rear. "Oh, then," he said, to my dismay, "you're some kind of woman." I was proud of my broad shoulders, my big boots, my brother's old flannel shirts—I was proud that when we lay them on the floor my jeans were square, like my brother's, not teardrop-shaped as women's were. Nobody was shaving; only in front were things all wrong. What drew these straight boys to me in a state filled with Farah Fawcett impersonators is as tangled an erotic thread as my own vague attraction to a scowling, hard-bodied black female track star.

Years later, one of my old women friends would haltingly confess her terror of being found out as a lesbian. Her whispers over boys and dating jealousies had been the most obsessive and the most artificial of all. Later still, she'd say she had decided to "go straight," telling me that her fear of even holding hands in public with someone she loved was too great to bear. I said, "What happened when you used to do it?" She said, "Oh, God, I'd never try doing anything like that. It would be too dangerous."

Another fell in love with a gay man. At the party celebrating their wedding engagement, I tried gently to ask how they would handle his interests. I didn't know why I cared so much. They smiled into each other's eyes. "No," she said, "we're really in love with each other. Jerry's straight now."

It never occurred to me that my friends didn't want to be monsters. Monsters were obviously the good guys. I knew the peasants with torches didn't like us, but then nobody who loved me was a peasant with a torch, because if they were, they'd despise me like the jocks and the cheerleaders did. Besides, the jocks and the cheerleaders hated my friends, too, so my friends must be monsters. My friends had other ideas. I wouldn't see myself as a woman, and they wouldn't see me as either a monster or a man. I seemed resolutely opposed to that benchmark of adulthood, dating. The only category left was child. So, though I was ahead of my grade in academic work, I began to be left back in the rest of life.

The problem got worse as I got older. The only adult roles for people in our society are *male* and *female*. Regardless of body type or gender identity, if a person can't fill either role for any reason (slavery, sterility, poverty, incarceration, transgenderism, sexuality, career choice . . .) there is no adult category. What is left is to be either a child or a nonperson. This may have something to do with how gender and racial stereotypes work—especially between men and women, and blacks and whites in America, both relationships fraught with authority and sex—and why there are so many gays and lesbians out there calling each other "boy" and "girl" and running around looking like Peter Pan. Personally, I would have given ten years of my life not to be Peter Pan.

One August day when I was almost thirty, I was sitting on my lunch break wondering how the hell to tell the union I couldn't support a family on my part-time salary, without my boss finding out and getting me fired as a troublemaker. I'd only started work June first, but I was getting desperate. A friendly coworker sat down and said, "So, what are you going to do once the school year starts?"

By the time I got out of high school, even Ivan and my closeted lesbian friend had started gay dating. They'd just taken a little longer. The stereotype of the lonely queer implies that queers are lonely because they can't get a date. Queers are lonely because everybody else can't stop getting dates, gays and lesbians included. The friends who stood outside with me while everyone else played Romance were a motley assortment of queers—

queer in some larger measure than who they would have sex with, queer as in nonperson, queer as in *monster*.

I was left with two unshakable friends. One was a man whose beauty was more shocking for the fact that he had no idea of it, a gentle, dirt-poor kid who came to school each day in red eyeliner, safety pins stuck through his ears. Ivan hated him. Together we were herded into a packed hall where we would be forced to watch well-scrubbed blond Christian boys and girls dance to uplifting wholesome songs extolling the virtue of family values. After five minutes Jeff and I looked at each other, and without a word we slipped together behind our seats, climbing down twenty feet of interior scaffolding to escape the guards. Ivan stayed, sharpening his parody, his clothes unwrinkled. Though at eighteen Jeff had taught himself four languages and wanted to become a translator, he was dyslexic, lived in a trailer, and put safety pins in his ears, which meant he'd been told he was too stupid to go to college. He joined the army. After high school I never saw him again.

Rick became a medevac nurse with a talent for psychotic girlfriends. In a tall blond country we were both short, dark, slight, with an identical taste for thousand-yard stares, black and-white movies, and leather jackets. We used to be each other's evil twin. Late at night, we'd walk the deserted streets together, rolling dice to determine the direction of our progress, or drive the deserted county highways, chasing stars. We'd stretch out—somewhere east of Laramie—on the warm hood of his 280Z, watching for the straight undying trails that marked the distant eyes of satellites.

One night, as we stood together on some nameless gravel drive, Rick stretched out his arm and pointed at the dark horizon, where a star was rising, blinking red and silver lights. "Look," he said. "The plane to Lisbon." In ten years of friendship, I don't think we ever touched each other. It was our unspoken rule. Rick was my reliable buddy.

And, in all those years, I don't really know how my friends saw me. I never tried to pass as a woman—my last dress came off when I was three years old, my last skirt at thirteen, when I realized that, though my stepfather had explained kilts were unisex in Scotland, this was Nebraska. By the time I was seventeen, I'd gone off to college where I could get my own Jockey shorts. Curiously enough, in a culture that kills men for wearing lipstick, nobody ever said a word. Though men seriously seem to think their dicks will fall off if they put a dress on—I certainly did—womanhood isn't negotiable. But if womanhood isn't negotiable, people still got the idea early on that there was something odd about me.

I think we all played a game of Twenty Questions. It's animal. It's too nice to be a monster and too old to be a kid. It's clearly not a man but not really a woman either. Oh, they said, it must be a lesbian.

I never really noticed what they thought. My game asked different questions about myself and came up with different answers.

I thought I'd figured out about men and monsters. Men and women were *adult* and *human* and had romances in various combinations. I couldn't be a man in the human world, and I wasn't a woman. I was a monster. And monsters don't get romances. If they're very, very lucky, they might get a reliable buddy. I've been a monster as long as I can remember, for reasons that have varied wildly—men, gay men, transsexuals, child prodigies, poor people, scientists who study bugs and sex have all been considered monsters. But gender did enter into the question. True to my pedigree from *Frankenstein* to Mr. Spock, I was a monster who would be a man, without knowing what being a man was. There was no way I could know. Being a man is a role an adult plays in the world, and both the adult and the world have to agree on the role. So I set out to make a life for myself outside the world. And if in Nebraska I could only be a disturbed and disturbing child, Peter Pan's evil twin, I was an adult the moment the door to any classroom shut. It was the alchemical miracle of the ivory tower. There, I hoped someday to be reduced to a pure brain suspended in the rarefied atmosphere. The academic world is happy to advertise a dream country of equality, where men, women, and monsters might finally see each other without prejudice, through the roles of *teacher, master, student,* and *scholar*—uncomplicated roles, of course, and untainted by the other roles we play. Heaven is a happy land of brains without bodies.

Or you could have a reliable buddy.

For years after I left for college, every time I was in Nebraska I ended up at the wedding of another former friend. Only Rick remained, reliable, still single. I never knew a man who had such hard luck with women. We'd walk all night or sit in his apartment watching movies and drinking ("Drink good!") while he'd tell me about his latest breakup, I'd commiserate, and we'd say, "Fuck 'em" and laugh. Rick could go through a bottle of Scotch and articulate perfectly, though he couldn't stand up. I'd slur like Donald Duck, fill the glasses without spilling a drop, walk a straight line with the best of them. We used to joke about it; if the cops ever showed up, we'd hold each other and pretend we were one functional human being.

One summer night the dice brought us to a children's playground. We climbed the slides, swung pensively on the swing set, side by side, never touching. After a while he looked over at me and said quietly, "You know, it's a damn pity you're a lesbian."

The word sounded like a tin horn, and it surprised me. "I'm not a lesbian," I said, intending to finish, I'm gay. But what's the difference, anyway? What would be the point?

"You know I don't give a damn whatever the hell you are. I'm not a bigot. I'm not saying you shouldn't be that way or anything, I know it's not a choice. It's just you and me, we . . ."

He looked away. I remember the pattern of the rubber tiles, like a puzzle underneath my feet.

Rick said, "I didn't mean pity for you. I meant pity for me."

I didn't say anything. There wasn't anything to say. The thing just sat there, between us.

After a while I said, "Yeah, it's a damn pity."

I still hear from Rick every now and then. He finally found the right woman, fell in love, quit drinking, got married, settled down, helped raise some dogs and a couple of kids. For the first time in his life he seemed happy. Love gets strange. Rick used to tell me, "You're my best friend. I know I can count on you. If you ever find out I've got a ranch house in the suburbs with a wife, two point two kids, and a dog, come down there and shoot me."

So I went to college. I was young and full of happy visions of my future as a brain in a glass globe. And once again, something was wrong. Dormitory life was less a brain barracks than nine months of summer camp. Thinking fast, I found myself a queer alliance. My latest blind hermit was such an impossibly exaggerated mix of swish and nerd that no one knew quite what to make of him; Paul could have minced straight off the screen of a forties movie. We got along famously. Paul's nearest modern relative was Pee Wee Herman, and in an era when Pee Wee's creator made headlines jacking off in a gay porno theatre, the world had found a special meaning for the word "sissy." Paul's particular queerness was a mystery to everyone for years, including him. It didn't occur to us that he might be queer because he wasn't gay. As a gay lesbian and a straight faggot, we were equal monsters, equally roleless and out of place in the human world. We did the only sensible thing under the circumstances; we moved in together. A monster family, we gave each other books instead of roses, all-night conversation instead of sex, and, in hallowed queer tradition, pets rather than babies. Paul was the first person I ever told about my little problem. It wasn't that I'd never tried to tell anyone before. In my early teens I'd talked first to my mother.

"Mom," I'd said, "there's something wrong."

"Physically or mentally?"

"Physically."

"Where do you hurt? Do you feel sick?"

"Um, all this *stuff* that's happening . . ."

She looked enormously relieved. "Oh, honey," she said, "it's normal to be shy about things right now. Your body's going through enormous changes, and . . ."

"No, that's not what I mean. I mean it *feels wrong*."

"Wrong how? Do you have cramps? Nausea? Nipple tenderness?"

"Yeah, something's really wrong, I'm really sick . . ."

"Okay. Everything's going to be fine. Just tell me your symptoms. Many women have these kinds of problems, you know . . ."

"No. It's not like that."

"You remember your friend Amy went to the doctor for medication, and now she's fine."

"No, it's not like what Amy had at all."

"So what are your symptoms?"

With intense embarrassment, I managed to get my symptoms across. Mom looked relieved again. "Oh, honey," she said, "you're fine. There's nothing wrong with you at all. It's all just part of being a woman."

Oh, hell, never mind.

When I told Paul, I was a little older. We'd been having a discussion about women.

Paul said, "Women are wonderful. There's the companionship, the non-violence, the shopping. I just love being with women! No bald spots. None of this awful hair. And those nice breasts." He cupped his chest experimentally. "It would be so fabulous!"

I said, "Tits, reproductive systems, babies. It sucks."

Paul looked sad. He said, "You mean you don't like having female parts?"

I managed to tell him, at length, that the thought of spending the next forty years of my life wandering around with a full set of female organs made me want to puke my guts out.

Paul had undying faith in two things: technology and condiments. He sprinkled another flavor packet on his ramen noodles, brightened visibly, and said, "Well, then. You're a grown-up. You can just have them taken out!"

Since I had no money and was not yet eighteen, Paul and I worked out a deal. I would help him buy those lovely slacks you can only find in women's departments if he'd help me tell my mother I wanted a little surgery. We could just explain everything simply and clearly, Paul thought; I had these extra organs that I wanted taken out.

He got the worse end of the deal. After the screaming died down, it was clear that my mother's perspective on the suggested solution was somewhat different from Paul's and mine. She wouldn't send the police to get me as long as I tried counseling. And our idea had seemed so simple, so reasonable.

However, it's hard to keep a good brain in a glass globe down when there's a library available. A little research later, I had discovered that birth control pills, properly applied, would eliminate those pesky hormone cycles, which led to the spectacle of Paul and me in an low-income family planning clinic, both in high drag, confessing our undying love. Though I was doubtful that either of us could pass as at risk for breeding, the long-suffering staff sent us off with the desired medication and a slow shake of the head.

But Paul's indomitable effeminacy was starting to get under my skin. He didn't seem to know how to work, fight, yell, take what he wanted;

where had his mother been? "She told me to marry rich," he said sheepishly. What was worse, he seemed to flourish reedlike in this fashion, passive, demanding, endlessly optimistic, endlessly resilient. Worse still, though nobody seemed inclined to modify the opinion that we were both flaming queers, everyone had decided Paul was my *boyfriend*. Of course we weren't fucking; hey, you think I'm some kind of a swish or something? You think I'm the kind that would fuck with *men*? That's better. What do you mean, we spend a lot of time together? Well, the poor bastard's got to have somebody looking out for him. (Friend good.) Say it again, buddy, if you want a hole in the head.

The difficulty of sorting love neatly by fashion had reared its ugly head.

"Hey, Paul, I'm thinking about doing some traveling."

"Oh, wonderful! I'm just about fed up with this anthropology program—they want me to go live in some awful *village* somewhere, with dirt and bugs, doing kinship diagrams. I mean, who *cares* about kinship? So, where are we going?"

"What do you mean, we?"

Paul looked stunned. "When would you be back? What would you do?"

"Look, I don't need you."

"Why do you say things like that? It hurts me when you say things like that. I need *you*. Isn't that okay?" His eyes began to fill with tears.

"For Chrissakes, Paul, be a man."

I started to walk away. Paul, frantic, grabbed my arm, begging me not to leave, to at least *talk about it*. I was mortified.

"Leave me the fuck alone," I hissed. "Come on, Paul, that woman is *looking at us*."

And suddenly she was there, a well-dressed yuppie clinging to Paul's other arm, screaming incomprehensibly, a total stranger. He still clung desperately to me, and as I swung around and shoved Paul away, her words suddenly came clear.

She was screaming, "What do you think you're doing to her, you bastard! Leave that poor woman alone! Do you think a woman is any man's property, that you can drag her around like a dog? Well, you can't! Did you hear me? You can't!" I'd hit him hard, dead center, and I caught one flash of his terrified eyes as he stumbled backward into a plate glass window.

Everything went very quiet. Paul rebounded out of the falling shards, gray with embarrassment and terror, miraculously unhurt. I rounded on the woman, balled my fists, and bellowed at the top of my lungs, "LEAVE US ALONE! WHY WON'T YOU ALL JUST LEAVE US THE FUCK ALONE!"

Things got much better after that. Paul and I stayed together for the next ten years, secure in the knowledge that, however strange our form of love was, we were monsters together, and anything the rest of the world had to offer either of us would certainly be worse.

The part of any monster story where the monsters live happily together in the castle usually ends up on the cutting-room floor. We did live happily together, Paul and I. Fast forward through the montage: Paul concocting gourmet Thai delicacies from plain label fish sticks, me going to graduate school, Paul and I walking proudly together in the pride marches where nobody's group seemed really appropriate, laughing, holding hands.

Though there were only ten students in my graduate department, they'd begun to date each other at wine-and-cheese parties. After two departmental weddings and six and a half years of higher education, it finally dawned on me that everyone else was in graduate school to become a professor, while I was there to become a brain in a glass globe. So I got out and immediately found a great job whose only drawback was an almost total lack of income. There were all kinds of people who didn't quite fit in anywhere. We made plenty of friends.

One day I flew home from yet another Nebraska wedding feeling a little pensive.

"Paul," I said, "do you ever feel like, you know, something's missing?"

Proudly opening his first bottle of Malaysian banana ketchup, Paul gave me a blank look. "What could be missing?"

"Oh, I dunno. Sometimes I feel like such a little kid. I've got a real job now and everything, but, you know, something's missing—I don't mean bullshit like two point two kids and a suburban ranch house or anything, just . . ."

39

"You've got me," he said, with a hint of uncertainty.

"I know. I'd sure be shit out of luck otherwise."

"Here, I bought a nice jar of green curry paste. Smell—you'll love it."

"Paul, did you ever do dating?"

"Ugh, *please.*"

"Yeah, I know, me too. I was just thinking about having some kind of relationship. What a stupid term. Like you and I don't have a relationship. God, I must be having creeping envy for the breeder lifestyle, and here I thought I had high morals."

"Well," said Paul finally, "I suppose you and I could, you know . . ."

For years, Paul would return despondently from visits to his conservative parents, break out his sissiest clothes, and put on something flamboyant. Then he'd turn to me and say, "How do I look?" I'd take in the billowy silk shirt, under which his narrow chest showed every rib, an insectlike economy as familiar and disconcerting as a mantis in a petticoat. He'd always say anxiously, "Do you think I look fat?"

For years Paul would sometimes fall asleep with one arm around me, hand cradling a breast. Each time I would replace his hand in some comfortable location, on my shoulder, around my waist, cupping my shoulder blade and its handle of flesh. For years, asleep, his hand would be drawn back magnetically to that breast, and I'd move it again. Over and over, for years. We looked at each other.

"Nah," I said.

"You're right," Paul said. "It wouldn't work." And if he seemed a little sad, I didn't notice.

Around this time we made friends with a Greek god. Actually, he was a dude from a little town in Ohio, which he remembered with great nostalgia; he only looked like a Greek god. Randy, of course, was straight. He was my buddy, just like Rick. Not that I was in love with him or anything. Of course, it did occur to me—I was seriously into effects makeup by then—that what Randy really needed was a pair of high black pumps with the heels cut off, a set of fishnet stockings, tied thickly over with hair, with a slit at the crotch to allow his dick to dangle for a seamless naturalistic effect. I'd rouge his lips and nipples carefully, provide some impressive horns, and he'd be a perfect satyr. This plan seemed completely workable. When Paul protested that it sounded just a little blue to him, I reminded him with some sharpness that I was an artist, after all. Ultimately, I decided that Randy was unlikely to go for this concept in costume and shelved the plan. Randy's problem in life, I thought, was that he didn't want to admit he was a monster. One night, at about two in the morning, we got into an argument about it.

I asked him, "What would you do if you could do anything? I mean anything, even something impossible."

Randy said, "I'd go back to high school."

This was not the answer I was looking for. I didn't know what kind of answer I was looking for, but I sure as hell knew this wasn't it.

"Why the fuck do you want to go back to high school? High school is where they send you if you've been too bad to go to purgatory."

"No, I mean go back as an adult, knowing what I know now."

I stared at him. "I used to meet these grown-ups who'd say, 'Enjoy high school, kid, those'll be the best years of your life,' and I'd think, 'If it's true, just shoot me now.' But I guess you were captain of the football team or whatever."

"No, I was the fat kid. Everybody hated me."

(The fat kid? Randy? The Greek god Randy?)

"If I could go back now, I mean be myself now, but fifteen again. I know how society works, the roles and everything, how to get people to like me. I could be the most popular kid in the whole damn state."

"Randy, *think*. You'd have to go through fucking *adolescence* all over again. Don't you think things ever get any better? Isn't the life you've made yourself now worth anything?"

Randy said, "I like my car." He had a spotless late-model Buick sport sedan. There were two other cars in our peer income group, an antique Impala whose exhaust vented through the back seat, and Ken's truck, with a manual shift, under the hood, with a rag around your hand.

Then Randy said, "My mom died when I was seventeen. Dad went a few weeks later."

"Hell, Randy, I didn't know. I'm sorry."

"No, it's not just that. See, I was the only kid, so I got all the money there was, but I didn't really know how to be on my own. I'd come home from school and I'd be standing there trying to figure out how to cook, hell, how to get food into the refrigerator in the first place. Everybody

41

else was still calling their folks for permission if they were going to be late for dinner. I ran into a leather worker and I had a pair of custom boots made. Full elk hide, laced up to the knees. Then I went out and bought a car. And that was it. The money was gone, and Mom, and Dad, and I was out of high school by then. So I drove up here and got a job."

After a minute he said, "It wouldn't work going back, I know. Even now that I look like this I still know I wouldn't belong, like people would catch on. I don't even know what the hell there is to catch on to. People look at me and I'm still thinking they know something's wrong, even though I'm not that fat kid anymore. I look normal and I still don't fit in. It's inside me somehow."

"You want to be normal? Like everybody else, like the people who hated you because you were different? You want to be like them?"

He said, "I don't know what I want. Maybe I'll move to Chicago, go to college. I always wanted to be an actor. I don't want to be the captain of the football team. I want to change everything. My best friend back in Ohio said you should do everything you really wanted to do. That sounded so right, but then he said thinking about anybody else was a cop-out; you were giving in, compromising yourself just to conform to society's idea of what you should be. If you did that, he said it meant you couldn't be following your own path, doing whatever you wanted to do. And, I mean, he had a point, but then he quit washing his clothes. He started getting really weird, arguing with everybody all the time. He looked like a homeless person. Nobody would talk to him anymore, he wouldn't take a bath . . ."

"Randy," I said, "if not bathing isn't what you want to do, you get to bathe."

He said, "I don't want to go crazy."

I can see him clearly, sitting there: head tilted up, tears trapped inside his clear blue eyes, shoulders back, chiseled chest, the muscles tense in his firm jaw line, the ironic, incredibly lush lips, one small delicate scar on the knob of his chin.

I said, "Sometimes I feel like somebody with nowhere to live; I'm walking down the street, and it's winter. I'm hungry and it's cold and I'm looking up at all the houses, through the lighted windows. I'm looking into one and inside I can see a party going on, men and women dancing together, eating from big tables full of food. They don't look hungry, but like they're eating just because they can, because everything tastes so good. People look like they're laughing, and I know there must be jokes, conversation, music. Everything looks so beautiful, so bright, so warm. And I know what I'm seeing is probably nothing like being there, because I've been to parties and they're full of miserable people pretending to enjoy themselves. I know there's probably even somebody in there looking out at me and wishing just as hard that they were out here, alone in the beautiful quiet street with the snow and the moon, watching the lights. I know that, and it's still not good enough. I feel like that all the time. I don't know what it means."

Randy said, "I don't feel good. I have to go home."

For a while after that night I called Randy a lot. Sometimes I called him at odd hours; when he got a new girlfriend I thought about sneaking over in the middle of the night and painting his burgundy Buick—bright colors all over—but I didn't. I wanted to save somebody. I thought it was him. Eventually, Randy disappeared. He'd told us all he was planning for school. One night he cleared his apartment, drove off, and never came back. Maybe he went back to Ohio, drove that car off a highway bridge over the Mississippi, went to college, became a big actor in Chicago. I never found out.

For a while after Randy I tried dating girls. It seemed vaguely as if I ought to do something. Every once in a while I'd call up someone from a personal ad; a normal, nice-looking woman would show up to meet me in an Italian restaurant, and we'd order a carafe of red wine, even though she usually drank white wine and I usually drank cheap vodka, because this was a date, after all. And that would be it. I'd go home feeling more or less satisfied that I'd done my duty, whatever it was. On my first date I spent the entire evening talking about my job. Since my job at the time was skeletonizing animal carcasses, this might not have been the most diplomatic choice of topic. She didn't call me back.

My second date spent the entire evening talking about rape. Apparently, all men my age were *college students*, drunken football linebackers who cruised the streets in rape gangs with their fraternity buddies. Feeling more than a little uncomfortable, I explained I had recently been a college student myself, still lived happily in a student neighborhood, and was honestly quite sure that not all young men were rapists. Her only response was to drive me home, refuse to allow me out at my corner, pull her car into the driveway, and stand guard with the engine running until I made it safely inside my door. I didn't call her back.

The vocal hatred and fear of men was a familiar routine. For some reason most nice normal young women took advantage of any time alone with me to mention that they'd love to be rid of men. The constant surrealism of this situation was something I dealt with by avoiding women whenever possible and explained to myself as a result of a knee injury that required me to wear Birkenstock sandals, causing them to mistake me for a lesbian. I thought perhaps if I only had more manly footwear, maybe combat boots or something . . . Anyway, so much for dating.

I didn't miss it; I had a lot of friends. Nicky, who drifted in from England in a flapper dress and a Louise Brooks haircut, with her husband and their lovers, male and female, blew open our midwestern sense of possibilities and drifted out again. Nigel, the sharp, strange man I'd loved to work with in the theatre. He'd played a woman with enormous intensity and conviction, and I'd played the male lead opposite, her lover. We'd been good together. Lots of tension, lots of chemistry. Soon afterward, he wrote a play in which everyone's destiny turns out to have been written in their genes. Then he was gone, too, moving away to become a geneticist. I wrote Nigel once, to talk about things, problems in theme and meaning in his last play. He wrote me back to say I had mistaken his interests; theatre was merely entertainment, but science was truth.

I didn't need a steady date. I missed Nigel. And Nicky. And Randy. And Rick. I just needed some friends.

Every few years the town we lived in would get old. It would seem as if something were missing, and Paul and I would pack up and move on. You could get used to it. One night Paul and I were stretched out on his big bed, eating junk food, watching reruns of *Miami Vice*, and chatting up queer subtexts in old TV shows. Suddenly I thought, *I could live like this for the rest of my life.* Somewhere, vague but clear, I heard a little warning bell. The little bell always says the same thing. It says:

The worst thing that can happen to you is to realize on the day you die there's something you haven't done, an experience you needed very much, something important for you to see, to know, to do, but it's too late. Whatever that thing is, do it, and soon, because no matter how badly it turns out, that's not the worst thing that can happen.

"Paul," I said, "I can't stand it any longer."

"Can't stand what?"

"I don't know. I'm moving to Los Angeles."

"What for?"

"I'm tired of the way everything is here: the people, the culture, the weather. I can't live like this forever, like a student, like nobody, like a kid. I want to be in another place."

"How about San Francisco? asked Paul hopefully.

"Oh, yeah, the gym-toned bleached blond beach clones are going to love us. We'd both be Mr. Popularity down there."

Paul thought for a minute. "Wait a year for me to finish my degree and I'll go with you. Walter Williams is at USC. He wrote this *interesting* book on the berdache tradition."

"What's that?"

"He researched stories about traditional Native American societies that had roles for men who cooked and wore dresses and for women who were accepted as men."

"I heard it was only men who were women."

"No, he says it went the other way, too."

"Yeah? Really? What else does he say about it? Maybe I could go back to school, take a class . . ."

"He says whites didn't pay as much attention to the lesbians, because of patriarchal male prejudice against women, but the traditional cultures had this special, valued place for lesbians, too."

"Whatever. I was going to write the L.A. County Museum about jobs. If I just had a high-class, professional-salary job, that would fix everything. So if I wait a year to contact the museum, you'll come along?"

"Sure," said Paul. "Shrimp chip?"

I bought a copy of the book, called *The Spirit and the Flesh*, anyway. There were certain parts I read with great interest. In these sections the author talked at length about people whom everyone called "she," people he was sure were *actually men*. What made them so different from other guys was that they were *gay* men. See, normal people think the same thing that makes you like guys so much makes you effeminate, so everybody treats you like a woman.

Aha!

The book told me how our society despises these people—*nadle*, *alyha*, *berdache*—people who aren't *normal*, neither flesh nor fowl nor good red herring. I'd started to do a lot of reading about homosexuals. Where I'd gone to college in St. Louis, Missouri, the only book in the library that mentioned homosexuals and wasn't locked up behind the librarian's desk was called *Psychopathia Sexualis*, printed in black-letter gothic, vintage 1886. It had said too much sex with other men would turn you effeminate; there were case studies of men who'd gone soft, grown breasts, turned into some kind of abnormal not-women-but-not-men. Now, in modern, socially informed, scientifically accurate books, I found out the Japanese don't care who you fuck, as long as you hold down a good job or make a decent home, get married, fulfill your responsibilities in the social contract, make your family proud, have children and carry on the next generation. You know, be part of something beyond your own life, something more than just a student, a nobody, a kid. Be part of something that matters. Something that lasts. That's what's important. A real homosexual is somebody who cares more about boys and girls and who they fuck, more about being different, than about the fact that they're turning their back on the whole rest of the world.

Walter Williams said there were whole societies of people who believed the lives of people who weren't *normal* mattered, that we could have a role in the world, be part of something beyond ourselves, an important part, a necessary part. The same year I went to see Vito Russo talk about his book *The Celluloid Closet*, on queer images in film. Afterward I stopped to chat with him. We ended up talking about monster movies. I wanted to thank him for the book, which I kept beside my bed to remind myself I wasn't the only monster in the world. He looked straight into my eyes and said, "That's why I wrote it. I wanted to do something for my people." This man looked at me and said *my people*. I wore his words next to my heart for years, like a Saint Christopher medal.

I said, "I wonder why queer people like monster movies so much. There's something in that."

He said, "I think so, too."

"Maybe you should write a book about it."

For a moment he looked very tired. I didn't know what AIDS was. Then he smiled at me and said, "Well, maybe you could write that one instead."

Two years later I'd stand on Hollywood Boulevard on Halloween night and realize that people love monsters, need monsters, that even the peasants with torches can't survive without them. Then I'd forget again.

Walter Williams said he understood about the monsters, the in-between people. He told me he knew the truth—these people were actually gay men because Mr. Williams was a gay man, and he found them very cruisable. Their flat chests, slender, muscular brown limbs, jaunty penises, twink faces, and sassy feminine attitudes struck him as familiar and exciting. Meeting Mr. Williams's gold standard neither for hot body nor for camp attitude, I felt rather depressed to discover that I could not be a gay man. Oh, and there was a little section in the back of his book about "Amazons" ("it is a status specific to women that is not subservient to male definitions"). He explained that these were women-loving women. The important thing to remember was they had nothing to do with the in-between people he'd been talking about. They had nothing to do with men. Nothing at all.

In the small print I did find a brief mention of some tribes' acceptance of their "gay men" sleeping with women and one story of a "lesbian" who slept with men, a practice the author explained as the tragic result of alcoholism and colonial male exploitation, ending in suicide.

Ah, who needs dating?

Rebel without a Cause

A year after moving to Los Angeles, Paul and I both fell in love. At about this time, I realized the reason I moved to Los Angeles was that when you fall in love, you're supposed to end up at the Griffith Park Observatory. Like most of my other substitutes for wisdom, I learned this one from a movie. On a winter day when I could escape the tourists, I took my car up the hill overlooking Hollywood, sat down beside the statue of James Dean, and I cried, and I cried, and I cried. And even then I suspected that I was no more or less happy than anyone else. Only I was twenty-six years old, no one had shot me to death in front of Griffith Observatory, and now I didn't know what in the hell to do. Dying on schedule is so much easier than outliving the script written for you.

We'd been in LA for less than a year when we realized Paul wasn't gay. This remarkable discovery came about when, at the age of twenty-nine, he found the first woman willing to have sex with him. The woman Paul took up with was *normal*, with polyester stretch pants and one burning ambition. Sitting on our couch one night, Brenda told Paul she was moving to Phoenix.

She said, "Paul, I want you to come with me. I want to get married. I've given up every other dream in my whole life: marrying rich, becoming a princess, having lots of children and a ranch house in the suburbs. This is the Only Dream I Have Left. I want a big church wedding and a cake with pillars and a white dress with yards and yards of lace and a veil and little flower girls. I don't even care who I get married to, as long as I can get married."

My buddy Dawn, who looked just a little like James Dean, later confessed the answer that sprang to mind was suggesting Brenda take a quick trip to Tijuana. I had no idea humor, or even sympathy, might be an appropriate response. Instead, I waited panic-stricken for Paul to say no, and Paul kept putting her off for a week and looking pensive.

This was the pensiveness of a man who had spent his entire life in a state of enforced celibacy contemplating a future of unlimited nookie. Unfortunately, I assumed it was the pensiveness of a man who had just discovered he'd rather be normal than a monster. The funny thing is that two reasonably intelligent people could find these concepts so easy to confuse. Suddenly Paul and I were standing on opposite sides of love, which is only the dream of not spending the rest of your life alone in the castle.

Paul said, "She gave me flowers."

I said, "Paul, they're plastic. She gave you plastic flowers."

And Paul said, "But they're flowers."

I had seriously underestimated Paul, a man capable of accruing a hundred thousand dollars of unpaid debts without ever having met a cop, a lawyer, or a former professional boxing champion.

He said, "Do you like Brenda?"

I said, "She's all right, I guess."

"Well, why don't you come with us?"

"If you haven't noticed, I'd be kind of an extra wheel."

"I love you, you know that. Now all we have to do is figure out what you could be to Brenda."

"Christ, Paul, I don't know. She's so damn *normal*. I don't want to live in a place like Phoenix."

Paul pouted. "Brenda's got a whole household in Phoenix. They're all pagans. Now tell me that's normal. There is absolutely no reason why we can't have an *alternative family*."

He analyzed the situation and decided the recipe for total happiness was for Brenda's unlimited nookie potential to be extended to me as well. One night Paul invited her over, thoughtfully provided us with a condiment tray and a quart of Stolichnaya, put on some tasteful mood music, and disappeared.

And so it was that my introduction to sex involved drinking in order to fuck a woman I didn't like, who was blind drunk because she didn't like me. This much of my sexual experience, at least, is completely normal. Afterward Brenda had something of a revelation; somewhere beneath the alcohol fumes, she realized she had been touched by a monster, and she spent the following hours in a shrieking panic, terrified of contagion. I was a little relieved. It was the first thing she'd done all night that seemed appropriate to the situation.

Sometime during the night Brenda passed through her crisis of faith and emerged untouched. And so it was that the next morning, teary-eyed, she came to me with touching thanks for the lasting, important role I'd just played in her life. She assured me she'd never forget my part in the ritual she'd chosen, that ultimate initiation into femininity with which she had forged a new and deeper relationship to her Goddess.

"Uh, Brenda," I said, "I'm afraid I have to tell you something."

When I was seventeen, at college, I found the script that was written for me. It was, unfortunately, written in 1955, a James Dean movie called *Rebel without a Cause*. In 1982, when I first saw it, nothing better had come along. I wouldn't celebrate how far we've come since then just yet.

From the man whose cheesy bronze bust stands at Griffith Observatory I learned a lesson that saved my life, at seventeen:

You can become so obsessed with proving your manhood that you will get in your car, a seventeen-year-old with a whole life ahead of you, and another man will get in his car, a seventeen-year-old with a whole life ahead of him; you will gun your engines straight toward a high cliff under the impression that whoever stops first is less of a man, and the winner is the guy who dies.

Watching some fifties idea of a hot sports car disappear slowly into the Technicolor sea, I finally got it through my head that proving manhood is a game you win by not playing. And if that had been all the movie said, maybe my life would have been a little different, but this is Hollywood, so the man who walked away from the game was beautiful and blond, with a chiseled chest and a firm knob on the end of his chin. He could walk away because he looked like he had nothing to prove. He looked nothing like me.

This movie had not two but three main characters: a man, a woman, and a third, played by Sal Mineo, who did look like me. This other was a man but something else—smaller than the man, softer, like me. American but something else, a stranger but not a foreigner, like me. White, but something else, darker in that blue-eyed world, like me. More scientific, more carefully adult, but something else, something that kept him helplessly estranged from the love of men and women, fixed him as an alien child, like me. I knew what the something else was. The dark soft strange lonely thing is *monster*. And here for the first time I saw myself explained. I didn't look like other men, but I didn't look like Frankenstein's monster, or a vampire, or the Invisible Man, either. I didn't look like all the other social monsters I had seen on the streets or in picture books: black people, bearded ladies, dwarfs and conjoined twins and tattooed men. I didn't look like anyone because I was some kind of hybrid, like Sal Mineo in *Rebel without a Cause*, like those berdache Walter Williams said I wasn't good-looking enough to be, like those men in the *Psychopathia Sexualis* who were transforming into women because they fell in love. Because they fell in love with the wrong kind of person. Half monster and half man. At the end of *Rebel without a Cause*, the man and the woman walk off into the sunset together, and Sal Mineo's character goes crazy and the police shoot him to death in front of Griffith Observatory.

I was falling in love.

After Sal Mineo's character dies but before walking into the sunset with Natalie Wood, Dean stops for a moment by the pathetic corpse sprawled across the steps. Kneeling by the body, he reaches out on impulse and zips up the dead boy's jacket, gently, tenderly, so he won't be cold. This image is the first clear memory I have of romantic love. Three weeks before I found myself at the observatory, I was sprawled on my apartment floor, Los Angeles in August, my head against a chair leg, weighing the odds on how long it would be before I either started to feel better or passed out uncomplainingly from smog and heat exhaustion. Something touched me gently, something lovely and cool. I opened my eyes and saw James Dean reaching out on impulse to press a cold can of soda, gently, tenderly to my forehead. And not only was I alive, I was all better, and a little angel had just fluttered down and painlessly removed the top of my head.

That James Dean had breasts was a minor detail compared to the can of soda and the cherubs. Fashion is built out of appearances, but style comes straight from love. And if we had been really stylin', I could now be saying we immediately drove to the observatory, pulled each other up from those marble slabs, and walked off into the sunset together like James Dean and Sal Mineo, but Hollywood isn't *Hollywood*. So the revelation that I could no longer pretend I didn't need to ride my little scooter up to James Dean and say I was madly in love with him came to me at three in the morning

51

in a Kentucky Fried Chicken on the freeway home from Phoenix. Oh, and James Dean went by the pronoun "she" and was living with a man who wanted to get married and buy a condominium in Antelope Valley at the time.

"Paul," I said, "I can't stand it anymore."

"I know *exactly* what you mean. I can't stand Brenda, I can't stand her family, and the Phoenix phone book has 316 pest-control agencies and one bookstore. I don't care if I have to spend the rest of my life as a *monk*; as long as I live I'm never setting foot inside another mall. So you needn't worry about a *thing*."

"That's not what I was worried about. I'm never taking you back there anyhow. But I think Brenda's fairy cousin dosed all that coffee he was plying me with."

"What *was* that all about? I gave you allergy pills, and coffee's not going to help your hay fever . . ."

"He was commiserating with me over Brenda. I told him I hadn't been crying. He wouldn't believe me. All their coffee was Snickerdoodle Almond Creme; he could have filled it full of Everclear and I wouldn't have been able to tell. And I don't think those were allergy pills you gave me."

Paul checked his pockets. "Oh, here are the allergy pills. You're right, they must have been the No-Doz."

"I think I'm going to sit right here until the table stops moving."

"You do look a little peaked." He eyed me critically. "But we're not moving to Phoenix. I'm even dropping Brenda. See, everything's fine now. What's wrong?"

"I'm about to strangle you in a Kentucky Fried Chicken, and I'm in love with Dawn."

Paul looked thoughtful. "I've always been very *fond* of Dawn . . ."

"One more word and I'll kill you now, I swear."

"All right, all right. Well, why don't you talk to her?"

"Paul, she's got somebody. She's got the life she wants. I'm not going to mess with that. And you can live in a Wal-Mart with Brenda, I don't give a damn. I'm through with love."

Dawn was a reliable buddy. Reliable buddies aren't the kind who go in for, say, just at random, Goddess worship. And the glimpses of that life I saw were clear: a small room, solitary night work, a pair of small brilliant eyes in an impassive face, a tall, spare figure walking up Sunset Boulevard at three in the morning, observing everything. The man who shared that room was an idiot who worked in the daytime; he'd arrive like a visitor in the evenings, pronouncing his opinions on the secrets of the universe. And across the room those wonderful eyes would glitter on the way out with the same secret amusement reserved for Paul and Brenda, for frightened women's' warnings about dangerous night streets, for beckoning men lonely for a beautiful boy to share a few minutes or a night, for all the world's desperate and amusing conundrums. Here, for the first time, I saw the life I had imagined for myself as a child: a life as detached and perfect as a snowflake, a self-built castle as clear as ice. It was too perfect to touch. I watched from a little distance, as close as I dared, and mourned the mess I had made of my life.

Once I visited the citadel by the sea where Dawn worked, and a casual wave of the hand conducted me past the sealed gates of the Rand Corporation.

"Do you want to break for dinner?" I asked cautiously.

"I don't often think of it when I'm working. Red Hots and coffee is fine."

"I'd like to go down to the ocean," I said. "I like to watch the sunset."

"The ocean? Is it far from here?"

"It's a block and a half from the front door," I said, a little startled.

"I'd like to go with you. I've never seen the ocean."

We stood on the beach for a long time, one watching the sun, one watching the other.

"Hey," I said suavely, "it's the same color."

"What is?"

"The hair on your cheeks and the light. That's really beautiful."

My buddy turned suddenly away, crouching—impossibly—in shame.

"I'm sorry. I should have shaved today, I'm sorry."

I was bewildered. "No, I didn't mean to say anything . . . I just thought it was beautiful. Really. That's all. It's okay."

We watched the ocean for a while.

After a while Dawn said quietly, "I always wanted to be beautiful."

Oh, I thought, you are beautiful.

53

"I used to think I always wanted to be a beautiful little Japanese girl."

"Why the hell would you want that?"

"I don't know. You've got kind of a different idea of what beautiful is, you know, if you like facial hair instead of little Japanese girls. I thought if I just looked like those anime girls, my life would be wonderful."

I said I thought there was nothing wrong with little Japanese girls, but James Dean, for instance, was beautiful.

A few weeks later the inhabitant of the perfect castle I had imagined sat on my couch and said quietly, "I hate my life."

All I could think to say was "Why?"

"I work second shift making Xerox copies in a windowless basement. I can't stand my boyfriend Brad, and the best thing I can say is he's not around much so if I die nobody but my cat will care and it will be a week before they find the body."

Oh. I hadn't thought of that.

The first thing I said was, "I'd notice. I'd care."

My buddy looked at me like I'd just thrown out a life preserver and said, "I guess I meant before. I never met people like you and Paul before. I want to leave, to change everything, but I don't know how. If I keep going like this I'll be stuck in a condo in Antelope Valley, and one day I'll go crazy and axe-murder the entire suburb. I don't want to pretend to be normal any more. Can you help me get out?"

"Sure," I said, as casually as possible under the circumstances. "I'm your friend."

So Dawn informed all and sundry that the future didn't look like a condo in Antelope Valley with the boyfriend Brad, it looked like a single apartment in Hollywood. Meanwhile, the ex-boyfriend Brad informed all and sundry that this madness was the result of "a Sapphic Initiation," and I remembered Brenda had mistaken me for a Goddess and thought, if you're going to give up on love, boy, now's the time to decide.

All day I sat at the observatory on the hill above Los Angeles and watched the gritty, tangled, loud brown streets line themselves up in symmetrical white rows. From this distance they seemed shining paths, leading conveniently straight to an invisible but promised perfect beach, one you saw once in a movie, although down there it will be impossible to find. Behind me all day long the stone eyes of famous scientists—each wart and wrinkle smoothed into the same art deco heroic mold—stared out over us all; stone lips unmoved, saying nothing wise. The mouth and eyes of James Dean's bust are open but hollow, with nothing inside. When it got cold and dark and the cops still had not shown up to shoot me dead before that magical bronze door that leads to the secrets of the universe, I figured it was time to get a life. I drove back down the hill, called my buddy, and mentioned that we could catch a cup of coffee after work; I'd take care of the drive home.

In front of a crumbling apartment building on a steep hill above the Hollywood Freeway, I stood on the brake of my car for an hour and a half and carefully explained to my soon-to-be-former reliable buddy that I'd fallen in love—I, a monster. Then I waited quietly for the next scene, in which the object of your affections screams and runs away, making side bets with myself as to whether I'd soon be dodging peasants with torches.

"Oh," said the object of my affections, "okay."

Okay? What kind of answer was "okay?" What was wrong here? Hasn't anybody read the script?

Nothing happened for the longest time. Finally I said, "Um, so what do you want to do now?"

"I'll have to think about it."

"Well, for instance, should I go away now and never come back?"

"No." Puzzled expression. "Why would you do that?"

"Oh," I said suavely, "no reason."

Then I went home and looked frantically through all my monster stories for anything even remotely like what had just happened. No screams, no peasants with torches, no passionate soul-saving embraces, no fuzzy sunrises and violins. Nope, nothing like that here. Wait a minute, here's one:

Once upon a time there was a king. One day he was terribly wounded. Everyone felt awful about it, because what happened to the king was an accident; there wasn't any heroic battle story to tell, or an evil enemy to take revenge on, or a martyr's crown. What was worse, he'd lost his balls in the accident, which was just too embarrassing to mention. Besides, if you talked about this problem, it would come out sounding like a bad joke instead of being really tragic. And it was really tragic, because the wound just wouldn't heal. The king was completely fucked up, but for some reason he wouldn't turn up his toes and die, which was a problem all by itself; even though nobody really wanted him to die, life gets awfully inconvenient when your whole country's got to deal year after year with this same damn fucked-up king. Specialists were called in: doctors and brave knights and learned philosophers. They'd arrive, and everyone would turn out, carrying the dire and terrible instruments of the accident on shrouded poles: the Jockstrap of Mourning, the Sports Car without a Driver, the Gene of Woe. Each specialist would carefully examine the instruments, nod sadly, and diagnose The Problem. Unfortunately, none of these excellent pronouncements seemed to do anything for the king. His only comfort was a prophecy that, someday, a knight would arrive with the power to heal his wound.

One day this strange-looking person shows up, not looking, talking, or dressing anything like a knight. In fact, this knight is a complete Fool. The fool walks unannounced into the room, where everybody's parading around in an elaborate ceremony, with the king wrapped up in a thoughtfully darkened corner, tears running down everybody's faces, and says, "What's everybody upset about? You there, in the corner. What's your problem?"

A hush falls over the room. Everybody's scandalized. The king looks up, and there's something about this idiot—no pennants or lances or warhorse or impressive family crest but something, well, noble—so he screws his courage to the sticking point and says, "I've got no balls, and the wound won't heal. I'm miserable, my kingdom is going completely to hell because I'm sitting around with an unhealed wound, and I don't know what to do."

"Oh," says the fool, "well, okay, then."

And everything gets better after that.

Maybe, I thought, I just told someone about myself, and they believed me. Now why would anyone do that?

A few nights later I get a phone call. The voice on the other end is grieving and riven with panic. It's Dawn.

"Listen, I have to tell you something right now. The other night you said you felt like you were lying to everybody about who you were, even though you didn't want to be lying? You know how you said you were a monster?"

"Yes," I said, steeling myself for the inevitable arrival of peasants with torches.

"But it's not you . . . I mean . . . it's me. I'm the one who's lying. You shouldn't want to be with me. I told Brad that I'd stay with him when I really didn't like him, and then I left."

"It was okay to leave Brad. You thought Brad was an asshole. I don't know why you hooked up with him anyway; what are you upset about?"

The voice on the other end of the phone said, "I didn't want to get involved with anybody I liked. I didn't want to mess things up with a reliable buddy. That's why I don't know what to do about you."

"Look, we like each other. We like to go places together, to spend time together. We can talk to each other. Remember when we went to that old house together, you and me and Paul?"

"Yeah, I liked that."

"You don't want to mess that up. I don't want to mess that up. Nothing has to get messed up. So what's your problem?"

"You don't understand. Everybody thinks I'm just this ugly woman, but I'm not. I'm . . . I'm not . . . I'm not really a woman. I'm sorry. I used to try shaving really close, plucking my eyebrows, wearing makeup and dresses, long hair, but everybody on the bus thought I was a drag queen. So I stopped. But I'm not really a man, either. It started happening when I started growing, I sort of got both. I'm . . . I'm some other kind of thing, I'm something in between."

"Oh," I said happily, "okay."

"Okay? What kind of answer is 'okay'? Don't you understand? I'm a monster."

"Well, okay, then."

"You mean I should leave and never come back again?"

"No, of course not. Why would you do that?"

"Monsters are bad."

"Who told you that?"

"Everybody, everybody knows that. Brad, and his friends, and my folks . . ."

"No, no, monsters are the good guys. Honest."

There was a sniffle from the other end of the phone. "I don't under-stand. I'm at work, I shouldn't even be talking about this . . ."

"Listen to me. I'm going to come get you. We'll go home, and I'll tell you all about it. Brad, and Brenda, and their loser friends, and your folks, and all the people here, it's just like where I was before. They're all just peasants with torches. But you don't have to give a damn what they think, ever again. You sit on the steps outside the front door at Rand, and don't forget to zip up your jacket so you don't get cold. I'll be right there."

"Okay," Dawn said, "I'll be here."

And that's how it was.

Burying Ophelia

About the time I met Brenda, I was interviewed for *Reviving Ophelia*. I'll be the first to admit that, like initiating Brenda into higher levels of Goddess worship, telling women how to raise healthier daughters was not the brightest idea of my life. What can I say? Somebody asked me. I've got fantastic opinions on hydroponic shrimp ranching, too, if somebody would only ask me. I've got a button on my bedside table that says, "I joined AA for the open mike."

One day during a visit to Nebraska, my mother asked me if I wanted to be interviewed.

"Of course," I said. "By the way, what about?"

"I have a colleague who's writing a book about mothers and daughters."

"Oh Lord, not another of those sappy *family* books. Do we get to pose in front of a Norman Rockwell print with matching gingham dresses and a doll that looks just like me?"

"No, no, this will be a very serious book. The author's a clinical psychologist exploring issues in the development of women."

"Well, as long as it's not one of those goddamn *gender* people—men are from Mars, women are from Venus, the writer's from Fozbeen, Planet of Reactionary Pseudoscience."

"Look, you don't have to do it if you don't want to."

"No, really, I'm looking forward to it," I said, rubbing my hands together briskly, mad-scientist style. "It ought to be interesting."

After all, in all those cheerful ads for cake mix and laundry soap, the housewife may hold up the box of Tide, but the last word still comes from the Voice of Mister Science. That a full-grown adult who presumably ought to know better can still see himself as Mister Science had, in my case, a lot to do with Los Angeles.

The most important thing to know about Los Angeles is that there's a man in my hometown who rides around all day on an old Schwinn bicycle, which he thinks is a Peterbilt truck. He's got a little air horn on the handlebars, and as he pedals slowly around town, he'll give a blast on the horn every once in a while, lean out the airspace that corresponds to a driver's side window, and call helpfully, "Look out, lady, truck comin' through" or "C'mon, gimme a lane, guys, I'm behind on my logbook and them strawberries got to get to Cincinnati." In my Nebraska hometown, people who know him will call out, "Hey, Milt, keep 'em rolling" and give him free donuts and coffee. In Los Angeles this man would be dead.

Folks like Milt don't live long in LA. The mean streets of the big city don't kill them. What kills them is there is no community of homeless truck drivers over forty suffering codependent relationships with transportation equipment. You're supposed to have a demographic. If there were five hundred guys just like him, Milt would be fine in LA. If there were a thousand, he could be getting rich running a specialty truck parts store in Burbank for the Peterbilt-Schwinn community.

At the time the author was gathering interviews for *Reviving Ophelia*, I was living in Los Angeles, a man without a clique. In the happy days when Paul and Brenda roamed the malls of Burbank, I saw clearly that the world had no place for folks without a demographic. This was before the Internet, that modern refuge of brains without bodies.

Another thing I noticed living in LA was that it was a lot more like my Nebraska hometown than I'd thought. I've been told that, as the incubation chamber for the American film industry, LA makes itself the mirror of our national convictions. I hope not.

If you see no place for yourself in the world around you, you can just walk away. But the thought of spending my golden years in a shack in Montana laying crush traps for invaders with stacks of old newspapers held little appeal. Call me a social butterfly. The other option I found was objectivity. If you have no place in the world, you can always claim yours is the only unbiased viewpoint. For instance, most of what I'd heard from women about gender seemed—to put it mildly—biased. Working at the LA County Museum, I filled stacks of fifty-pound boxes—cans of old paint, chunks of pitchblende, fiberglass—for basement crews of black guys working through the September heat in dust an inch thick, without masks, doing temporary work at minimum wage. Since I was white and had an employee tag and did not want to spend the rest of my life in the basement, at lunchtime I'd run my head under the sink and go eat with a dozen middle-aged white women with air-conditioned offices and salaried jobs and ranch homes in Encino who talked endlessly about men, those bastards who had all the money and the respect while women busted ass and got the short end. This was basically life in California. I did not develop a high opinion of women's objectivity. It seemed obvious to me that I was a more objective observer of their situation and could teach them a thing or two about women's experience. That my objectivity on this subject was untainted by any bias—like, for instance, actual women's experience—was a point I considered to be entirely in my favor.

Which is how I spent four hours explaining women's experience to the author of *Reviving Ophelia*, without the slightest suspicion she might conclude I was a woman—unless, of course, she was extremely stupid. She was very patient with me.

I decided to subvert her purpose to my own. I'd hammer out a media-friendly sound bite for people like me and sneak it into the book. I'm not sure what I thought my demographic was, but it seemed to be what happened to bright young folks who couldn't work jobs requiring suitable office clothing. These days I would call it poverty. But all I knew at the time was that I was gonna start that Peterbilt-Schwinn place in Burbank, by God, and I was going to do it with my bare vocal cords. As I said, this was before the Internet.

Six months later I was ambushed by the results. The draft of her interview arrived the same week Brenda and Brad both decided I was an ideal leader for Sapphic Initiations.

Our names had been changed to preserve our privacy. But where the hell had "Rachel," this "woman in the pink shirt," come from? What woman? There'd been no woman over there; that was where *I* was sitting. Where were my *small*—not *large*, damn it—stylish glasses, my shocking queer-pink West Hollywood Lycra tank shirt, the hardbody gym-boy physique, the latest I'm-a-surfer-honest-it's-not-hair-gel haircut? A vase full of sparkly flowers? My mother looks like Susan Sontag? And what the hell's this business about "lighting the way for girls like me"? I said *people* like me! This "Rachel" had sprung full-blown from the imagination of the author, I thought furiously, and she was putting my words in her mouth. I literally had no idea why anyone could possibly have represented me in this way, except as the endgame in a literary conspiracy to re-create me in female shape as a palatable message for readers. I was furious at this subverting of my subversion. I fired back a long series of corrections. I told her she was creating a false image of what everything had looked like. The room, the people, me. Me, me, me.

A week after Brenda had tried to use my body for Goddess worship, I was staring for the first time at a picture of what reasonable, intelligent, experienced people saw when they looked at me.

This was when I used the word *transsexual* to describe myself for the first time, in response to the looming danger that I might appear before the world as a revived Ophelia.

But I still used the word as something I was not, because as far as I knew a transsexual was a kind of woman. Everything I had ever seen— from *Geraldo* to the latest from the radical queer press—made the gender of transgender very, very clear. Transgender, like all gender, was about women. Women good and bad, real and fake. I supposed there could be ridiculous women who thought a fake mustache was masculine, a corporate monkey suit was powerful, and wearing them was what made somebody a man. Women had strange fantasies about men. No surprise that transsexuals were women. Being a man is for real.

So I told the author of *Reviving Ophelia* that, though I was not a transsexual, I felt very seriously that I couldn't be responsible for her telling her readers I was a woman. Could she tell them I was something else, perhaps? Oh, and please don't tell my mom.

The author of *Reviving Ophelia* knew a can of worms when she saw one, and she knew her work well enough to remove my interview from the draft of the book. So we laid to rest the ghost of Ophelia, or rather Rachel. I hadn't liked the way Rachel looked sitting in my chair, and by God, I never wanted to see Rachel again. I decided the ideal way to solve that problem was by simply not looking. It's only women, after all, who ever think about being looked at.

Not Coming Out

"Hi, Paul," I said. "Boy, what a beautiful day. Look at those trees. When did everything get so *nice*?"

Paul gave me his best Disapproving Look. "Your mother called," he said.

"What did she have to say?"

"She wanted to know where you were."

"Okay," I said, somewhat confused. "What's the problem?"

"I told her you were out with Dawn." Paul pursed his lips and looked thoughtfully at the ceiling. "Oh, yes, *Dawn*. She seems to be seeing a *lot* of her friend *Dawn* recently. So, Paul, what's *Dawn* like? Is she *nice*?"

"Oh. Psychic Mom Powers."

"She wanted all the gossip."

"Paul, what the hell did you say?"

"Nothing! That's the *problem*. I felt *terrible*. She *trusts me* for all the details; out here I'm her only source. You have no idea what it's like." Paul put his hands on his hips and said sternly, "You have got to tell her about Dawn."

"What about Dawn?"

"Everything."

"That's none of my business. If Dawn wants to tell my mom the story of her life . . ."

"That's not what I meant. All about you, then."

"What about me?"

"You're evading the issue."

"I am not. Just because, um, uh . . ."

"You're madly, passionately in love."

"Uh, yeah, that. Anyway, it doesn't mean anything about either of us. I'm exactly the same person I always was."

"You didn't used to hum."

"Look, Paul, none of this 'I'm a new person!' bullshit. No 'I was incomplete without you!' I was plenty complete already, thank you very much."

"What's wrong with admitting you're soul mates?"

"Paul!"

"Oh, all right, but the next time she calls, don't ask me not to tell her all about it."

Faced with the picture of Paul spinning hordes of pink cotton-candy cherubs all over my carefully polished fuck-you image, to my *mom*, of all people, I sat down and tried to face the problem.

If I told my mother I was in love with Dawn, she would think I was a lesbian. Well, she already thought I was a lesbian. Everybody always thought I was a lesbian. Women seemed to want to give me things, be my friend, help me out, and worship me in a deeply satisfactory recognition of my many superior qualities. Of course, women said I was superior because I had finally achieved freedom from contaminating Maleness. Ugh. I never had sex with women, never had a girlfriend, I didn't even *like* hanging out with women. I even told people I was gay. Nothing I did seemed to have any effect on people's idea that I was a lesbian. I never could figure out why. My mom loved lesbians, which people thought was great for me.

And if I told my mom I was in love, she'd think *Dawn* was a lesbian. If there was anything worse than your mother thinking you were a lesbian, for Chrissakes, it was your mother thinking your lover was one. I mean, what did that say about me? No, we definitely weren't going there.

Of course, as Paul had gently pointed out, the obvious alternative of just not telling my mother anything could easily be stretched out for a few more days. Weeks. Years. The rest of our lives. Having chosen this alternative in his own life, Paul could spot it coming a mile away. No, we definitely weren't going there, either. Losing touch with my mother was about the only thing I could think of that was worse than her thinking Dawn was a lesbian.

Eventually, a brilliant plan struck. Since neither Dawn nor I were lesbians, the *actual issue* was that Mom would think she was the *mother* of a lesbian. Yes, this whole identity business was clearly her problem, not mine. Aha! In a stroke of generosity, I decided to offer my mother the option of maintaining separate but equal universes. I raced down to West Hollywood, purchased a glossy anthology of essays by the mothers of lesbians, and sent it off to her along with a note to make sure, one more time, that she didn't think I was a lesbian. There. I knew she loved books. I didn't open the book, much less read it; I didn't care to know what was inside. She could come out as the mother of a lesbian if she damn well wanted to; that was her life and her business, not mine.

On the hottest July morning in her town, Sarah's mom sprinted over the hot sidewalk to the metal mailbox and pried open the door, pulled out the mailer stuffed behind the Visa bill, and raced back to the house shaking her burnt fingers. The mailer was from Sarah, good news. She pried off the three staples instead of pulling the red tab and discovered inside the glossy book written by a group of mothers. Good. She was a mother. For a long time Sarah and her mom had exchanged interesting books, mostly about science. She put away her manuscripts and read the book. After a while she understood that the only two things these mothers had in common were lesbian daughters and not being writers. The essays were sappy, silly, conventional, and badly written. If Sarah had meant to come out as lesbian to her mom, this book was a bad way to do it. She remembered stories from her own youth in which the parents of her friends told them about sex by leaving a pink or blue pamphlet on the dresser. She'd spent a lot of time telling Sarah about sex. In person. Without metaphor and with diagrams and correct terminology. The fact that Sarah hadn't been interested hadn't affected her mother's diligence at all. Obviously Sarah as an adult didn't think that her mom knew anything at all about lesbians. And worse, Sarah thought her mother would have the same kind of response that these mothers had. Sarah's mom was really pissed off.

So Sarah's mom sat down and began to write a thank you letter in response. She chose a scroll of beautiful laid paper from the going-out-of-business sale of the local printer. Her best ink pen. A big envelope without a clasp, with a glued flap. This is what she wrote:

22 July 1991

Dear Sarah,

Your coming out letter and the gift of the book are important to me in several ways. But I'm angry at the responses of some women in the book (especially the Jewish mom, who is NOT ME or my community of Jewish women. Did you know, for example, that Susan Jacobsen, one of my best friends, who died and was buried as an Orthodox Jew, was gay?) and angry at your assumption that the issues central to lesbian identity are not and have not been (WITHOUT your ever asking ME) central to my own life.

I love YOU and what and who you are. I've cherished and protected you (not always well) as you are and will be and raised and supported your nature since you were conceived. Who and what you are I've been witness to for twenty-six years, one of the major pleasures of my life, and the one that draws my attention most truly, as you—or anyone—can see in my WORK. The complex blend of Sarah always delights and teaches me. You ALWAYS have and ALWAYS will have my total interest and support. You.

I'm sad you won't have (or raise) a child. Your child might have advantages other children don't. But I'm not VERY sad. I hope and expect you'll have contact with some kids along the way. Or not.

I'm sad not to have known your identity as male-identified in a lesbian culture that insists on another configuration these days. I don't believe you won't find companions who are women and can be your friends but I see the problem more clearly now. (I've always known you were male-identified, of course, but not that you were trying to find . . . what? Acceptance among feminists who embrace what you deplore.)

Please remember the circle of stories you bring again and again to my attention: take heart and believe that just as you were born and grew to be Sarah at twenty-six, some other women are having a similar experience now. In LA, perhaps you'll find them. All women of ambition are male-identified in some major ways just as your friend Paul in his most flamboyant-sock mode can be called female-identified.

I hope you'll find women of talent, intelligence, and good humor to love and/or hang out with.

Hilda never sent this letter. Years later we found it in a pile of papers, still sitting on her desk. When she handed it to me, she said she'd meant to write more at the time, but whatever was left unsaid she couldn't find a way to say.

Psychological Considerations

Two worthy citizens of the Land of Fools were talking together.

"Do you know," said the first, "that whenever I read the multiplication tables my head starts to swim?"

"But this is amazing!" shouted the second, "because the very same thing happens to me when I run any distance."

Unable to see any common explanation for the two happenings, they took their experiences to the Very Wisest Man of the Land.

The Very Wisest Man said:

"It is obvious that both numbers and running were invented by an undesirable person, and his influence still subsists in them—therefore shun both!" | IDRIES SHAH, The Magic Monastery

When I was about ten years old, I found a tree on my way to school. It had a big flat branch shaped like a swing, conveniently at swing level for a ten-year old. I was extremely grateful to this tree for providing me with such a friendly seat in a state where climbable trees were few and far between. We became friends, the tree and I. After a while, I noticed the tree had been giving me a nice place to sit every day for months, but I'd never given anything back. Real friends always give each other birthday presents. But when was the tree's birthday? Sometime in the spring, obviously. I put my head against my friend's trunk and listened quietly until the appropriate date presented itself. So, on the morning of the appointed day, my mother found me in the kitchen, mixing up a large bucket of liquefied fish.

"Honey, what are you doing?" she said mildly, through the odor of well-rotted pilchard.

"Oh, I'm taking a birthday present to my friend the tree. It took me a long time to figure out what to get. Regular presents just didn't seem appropriate. I mean, what's a tree going to do with a book or a yo-yo or a chemistry set? It's kind of like when your brother gave your mom a football for her birthday. But then I thought, aha—fertilizer . . ." I trailed off. Mom did not seem proud of my ingenuity. In fact, she was looking at me with the strangest expression, as if I'd done something wrong.

"You know," she said ominously, "that you're playing *make-believe.*"

"It is not make-believe. You know that tree with the funny branch on Valley Road, that's the tree I'm talking about. You must have seen it a million times."

"That isn't what I mean. You know that what you're saying isn't *real*, don't you?"

"I'm not lying," I said, starting to get mad. I hated it when people talked this way. "It's not my fault if you don't notice a real tree."

"But you know trees don't have birthdays, don't you?" By now, my mother's voice had that weird reasonable tone my teachers sometimes got, the voice of a person trying unsuccessfully to pretend they weren't personally upset.

"Yes they do," I said triumphantly. "They're alive, and all living things have to be born sometime."

"But they don't have a *birthday* . . ."

"Well, so what if I don't know whether it's when the root sprouted, or when the first leaf came out, or whatever. I mean, people's birthdays are arbitrary, too. Like this book said the Chinese only celebrate your first birthday when you're already a year old, or we could celebrate when the baby is conceived, but we don't." I waited for my dazzling display of logic to settle the matter.

Mom tried again. "How do you know that today is the tree's birthday?"

"'Cause it told me."

There was a very long pause. During this pause I suddenly realized something was Wrong. Capital W. I don't know if I understood how frightened my mother was. She said, "That's all very entertaining, honey, but you know this is just a story, don't you? You know that stories aren't real. Like the people you said other people can't see; you know they're not *real*, they're *imaginary*. You understand the difference between fantasy and reality? Don't you?"

And I said, "Geez, mom, of course I know. It's just a game. I made it all up, it doesn't mean anything."

I knew somehow it was absolutely crucial that I say this. But even as I said it I knew it was too late, because suspicion still lingered in her eyes when she looked at me.

Soon afterward I was taken to a child psychiatrist. He talked to me for an hour about what's real and what isn't, about how little kids make things up just to get their parents' attention, and how it was about time that I grew up.

On Sunday mornings at that age, I watched a show in which a man in a sober polyester suit talked about Jesus with a sock named Morty. Morty was dressed up as a mouse, with little felt ears. Morty talked in a high, squeaky voice and vibrated like a Chihuahua. The voice came from somewhere in the general vicinity of the man in the polyester suit, whose hair did not move at all. It looked to be made out of hard plastic, in the shape that you see in barbershop windows crowning a blank face, with the words "Men's Haircut" in block printing underneath.

What fascinated me about the show was that I already knew about men in gray suits with plastic hair who talk in the Very Reasonable voice of people who believe that being grown up means not listening at all. These were the people who knew what *real* was. Puppets weren't *real*. Many of the things I believed in weren't *real*. And here was one of them, on television, talking to a sock about Jesus. The sock was talking back, and everything was just fine, and his real reasonable voice was not changing at all. I knew this man could not believe in Morty Mouse. Morty wasn't real, even to me, but he was talking to it anyway. For months I kept watching the show in fascination, trying to figure out what was going on. I think my mother was briefly afraid I was going to become a southern Baptist.

I learned a lot from the man with the sock and the child psychiatrist. I learned *real* is a word that means "whatever the person who's bigger than you are says is true." I learned you can avoid having to ever go to the psychiatrist again if you just never tell anyone anything that matters.

Beyond my tree there was a field. Every spring I used to go there just to breathe an air so thick with flowers that the scent of each species was a voice speaking; each breath of all of them together slid across my tongue like language. I could taste what bees tasted. When my bike and I drove down the high hill by that field at a million miles an hour, I could stretch my hands out and feel what made birds fly moving underneath my fingers. In these moments there was no more reason for anything. No cake, no ice cream, no movies, no toys, no presents, not even books, nothing better than this. This was one of many things I never told anyone. By the time I found out it's also what happens when you fly in a front flip off somebody's shoulders, I was thirty-eight and pounding my head against the wall because it had been so many years since I remembered how to trust myself or anybody else that much.

One of the things my mother never told anyone was why her brother was dead. He was the family genius, the only son who'd flown off to war, walked into Buchenwald with a rifle when he was sixteen, and come home alive to become a professor of physics. When he was forty, he killed himself with a rifle after his release from a mental hospital. Since schizophrenia doesn't usually show up for the first time at forty and then disappear, I assume he had what they used to call hysteria, then shell shock, then Vietnam syndrome, then post-traumatic stress disorder. But my uncle has been dead since the sixties and no one really knows. The popular science books from the days of my mother's childhood have impressive-looking charts of family histories: "Woman from insane family, married artist with deviant tendencies, son criminal, daughter insane. Children sterilized for the public good." "Insane, violin virtuoso, married woman of high IQ, one son deviant, one son a suicide, daughter nervous, with artistic temperament. Sterilization recommended."

My mother makes magazines and books. When I was growing up I used to watch her bring home piles of ordinary envelopes. Later she'd bring home sheaves of long paper she called *galleys*, a word I knew as the bottom of a ship, where the hidden slaves who powered the boat would row. Then, one day, she'd come home exhausted and triumphant, with a real book in her hands. She made real books out of nothing, out of poems, the kinds of words people never told anyone.

My father taught English literature at the university. I never saw him teach, but I remember him saying he liked Jane Austen. When I went off to college, my favorite teacher, David Hadas, assigned us a Jane Austen novel. It was the most boring book any of us had ever tried to stay awake through. One beautiful spring day when nobody wanted to be there, our teacher walked into class without a word, threw open all the windows, opened the book, and began to read. He read out loud, the way we hadn't been read to since we were children; his voice sank into confidential asides, bounced through dippy teenage words of wisdom, rose in breathless trills of outraged propriety. The dead words rose up and took on flesh. We grinned, we winced, we roared with laughter. I think this was the first time I realized what teaching really was; that my father, like my mother, made stories real for a living. I wish I had been able to watch him teach.

As a kid, I knew my mother was Jewish, and my father was Episcopalian. Episcopalian was a nice long word, but I had no idea what it might mean. I thought it might be related to the word "Caucasian," which had a similar sound. I knew "Jewish" was an ethnic group that involved having big noses (except for me), being killed by Nazis (except for me), and eating bagels. I liked bagels. Nobody else in my school knew what a bagel was. I told them proudly that it was an ethnic foodstuff. My mother carefully explained our Christmas trees were a *custom*, not a *religious object*, so I knew the Hanukkah candles were a custom, too. The only trouble with the candles was that my brother always got to light them, because the custom was the eldest son always lights the Hanukkah candles. When I was grown, my mother told me Hanukkah candles are actually always lit by the eldest daughter. She said she'd made the other story up because she thought my brother ought to have something important to do around the house. To this day, I've got no idea whether the lighting is supposed to be done by a son or a daughter, which is probably just as well. My mom's like that. For any situation, she usually has several versions available.

My dad had been a professor in Boston. Mom took his English class and fell in love with his teaching. When my mother married my dad, her family had a fit. I had a vague understanding of the problem; the word "Episcopalian" kind of sounded like "miscegenation," a word I'd learned from old science books as a term for what happens when people from two different ethnic groups get married. The old science books explained miscegenation leads to inherited antisocial behavior and insanity. I understood this explanation meant that my family was one of those things bigger people didn't believe in. Eventually, the university in Boston decided Dad wasn't suitable for tenure and let him go, which is why I grew up in Nebraska where nobody knew what a bagel was.

My dad came from a distant land called The South, where I thought Nazis hung people they didn't believe in from telephone poles. He'd escaped because of a man from a university. This man—a crippled man, my dad once said, who'd gotten out of their hometown and become a teacher—had driven back in a big black car, found my dad working at the gas station, and given him some kind of test. Dad took the test while the man waited, and after a while the man came back with an admission letter and a scholarship. That's how my dad went to college. Several scholarships later, he got a PhD and became a teacher. After Boston he become a professor in Nebraska. Later my dad helped me win a scholarship, too, so I could get out of Nebraska. My dad was very proud of me, but I never got a PhD. Several scholarships later, my fellow graduate students were getting married, setting office hours, and wearing suitable office clothing. Eventually, the university decided I wasn't suitable for the academic life and let me go.

In the scheme of things, I knew I was Jewish because of my mother. This idea made sense; it was kind of like a custody arrangement. I had never seen my mother go to temple or my father attend church; there was no cross in my father's house and no mezuzah on our door. It never occurred to me that things could be any other way. I'd never seen a Jewish temple, but I knew churches were the buildings with beautiful windows where the Art History was kept. And I knew faith as an excuse for swastikas painted on my high school and people shot dead in small Nebraska towns.

One of the stories my mother didn't tell me was that my parents married on the condition they wouldn't have children unless they raised them without religion of any kind. Closing the door on the issue was the only way they could find to keep two families with separate but equal convictions together.

Growing up, I thought joy and pain, right and wrong, real and unreal were concepts either for physics or psychiatry. You could choose whichever system of belief you preferred—the sciences or the humanities. I chose science, which seemed happily unmired in the messy business of humanity. I never knew there were thoughtful, knowledgeable people who believed in things you couldn't see, that the academic system and the scientific method were not the only tools to understand experience. My parents had no way to know I could fall through different cracks than the ones that threatened them.

The man my mother chose to grow old with comes from a fundamentalist Christian family. Every Christmas Eve we used to drive to the tiny Nebraska town where his parents lived to celebrate the holiday. There'd be a potluck dinner—potato casserole with french-fried onions, Jell-O with minimarshmallows—then a few presents, so as not to distract attention from the true meaning of the holiday, which involved family Bible reading and interpretation with the help of essays by Billy Graham. Dale's family is a group of decent, thoughtful, loving people who welcomed us into their home. Years ago I stopped riding along. I'm enough of a Nebraskan to have spared them introduction to the family I've made for myself. No point in making trouble. My two families, Nebraska and the West Coast, like my mother's and my father's, span a distance I fall between. The bridge of my body seems only wide enough to carry one person, and I'm not always sure about that. I'm also enough of a Nebraskan to refuse to be ashamed of either of my families, so I stayed away from Nebraska. Then there was the little gap occasioned by the problem of pronouns, then surgery. A couple more years for forgetting. Some things you don't forget. So one Christmas Eve I went back to Norfolk as if I were a single man, my Nebraska family's son; we drove past hundreds of farmhouses where lovely, plastic stars shine from the top of each abandoned windmill. The family there welcomed me into their home again. Nobody said a word against me. Nobody said a word about what had happened.

The same little vinyl tree sat against the wall, decorated with pastel cherubs in pajamas, paper tinsel, a cross made of olive wood from the Holy Land. Dale's father was a jeweler, as I've been; one Christmas Eve he proudly showed me the intricate cutwork of the cross. When I was a zookeeper he told me softly how he'd always wanted to see the Holy Land: its deserts and mountains, the scents of its herbs, the wild camels racing. He'd never seen an olive tree. I tried to tell him how they grew in California; the bright leaves' flicker dark and silver in the sunlight, their intense twisted reach upward, the ground around sprayed dark and pungent by their lovely, bitter fruit. That night he told me how he'd never left Nebraska, except for the war, how he was young and stationed in Hawaii and the first time he saw pineapples growing he thought a destroyer had brought

73

him to Paradise. How good everything smelled. He made the wedding rings for my brother and his wife, for my mother and his son. I made my own. I'm from Nebraska. What I can't make myself I do without.

The Nebraska relatives tape up Christmas cards on the wall behind their tree. That year I scanned them idly. One was a photo portrait of at least fifty people. Curious about what family could have so many members, I opened the card. "Greetings and God's love to our members," it said, "from Focus on the Family." Focus on the Family is a political action group dedicated to the eradication of homosexuals and other related deviants. Each year in the state where I live, they use their membership fees to support ballot measures to make it illegal for me to have sex-change surgery, get married, raise a child, rent an apartment, do service work, teach, or have contact with children. I didn't say a word against them. I didn't say a word about what had happened.

Nebraska has a fragile peace, maintained by silence. When that family's firstborn son came to them at seventeen to say his dream was to play the rock-and-roll guitar, they cast him out as a sinner. Or so my mother says, who married him. There have been a lot of years for forgetting since then, and nobody who was there would ever say a word about what had happened. My mother told me Dale's father eventually told him he was wrong about the casting out, and he was sorry.

My mother told me Dale's story the way she told me my dad's stories, my stepfather's stories, all the family stories I ever knew. In Nebraska guys don't talk much. I never would ask, either, the way I'd never bring a gay lover to Norfolk at Christmas, or leave him behind me like something shameful, or tell anybody anything personal, like writing all these stories down. When my mom goes on about poetry, or my brother's quoting Shakespeare again, or I start deconstructing Charlie Chaplin, the former rock-and-roll guitarist sometimes turns to us and says, "Oh, that's just somethin' somebody made up."

I watch the muscles in his cheeks twitch from the pressure as his lips turn: up, down. Up, down, up, down, up.

When I was seventeen I told my mother I wanted some female organs removed. Eventually, we settled on the agreement that she wouldn't call the police to have me removed back to Nebraska by force so long as I went to see a mental health counselor. Since I figured my mother's high dudgeon was worse than any mental health counselor could possibly be, I arrived at my first therapy session and reluctantly described my situation to a taupe-haired young man who responded with acute confusion. He stared at me with his mouth hanging open for several minutes.

Finally he remembered what the university paid him for, rearticulated his jaw, and said, "What would a nice young girl like you want to mess herself up like that for?"

"Oh," I said casually, "never mind. I made it all up. It doesn't mean anything."

The saving grace of this encounter was that student health paid for only ten sessions. So, once a week, I'd nip down to the health service, the taupe young man would anxiously inquire into my mental state, and I'd tell him I was somewhat concerned about my tendency to be late to class, or that I could use some tips on final-exam stress management. As the last session approached, his confusion threatened to become terminal.

I'd say, "I'm sorry I'm so late. As you can tell, I've still got some time-management problems to deal with."

He'd say, "Do you ever receive instructions from inanimate objects?"

In my high school geometry class, Miss Buell once told us that on an infinite plane, diverging lines will continue to separate forever. Luckily, ten sessions isn't forever. I stared at the counselor.

"Like, say, a radio," he said. "Do you listen to the radio a lot?"

"Yes, I do. In fact," I said, struggling for convergence, "that's one of the reasons I'm late so much. I start listening to something special and forget about what I'm supposed to be doing."

"Something *special*," he said, brightening visibly. "Do you listen to voices on the radio?"

"Well, I hate opera, but otherwise, yeah, I'm pretty much into vocal music."

"Do they ever tell you to do things? Like, say, hurt yourself or other people?"

There it was, the Weird Reasonable Tone of Voice. Nature's warning sign.

"No," I said carefully, "I've never been fond of heavy metal. I don't like any of those bands with the makeup and the satanic lyrics at all."

I didn't grow up in Nebraska for nothing. Unfortunately, the taupe-haired young man didn't seem to be from Nebraska. He frowned in a Concerned Fashion.

"Makeup. I don't think I mentioned makeup. Is makeup something you have strong feelings about? How about satanism?"

"No, not really." I quickly decided not to tell him about the sparkly gray eye shadow vampire makeup and the werewolf prosthesis I once constructed out of first-aid gauze and hair clippings. He looked unconvinced. "I like Mozart's operas," I added helpfully.

"Do the voices continue even after you turn the radio off?"

"No. My radio works just fine." Right now, my radio was coming in loud and clear. It said, Danger, Will Robinson. Danger.

"You know that you're a perfectly healthy, lovely young woman. You know that what you want would only be hurting yourself, don't you?"

"Yeah, it was a stupid idea. I've forgotten all about it."

"I'm glad to hear that. But why would you want to hurt yourself?"

"I don't want to hurt myself."

"But why *did* you want to hurt yourself?"

"I never wanted to hurt myself."

"Have there been other times you've wanted to hurt yourself?"

"Look," I said, articulating the words slowly and clearly, "I don't want to hurt myself. I want to help myself. Maybe it was a stupid idea, but I only wanted to help myself."

I waited anxiously for any evidence that this concept had penetrated his hair.

"Have you ever considered suicide?" the counselor asked.

When he first started asking me if I'd gotten the surgery idea from my household pets, or maybe the invisible conspiracy from Venus, I started doing a little checking up on my counselor. My investigation consisted of asking friends at the dormitory. In spite of this approach, I came up with two useful pieces of information. One was that my ordeal was limited to ten sessions, *unless the health service could determine you needed intensive therapy, in which case you could be sent to a mental institution.* The other bit of information came to me by sheer chance. When I told one friend I had a therapist who seemed to be manifesting fixed delusions, she took me aside. It turned out she had survived a bout of anorexia and knew something about the mental health system.

She said, "Never tell him you've thought about suicide. Ever. Never tell him you've thought about hurting anybody, not even if it was the third grade teacher who made fun of your macaroni project."

"Why?"

"Counselors try to get you to talk about feeling bad. Some counselors can be really subtle about working you around into admitting you've thought about dying."

"But everybody's felt like picking up a gun sometime, or had a really bad day and wished the ceiling would fall on them, or whatever. It's not like actually planning to blow your brains out."

"Maybe everybody feels it, but if you admit it to a counselor, they can say you're a danger to yourself or others. They can put you in an institution."

"I wouldn't sign the papers."

Suddenly I realized I wasn't sure whether my mother could have me committed against my will. Six weeks before I wouldn't even have raised my voice to someone who suggested the possibility. It would have been as ridiculous as suggesting she'd threaten to have me kidnapped by the police, which is what happened when I'd told her about my plan to have some female organs removed.

My mother and I yelled a lot as I grew up; keen minds often sharpen themselves on each other. Fighting was a kind of communication I'd learned to trust. It let you know exactly where the other person stood. Before the fighting started, in the senseless tangle of trying to "talk about it," I'd asked my mother why she wouldn't give the approval that could let her minor child have surgery. She told me she was doing what she'd always done: protecting me as the mother crocodiles and tigers she wept over on the nature specials protected their young. She was protecting my future self—a lovely, free woman whose greatest moment in life would be to bear witness to an everyday miracle: creation, life rising up and taking flesh out of her own body.

When the fighting began, my friend Paul was cast as the villain, an Evil Man. My dangerous desires were his fault, and she would stop at nothing to protect her young. I leapt into the fray with joyous abandon. Did she think she'd raised a submissive little family-values wife, who'd let the first guy that came along decide what to do with my body? No, she admitted, that didn't sound like me. Perhaps, she said carefully, I was having a hard time, a little mental problem.

Having triumphantly wrestled the specter of Paul as Great White Hunter to the dust, I raised my dripping jaws to discover I was the one my mother was now looking at. Crocodiles and tigers defend their young to the death. I sat in the dormitory's cheery blue vinyl institutional chair and watched little pieces of my world flake off and fall away. Could my mother sign commitment papers? Would she?

"That's the whole point," said my friend. "If a psychiatrist decides you're a danger to yourself, what your *mom* thinks doesn't matter. They don't need anybody's permission. Mr. Taupe Hair can just have you hauled off in the middle of the night."

Suddenly I realized "insane" means "believing in things that aren't real." And I remembered: *the bigger people get to decide what real is.* Mom's bigger than me, psychiatry is bigger than Mom. And we weren't playing kids' games anymore; this time when a psychiatrist doesn't believe me, they're not going to slap my hand and tell me it's time to grow up.

I said, "Are you positive?"

She said, "It happened to my best friend. She made some joke about a gun at school, and she was in the locked ward that night. It's not even about whether they think you need help. A lot of mental hospitals make their money by filling the beds and billing the parents."

"No," I told Mr. Taupe Hair. "I've never, ever thought about killing myself. I've never, ever wanted to hurt anyone else. I love my life."

At the end of this last session, he said, "Is there anything else that's bothering you? Anything you want to bring up? Anything you haven't said?"

"Nope."

He sat for a minute in silence. "If you feel you need more help, you know we can arrange it," he said, helpfully.

"No, no, that's fine. I'm fine."

"And if you come in at another time, your ten sessions start all over again."

"That's great," I said. "Just fine."

Finally, reluctantly, sadly, he looked at his watch.

"I guess that's all, folks," I said. I stood up. I'd taken the precaution of watching *The Great Escape* and had my route planned if he tried to stop me. I figured I could probably tackle him, get through the door, and steal a motorcycle before the SS arrived with the straitjacket. He didn't try to stop me. After I walked through that door to freedom in the guise of a perfectly healthy, lovely young woman (artfully sewn from blanket ticking and dyed with boot polish), he stood in the doorway and called after me: "Whenever you have a problem, think of me. If you ever get into any trouble, we'll always be here, waiting for you. You can always come back."

Fat chance, taupe-boy. Can't catch me.

But I did exactly what he said. I remembered. For years, whenever I had a problem, I thought of him. I attributed my escape entirely to lucky chance. Of course, if my parents had been worse than my mental health counselor, I might now be attributing my escape from horrific abuse to psychiatry. As it was, I had a responsible, loving, somewhat confused family who trusted in the mental health professions and a lousy counselor, so it would be twelve years before I ever told anyone my little problem again.

What shattered when I was seventeen was my happy assumption that I was something bigger people believed in.

I think my mother must have emerged from her brother's suicide holding two convictions found under the wreckage. One was that when I was in trouble I could always count on her, my blood, my family. The other was that if I had a problem, something personal and beyond the bounds of reason, I must quickly find a mental health professional. The small-town policeman of the soul would show me my way home.

The words that struck me were the only ones both my mother and the counselor had used: they wanted *to protect me from myself.* Abruptly up against the wall, I saw my family and society at large united only in the belief that me and myself were two different people engaged in a fight to the death. The shape of my condition would be war, a world war between myself and the image of me. The choice I would be left with was whether to make myself the enemy. I chose to side with myself and find my enemies in the world that saw me.

I saw people dedicate themselves to a particular vision of war, a battle between men and women. For years I watched this battle mirrored in every mental health professional I spoke to, on every date I went on, and in every face I met. Whatever else they knew or didn't know about me, people were sure of three things. First, that I was deeply involved in the gender wars. Second, that my truest, deepest self was the image they saw, a woman. And third, that any fight between a man and a woman—especially a pretty young woman with porcelain skin—must be between a dangerous sexual aggressor and his blameless, possibly helpless victim. If I flourished, I had done the impossible—triumphed over Men. If I floundered, the Man was to blame. My role was to be confessor and confidante of the terrible and secret fears people had about myself—the man, the evil Man, oppressor, rapist, killer. Like every other war, this one wouldn't end without blood and sweat and tears and scars, enough for everyone.

Luckily for me, there are assorted Other Forms of Counseling, unrelated to the formally defined Mental Health Professions demanded by university health services. I owe the fact that I didn't spend my twenties laying tiger traps for wandering therapists to one of these, a discipline called Neuro-Linguistic Programming. NLP counselors, like many in the Other category, have the wonderful combination of no social authority at all and a very impressive scientific-sounding name to attract millions of dollars in free-floating corporate seminar money. While I was studying the history of science, my mother went to an NLP counselor to overcome her fear of public speaking. He taught her an Advanced Neural Reprogramming Technique: once a week and before any public speaking engagement, she would imagine the crowd of imposing gray-headed academic gentlemen sitting in the audience without any clothes on. My faith in mental health assistance was restored.

So the next time I began to have a vague sense of choking on my limits, I found myself a guy with a cheap office and no sign of a medical degree.

"So," he said, "what seems to be the problem?"

"Oh, I don't know. I'm okay, even happy most of the time, but I just can't seem to get what I want most in life. It makes me depressed. Not like I've ever thought about suicide or anything."

"Okay," he said. "I believe you. So what do you want most in life?"

"Umm, uh, I dunno. Well, I live in this condemned building, and my job hardly pays minimum wage, and I just thought if I could get a little ahead, then . . ." I trailed off.

"Any chance you could get a raise?"

"Nah. They'd give it to me if they could, but the museum's got no money, and we're losing some more funding next year."

"Okay. Would you want to quit your job and find one with better pay?"

"No, I really love my job, it's the best I could ever imagine, and there aren't any jobs in this town with decent pay, except for corporate work, and I can't do that kind of stuff, I mean, the clothes and everything, and I wouldn't want to anyway."

"So what do you want to do?"

"You know what I think the problem really is? I mean, my situation isn't really bad. I think I've got seasonal depression."

"Could be. It's not uncommon this far north. I'll tell you what. Why don't you keep a journal of how you feel each day and correlate it with the weather. Come back and see me next week, and we'll have some more information to go on."

I returned a week later.

"So how've you been?"

"Oh, up and down. Down mostly."

"That's a strike against the seasonal depression theory. It's been sunny all week."

"Look, I'm sure that's what it is. My workspace doesn't have any windows, so I never get enough light."

"Can you move your workspace to an area with windows?"

"No." I was starting to get irritated. He acted like he was accusing me of something, even though I wasn't lying. "Look, I work in a lab environment. Depression runs in my family, there's nothing I can do about it."

"Well, then, let's talk about how you feel."

"Well, I feel like shit, but that doesn't mean anything. There's nothing I can do about it, so it doesn't mean anything."

"It certainly means something. It means you feel bad, and we can look at different approaches to help you feel better."

"Nothing's going to make me feel better. I've got a chemical imbalance. How I feel about it doesn't make one goddamn bit of difference, because there's nothing I can do about it."

He gave me a hard look. "How do you know?"

I was taken aback. As usual when I didn't know what to say, I got mad.

"You think if there was something I could do about it, I wouldn't have done it by now? You think I *enjoy* being like this?"

"Look, suppose you're right. Suppose 99 percent of your problem is genetic, or it's hormones, or whatever. That still leaves 1 percent of your problem you can do something about. You do something about that 1 percent, and you've taken some control of the situation. You're that much better off than you were before."

"Oh, boy, 1 percent. I'm excited."

"Well, 1 percent is better than nothing. It could be you can do something about 1 percent of your problem, or 10 percent, or 99 percent. You won't find out unless you make the effort. Your choice."

I walked out of his scruffy office after this session, furious at my inability to make him see the hopelessness of my situation. Not horrible, not intolerable, just hopeless. Hopeless, hopeless, hopeless. I never went back. I never asked him how you measure some unknown, improbable benefit against the pain of hope.

Soon afterward I decided to move to Los Angeles. Nobody tells me I'm not in there fighting, by God.

Unfortunately, Natural History is part of the culture biz, which was on the skids in Los Angeles. I had a quick introduction to life outside the ivory tower. After a couple of years I was paying my rent selling jewelry at Renaissance faires, which are Southern California's answer to the culture biz. My time was equally divided between work and leisure, both of which had a uniform code. The uniform code at work encompassed costume options from millennia of world history, requiring only codpieces and abundant facial hair for men and, for the women, conversion of the breasts into a quivering, gravity-defying tower of exposed flesh. The uniform code at leisure was West Hollywood Gym Clone. Needless to say, I fit right in.

I can't say whether the last straw was the growing disapproval of my customers for my fantasy office attire or the Saturday nights spent standing in front of the air vent outside the Melrose Baths, watching beautiful men my own age, wasted and miserable, tricking each other in the homey scent of warm clean laundry. Anyway, I ended up taking another run at the mental health professions, with the idea of discussing my vocation in the future. Counseling options in my income bracket were limited to guinea-pigging for the psychiatric social work interns at USC, who couldn't be licensed without accumulating a number of practice hours. If you're poor, your medicine, dental work, and mental health care are done by students for practice, if you're lucky enough to have a teaching school around. Otherwise you don't get any. It's a factor in this story that might be worth considering.

I arrived at my appointment in the friendly armed compound that is the University of Southern California and was directed to the basement of a nearby building. After filling out six pages of medical history on a little plastic clipboard, I strolled down the hall for my intake interview. Behind the door was not a psychiatrist's office or even a corporate NLP seminar. Behind that innocuous door was a room roughly the size of a small auditorium, whose walls soared upward, featureless except for a ring of mirrored black plate glass dimly visible in the darkness above my head, fifty feet of state-trooper sunglasses cleverly disguised as windows. The only light came from single bulbs suspended above solitary desks on the huge expanse of empty concrete floor and from the tiny scarlet eyes of surveillance cameras. "Oh," I thought. "I'm inside a Cylon." I turned over the last page pinned to my nice plastic clipboard to find a release form. I understood that I might or might not be being observed for educational or other purposes, by person or persons who would remain unknown to me. I understood my activities might be videotaped, my conversation recorded, for purpose or purposes that would not be revealed to me. I waived any rights to my image and voice. I had no objection. If I had an objection, I must leave now. If I stayed, the university would not be liable for any damages. I would not attempt to look at the windows. Underneath was a space where I signed my name. Then I sat down on one of the two empty chairs on either side of the nice office desk and waited for the smiling Nazi with a dentist's drill to appear out of the gloom.

After a few minutes she walked in, carrying a thick manila folder. My counselor was wearing a complete suit of baby-pink fleece. She had matching sweatpants and sweatshirt with a delicate white lace collar, and white little-girl Keds sneakers. Somewhere, with great ingenuity, she had found a little pair of matching white lace bobby socks. She was blond and blue-eyed, painted in the sheer and natural makeup colors of a baby doll, and apparently nineteen years old. She sat down, raised the manila folder in her best brisk office manner, and turned to me with a dazzling smile.

"Now, what seems to be the problem?" she asked.

As she raised the folder, I observed she was wearing a complete set of Lee Press On Nails, French Manicure. I looked at the perfect white plastic half-moons at the tip of each tapered finger. Clearly, I had made an error. I was in a Terry Gilliam movie.

"Oh, well," I said. "Never mind."

Actually, I made it through the entire session. We talked a little about my vocation.

"Well, the first question we always ask in career planning is what job have you had that made you the happiest?"

"My job as a preparator. No question."

Her unlined brow sent forth the brave suggestion of a wrinkle. "A preparator? What's that?"

"It's a position in natural history museums."

"Oh." Dazzling smile. "Well, what did you do?"

"I cut up dead animals, mostly. Local wildlife, but also exotics, you know, giant antelope, tigers, stuff like that. Did a twelve-foot boa constrictor once. Loved that job."

She struggled gamely through the rest of the session without her dazzling smile.

For a moment she considered my vocational information. Then she said, "Do you hear voices?"

"Nope."

"Have you ever thought about hurting anyone?"

I gave her my very best dazzling smile. "Never."

"Have you ever considered suicide?"

"Nope. I love my life."

At one point she mentioned I seemed a little resistant, even hostile, to the idea of her advising me. Knowing perfectly well what was the problem, I told her she was a little young for my issues. Which was perfectly true; discussing them with her seemed rather like discussing fucking with an eight-year-old—certainly a lousy idea, and probably a felony in Mississippi. I wasn't stupid. She couldn't catch me.

In retrospect, I think I may have been a subject of one of those psychology experiments where the whole thing is a setup and subjects are unknowingly recruited to see how they respond. Somebody up there past the black glass windows was tweaking coincidence, at any rate; it was all too perfect. By the time I got out, my rage had evaporated. I drove home pounding on the steering wheel, weak with laughter. For the first time in my entire life I realized my situation was funny.

No mental health professional ever asked me if I might be transsexual. I never heard one mention the words "transsexual," "transgendered," "sexual reassignment," or "gender identity." I came across the concept of transsexualism by the time-honored method of freaks; I moved to the big city and hung out in what used to be called the bohemian district, is currently called the gay community, and will probably get another name just as soon as Socially Acceptable Homosexuals finish distinguishing themselves from the queers. From watching the queers, I knew enough about drag queens to know that some of them had surgery so they could be women.

I only learned transsexual men existed because I had the flu. Bored out of my skull at two in the afternoon, I channel surfed into an image. It was the poor man's alternative to the mental health professions—though it's now called *Jerry Springer*, in my day it was *Geraldo*. What I saw was a woman in a three-piece suit and a plastic Men's Haircut, shielding her crotch with her hands as she trembled with tension and spoke in a high squeaky voice about how nobody took her manhood seriously. This was my worst nightmare. It was like driving past a car accident and watching the paramedics pull a mangled body from the wreckage that once looked just like you. Underneath this image, in glowing letters, was the word "TRANSSEXUAL."

What I didn't know then is how carefully images of transsexual bodies are edited out of existence. The producers of these shows are very careful to choose only people who can be easily identified by any casual observer as something *not like us*. Since transsexual men who've had surgery and hormone therapy are indistinguishable from nontranssexual men, the producers were reduced to finding people who, for some reason, lived as men without either surgery or hormones. Not surprisingly, they were defensive, frightened, angry, and looked and sounded just like women. Not surprisingly, I assumed this was all a transsexual man could be; this is, after all, the impression the program was designed to produce—*We're freaks, and we're unhappy, not like you.*

Though the second thing I discovered about transsexual men was that I must not be one, the first thing I knew now, however, was that they existed. This was at least a starting point for an investigation. So off I went to the one part of West Hollywood the Socially Acceptable Homosexuals avoided: the ramshackle community center where the hustlers and the freaks hung out. Sure enough, they had a support group for transsexuals. Hot damn. I signed up.

When I walked into that room I had no idea what I would find, but I was desperate with anticipation. Ranged around the table was a textbook series of female stereotypes: Country Crafts Girl, Church Basement Lady, Business Bitch, Tasteful WASP Woman. They all looked like men pretending to be everything I knew women were fighting against. I went in and sat down anyway, staring around at the panoply of walking stereotypes.

What I didn't bother to figure into my righteous indignation was that these were women who had only recently mustered the courage to walk down the street, and found the whole world responding to a man in a dress. A stereotype is a kind of camouflage; the eye finds what it expects to find, and passes over details. At the time, I didn't understand the difference between meeting someone else's expectations and meeting your own. My survival had always depended on ignoring everyone else's expectations, regardless of the consequences. Back then I didn't want to think about how high the price in consequences can be. Back then I didn't know how often, for such women, the price of believing in truth without consequences might be a knife in the belly or a bullet in the head.

Two of the people here did look different. One of them was a gorgeous woman with a badass rock-and-roll haircut; I wondered what the hell she was doing here. Maybe she was somebody's girlfriend, I thought. That would be a hell of a shock. The meeting came to order, and she opened her mouth and spoke.

"Everywhere I go," she said, "I'm terrified somebody's going to find out."

Find out? Find out what?

Slowly, painfully, I realized she, too, was transsexual. Nobody would ever have known.

"I could lose my job. My landlord's an old conservative. I'm sure he'd evict me. I play in an all-girl band . . ."

And I thought, honey, if you told 'em, they wouldn't believe you. What the hell are you worried about?

But somewhere deeper down I thought, if this is it, if this is the best it can possibly get—still standing paralyzed in front of the goddamn closet for hours every morning, still living in the prison of fear for what people will see when they look at you—then what the hell's the point?

I kept going to meetings anyway. The other odd woman out kept me coming back. She wasn't young or pretty, and she wasn't playing a stereotype. There was an ease about her that made her tall, spare body and her weathered face graceful, open, as natural as Norwegian ranch women in Cherry County, cow moose, the tiny flowers of cottonwood trees. Whatever she was, she was herself. She ran the meetings.

"Who are you with?" I asked her. "Is there a group, a society you represent?"

She laughed. "I'm the lonely lesbian of the Central Valley. I drive into town on weekends to do these groups. None of the social services people want to put money into this stuff, honey. There's just me, myself, and I, and the need. And what you need is to talk to a transsexual man. I wish Ian were here. He shows up sometimes; keep on coming, maybe he'll be here."

"What does he look like?"

"He's about medium height, brown hair, bald on top . . ."

"Bald?" I thought, God, shaving a bald spot in. That's desperation.

She laughed again. "He's got muscles like a bodybuilder, too. He's very handsome. I just wish he were here, or that he came by more often."

Each time, I walked in hoping to see a man, or at least the closest you could get among transsexuals. One night I finally saw one—tall, and so beautiful it hit me between the ribs like a fist. It never occurred to me that someone who looked like that could be a transsexual man; it was enough, in that moment, that a man could even *be* here, in the gender room. He opened his mouth and spoke.

"I know it's unlikely, I know what I look like. I've accepted what's realistic, and the limits of what I am and what I can be. But I want to be beautiful."

Oh, but you are beautiful.

"I want to be a beautiful little girl."

Drumroll, fist in the ribs.

That night I argued with the lonely lesbian of the Central Valley. "Why?" I asked. "I've got to do something about my physical problems, but why does it have to be like this: all these stereotypes, this misery, this bullshit about fitting in? All this stuff about how we've got to look normal, be John Wayne or little Japanese girls. I know you think it's bullshit, too. Why can't we make someplace in between, and just be there together? Why can't we do whatever we want? Why can't we just be *people*?"

She looked at me sadly. "Honey, if I had my choice, I'd be a Doberman pinscher. I think they're the most beautiful things in the world. But we're human beings and we come in two kinds. You don't get to choose but one or the other."

"Why the hell not? There's all kinds of people out there, dwarves and people with no legs and Siamese twins."

"Because every morning you get up and walk down the street, and people will look at you and say, 'There's a boy,' or 'There's a girl.'"

"Well, what if that weren't the only option? What if you were something in between?"

"If they can't decide which one you are, they get too uncomfortable to look at you or talk to you at all. That's a lonely way to live, sweetheart, and people don't like to think about it. No matter what you do, most of the time they're going to look at you and pick one or the other, and you've got to decide which one you want to live with."

Briefly, I imagined my options. They could say I was a girl, or I could do some things to make myself look less feminine and then they wouldn't be sure and it would depend on how I was dressed, and I'd have to spend the rest of my life agonizing about what kind of dressing and walking and talking and breathing was manly enough to convince people I really counted as a man. Back to the closet again.

"I don't give a damn about what other people think. I'm not going to do anything to myself for their sake."

She shook her head. "Oh, honey, I don't have the time. I've got fifteen people here tonight who need my help and know what they want. That's all it is. Sooner or later you have to decide what *you* want."

She turned back to the chalkboard, where the meeting topic said "Electrolysis." For fifteen minutes I listened to the transsexuals talk about how to eliminate unwanted facial hair. Then I walked away and never went back. I didn't know what I wanted, but I knew eliminating unwanted facial hair wasn't it.

She'd given me a thick stack of copies she'd made that said "Resource Guide." I went through it, looking for surgeons. There weren't any; she'd said something about rules that meant she'd had to include addresses and phone numbers for mental health counselors instead. So I looked up Mental Health Resources. There were books on meditation and information on the group I'd just left and a couple of phone numbers for "sympathetic counselors." I called the only one who wasn't a woman, a group practice in a liberal part of town.

"I'm sorry," said the nice voice on the other end of the phone, "that counselor is no longer in practice with us. No, we don't have a number for him, but a colleague of his did take over his practice. Shall I make you an appointment for you with him?"

I hesitated for a moment, unsure.

"Perhaps you'd prefer to see a woman?" said the nice woman's voice on the other end of the phone. "Many of our female clients are more comfortable with female counselors, and we'd be happy to do that for you."

"No, that's fine." I said. "Make me an appointment with the guy." And I thought, what the hell, I'll just walk in, tell him I'm a transsexual, and ask for referrals. If he'd have me locked up for talking about surgery, he wouldn't be in the resource guide. What have I got to lose?

So I went to the office, which looked like a fern bar, and sat down on a nice brown couch. On the other side of a nice brown desk was a nice blond young man with a California tan, who looked vaguely like the hero of a late-seventies movie.

"Hi," I said. "I got your name out of the transsexual resource guide. I'm a transsexual and I want to start looking at surgery, which is all fine with me. My problem is that I've never met a female-to-male transsexual, I can't find any information at all about what's actually involved in a sex change, and I haven't been able to find a surgeon I can talk to about what the options are. I figured that since you're in the resource book, you must know some of these people. My mental health is fine, but I really can't make any more decisions about how I want to live without some medical information. So, actually, what I need right now isn't counseling but help in getting access to information so I know what the possibilities are. Would you be willing to help me with that?"

To his credit, he recovered much more rapidly than Mr. Taupe Hair had. His twinkling blue eyes went wide briefly and he said, "Why would you think you're a man?"

I squashed a flash of annoyance. I was going to be reasonable, by God.

"Well, I didn't really come here to deconstruct myself. I'm comfortable with my beliefs and my sense of self as they are. I guess what I'm trying to say is that my manhood isn't really up for negotiation. What I need to figure out now is what to do about it. If you want to help me with that, I'd be really grateful, but if you don't, that's fine, just please say so now."

"No, please stay. I'd really like to try to help you."

"Great. The first thing I'd really like to do is talk to a female-to-male transsexual, somebody who's been through the process, whatever it is. Can you give me someone's phone number, or set up a meeting for me so they wouldn't think I was some random stalker?"

"Well, I don't really know anyone like that."

"Okay, actually, the thing I really need most is just a picture, just a photograph. That would solve a lot of my problems, answer a lot of the questions I have about my choices. If I could only find out what one looked like . . ."

"I don't really know where to find something like that."

I stared at him. "But the resource guide . . ."

"I guess that was someone else at the office. But we deal with a lot of sexual-minority clients, and I'm perfectly sympathetic."

"So how much do you know about transsexuals?"

"Well, I've never actually worked with one before, but I'd really love to work with you. I do psychotherapy, but I'm not a Freudian; I think his theories about women are discriminatory, honest. But if you'd rather see a woman . . ."

"No, actually, I would not rather see a woman."

"Actually, I'm a gay man myself, if that's any comfort. I'll talk to my colleagues, and maybe I can get you some of the information you're wanting. I'll see what I can do. Okay?"

"All right." It wasn't much, but it was something. Actually, it was all it seemed I could get.

"Good. In the meantime, why don't you tell me something about yourself? Just start at the beginning, with your childhood."

So I paid him fifty dollars to talk about myself for fifty minutes. He said very little.

He said, "So tell me about your first sexual experience."

I hemmed and coughed for a couple of minutes and then admitted that my first sexual experience, if any, would be in my future.

He said, "Well, how did you feel about your father?"

The next week I went back. Another fifty dollars. No referrals.

"Well, could you just find the name of a surgeon for me, then? I'm sure he'd have photographs I could see, former patients I could talk to, I mean, if there's surgery. Are there special surgeons, or do they just go to somebody who does breast reductions? Do female-to-male transsexuals even get surgery?"

"I'm not sure if I can answer something like that."

"Look, I'm not going to run right out and grab somebody off the street with a rusty knife. I read something about chest surgery in the medical literature. They said the results were disfiguring and dangerous, but I'd still like to see a picture for myself."

"I'm just a therapist. I may not be able to answer those questions for you."

"That's why I want to talk to a surgeon."

"Well, I'll see what I can do. In the meantime, let's continue where we left off last week."

"I don't really think talking about my childhood is very useful. It was

91

over a long time ago. I got some bad attitudes from my stepfather and had to spend time unlearning them. It was hard work, and I did it years ago. I'd like to move forward from here instead of back."

"You got some bad attitudes from your stepfather?"

I sighed. But he didn't really have any way to know I wasn't lying, and I was being reasonable, so I spent the rest of the hour explaining I'd figured out a long time ago that I did not want to be the Marlboro Man.

I went back the next week. Another fifty dollars. No referrals.

"So, last week you were saying you were often depressed as an adolescent?"

I was done with rehashing my adolescence. I said nothing. He said nothing. The dollars ticked by. Finally I said, "No, I've never attempted suicide. Now, can you please tell me something about where I go from here if I want to find out about transsexuals?"

"You've never attempted suicide?"

"No, I've never attempted suicide. I'm not thinking about attempting suicide. I'm not going to run out and axe-murder random passersby, and I don't hear alien voices telling me what to do on my radio. Are we done now? Can we move on to deciding what I can *do*?"

"It seems as if you might be feeling hostile about these sorts of questions."

I thought, if I strangle him it's going to look really bad.

Two hundred fifty dollars later, I'd made several observations. The first was that I still had no information and no contacts with anyone who did. The second was that every time I pushed for information, he'd begin carefully asking me questions about my feelings in the curiously stilted phrasing of someone reading a recently memorized textbook out loud. The third was that I was paying fifty dollars a week for this service, which would be two hundred a month that could go toward surgery, and a quarter of my monthly income. I took two last twenties and a ten and went back one more time.

"Look," I said, "I've been analyzing myself, my feelings, and my motives since I was twelve years old. I'm very good at it. I can analyze my situation all by myself. What I can't do by myself is change it. I can't figure out my options by thinking. I need your participation, your practical help."

I looked over at him. Silence. I tried again.

"I don't know why I'm this way, but at this point I don't think trying to find out why is productive. Queer theory says you don't focus on what causes an identity unless you want to cure it. I'm a functional human being, I'm not hurting anyone, at twenty-five I can safely say I am not going through a phase, and analysis isn't going to change who I am. As a gay man in the mental health professions, you ought to be able to understand that."

I looked over at him. Silence. Well, so much for solidarity. I dug deep and tried it one last time.

"I'm stuck in a place I can't stand. No matter what I say or do, or how I act, or anything about myself I try to show, people think I'm a woman. The harder I try to communicate that I'm not a woman, the more excited everybody gets about what a great woman I am. I went to see a bunch of transsexuals, and they're stuck in analysis, all these same obsessions with appearance, all this same sexist garbage about how men and women are supposed to behave that I had to learn my way out of when I was seventeen years old. What's feminine, what's really manly, how you're going to walk and talk and what you're going to hate and like, as if a person's less important than what clothes you're going to wear. But if I wear my leather jacket, people call me "Sir," and if I wear sandals they call me "Ma'am" and direct me to the womyn-only section of the universe. I end up doing this macho bullshit all the time, just trying to compensate. Trying to communicate. I hate it. I know it's wrong and it's wrong for me, but I'm *stuck* in it because of what I look like. Thinking about what's wrong doesn't change anything, it just keeps my head above water for another day. I close my eyes and I know all the assumptions people make, the things they say and do and think, none of it is real, but I can't get out. I have to live here, and I'm getting tired of fighting. Talking about masculinity and femininity and whether I played with trucks or dolls when I was a kid just makes everything worse. Pink and blue, trucks and dolls, it's all bullshit. Anybody can wear and play with whatever they want. It doesn't mean anything.

"I've become a feminist, and analyzed media images, and educated myself, and been to counselors, and deconstructed my childhood. I've experimented with my speech patterns, my hair, my clothes, the part of the country I live in, the social groups I hang out with. I've done everything I can do myself. I've gone as far as I can go, and it does not change my situation. I don't want to talk about it anymore. I want to get out of the situation. I want to *do* something about it." I was startled to discover that, for once, I wasn't crying because I was angry. I looked at him. "Now are you going to help me or not?"

He said, "I'm a psychotherapist. What I do takes time. It may take a lot of time, maybe once a week for years, but I really think you've already made some progress."

The next week I called to cancel my appointment with the nice liberal gay therapist.

He said, "I really think you need to reconsider."

I said, "You can buy a computer program that repeats the last sentence you say to it. If that were all I needed I could get it at Radio Shack for $19.99."

He said, "Last week was critical. I think we really made a breakthrough, an emotional breakthrough. You were crying, that's a very hopeful sign."

After a moment I removed my jaw from the floor. Finally, I said, "Honey, crying about it doesn't help. I've been crying about it for years."

"This is really a classic pattern," he said excitedly, "emotional honesty, then withdrawal. Fight to overcome it, now, we've just made an important breakthrough in the history of your family relations."

"Good-bye," I said. "Good-bye."

So now I was on my own.

Coming out as a transsexual is an intensive hands-on course in leading a transparent life, a glass house from which I have no business throwing stones. For most of my life, I can't say I knew how the destructive gap between my body and my sense of self might relate to the equally destructive gap between how I saw myself and how other people saw me. So I can't really blame the mental health professions for not doing any better. What I can say is my studies in the history of science taught me I live in a country whose mental health professions are the business of social lubrication: solving people's problems with each other in the guise of solving people's problems with themselves. Unfortunately, the familiar solution to people's discomfort with each other isn't to get rid of the discomfort but to get rid of whatever triggers it. Which is exactly how I was afraid psychiatry would handle me. And so, of course, that was precisely how I handled psychiatry.

That I got rid of my body rather than getting rid of my discomfort with it is the prime argument used against transsexuality. Do I criticize other people for taking the same route I took myself? But the convenient terms I hear each time my sex change comes up—that my former self "died" and a new one "was born," that I "love my new body," that I was "a man trapped in a woman's body"—all pretend I was two people or have had two bodies. I wonder why it isn't obvious that if I'd dealt with my discomfort by getting rid of my body, I would now be dead. I wonder who the second person I'm imagined as might be. Questions of authority over someone else may have different answers from questions of authority over the self and the body. But these are all questions of authority, and authority is an uncomfortable subject. We fight about abortion, and about the right of people who are HIV+ to control their bodily fluids as well. (And as an aside, it still pisses me off as a gay man that generations of us fought and died in this country to achieve authority over our own male bodies and desires, and this authority still does not extend in my own community to recognizing mine.)

There are a couple of very practical differences between my desire to solve the problem of psychiatry in my life and psychiatrists' desire to solve the problem of me in their profession. One point is that, with the authority produced by an MD degree, psychiatrists can treat uncomfortable people with drug regimens that cause permanent nerve damage, as well as making you drool and all your teeth fall out. These drugs are a replacement for the previous habit of treating uncomfortable people by lobotomy, the medical term for shoving an ice pick past your eyeballs and jabbing it around in your brain until you quit being so antisocial. Since the pendulum of medical practice has swung away from brain surgery with ice picks, and incapacitating doses of antipsychotic drugs are now reserved for the deeply uncomfortable, psychiatrists now frequently offer safer and more effective drugs like Prozac. These drugs can significantly reduce the misery involved in learning how to do things that won't make your psychiatrist uncomfortable. Of course, some psychiatrists are wonderful, and some even think of drugs like testosterone or Prozac as tools to reduce the misery involved in learning how to do what makes you happy.

If you ever have to have a psychiatric evaluation, you'd better find a psychiatrist who's wonderful, which brings up the question of whether you get a voice in who has authority over you.

I can call one or more psychiatrists crazy if they disagree with me. So can they. If I'm uncomfortable enough to do it, it's an insult. If they're uncomfortable enough to do it, it's a diagnosis, which gives them legal authority over precisely those aspects of my life about which we disagree. So, in my own case, I avoided psychiatrists. Some of them think I'm insane for wanting surgery. These psychiatrists, of course, are the ones who legally control my access to surgery; since psychiatric authority extends only over crazy people, psychiatrists who conclude I'm not crazy don't have any authority over what happens to me. If they don't, who does? Who will help me? And who will pay the price? These are questions of authority. Authority is an uncomfortable subject.

History creates its own madness. The worst psychiatrist I could have met in this place and time couldn't have destroyed my brain with an ice pick without violating the rules of his profession and probably the law. I could justify my fears by describing horrific contemporary "therapies," but that would be telling scare stories. Scare stories are to keep you from going into the woods, and as long as some of us still have no choice but to walk there, telling them is cruelty. It's perfectly possible that my fears kept me away from counseling professionals who would have helped me find medical help ten years earlier. It's certain there are other lives than mine, some of them transsexual lives, that have been saved by counseling or even by psychiatry. As part of my studies in the history of medicine, I read of lethal experiments performed by doctors on black patients at Tuskegee Institute. Though I was thoroughly disgusted by what was done, and shocked by how recently it was done, I remember wondering why so many African Americans still won't trust doctors, since it's their own health that suffers from these old suspicions. And while I wondered, I never abandoned my own first lessons, the madness of history I learned from being a fruitcake instead of from being native or black or even Jewish—to know what horrors the world's good people did and are doing to people who could have been you.

On my way to healing I made some detours that almost killed me. In the end my mother saved my life. Mostly, I figure the choices that led me into trouble were my own fault, the results my own responsibility. Sometimes I remember people who aren't transsexual also get sick and also make lousy decisions, but then I remember Mr. Taupe Hair and his schizophrenic girl who wanted to mess herself up, the social worker with her Lee Press On Nails and delicate disgust, the nice gay psychotherapist who could have easily found me the help I needed and chose to bury his head in his textbooks instead. I wonder if I might have been believed more often if people hadn't thought I was so pretty.

And if I were my mother's age, instead of writing this book in my garden with a beautiful body and the memory of a few narrow escapes, I might be sitting in an institution with a drool cup and a hole in my brain. It's a hard truth to forgive and forget.

Before my mother's brother died, he had two sons. The older one became a scientist. The younger one, my cousin Jeff, became a clown. Traveling in Europe, Jeff came across a Holocaust museum on the walls of which were photographs of Buchenwald. Looking closely at one, he saw his father's signature. His dad's photographs were something nobody in the family had ever talked about. Jeff and I imagine his dad, my uncle, walking into the camp, staring, taking pictures. I imagine a life in which the world would find me an everyday miracle, like a woman building herself a house in her own name, an office with brass plaques and awards and trophies with the state seal of Nebraska out of poetry, like an Arkansas pump jockey with a pencil in his grease-stained fingers quoting Shakespeare to the warm hood of a big black car, like those beautiful windows in which the word is constantly made flesh. I imagine a life in which I live in constant awareness of each everyday miracle: the scent of flowers, the flight of bees unlikely by the laws of physics, my own survival, the birthdays of trees. Sometimes I imagine my mother's brother died from this: he could not cease to bear witness to the everyday miracle—that one person will stick an ice pick into another's brain, war's horrific suffering. The world is what we make it and contains that much salvation. My brother married a Gentile from Germany. My cousin Jeff married a psychologist.

Surgery I

By the time I was in my teens, I had vague plans for surgery. I was never too clear about the details. My early theory was: you find a competent surgeon and tell them what you want done. They do it, and you pay the bill.

Things turned out to be a little bit more complicated.

Eventually, I figured out a very simple rule. Surgeons deal with physical problems. Psychiatrists deal with mental problems. Great. Only every time I told someone about my physical problems, they tried to send me to a psychiatrist. Apparently, if I ever wanted to see a surgeon, I had to lie about my problems. Since people obviously thought the truth was a mental problem, these lies had better be plausible, or I might find myself taking a quick detour to the Shady Home. So all I had to do was find a surgeon, lie thickly enough about my problems that they would be convinced I was radiantly normal, but thinly enough that they'd still correct the problems I couldn't tell them about. Hey, no problem. Moses talked to God, right?

When I was in graduate school my mother had a hysterectomy, which had been the first surgery on my shopping list. It took her a year to recover. Soon afterward she was diagnosed with cancer and returned to the hospital to have a breast removed, the second surgery on my list. Watching her recoveries, my enthusiasm for the surgical experience quickly waned. In a career that involved hard labor for hourly pay in the single digits, six months off for a major operation or two was hardly an option. This was my explanation for why I couldn't pursue those wonderful plans for surgery. Not that it wasn't true, as far as it went. It's just that excuses won't take you very far.

It might be more relevant to say that, red-blooded American boy that I was, I had learned from endless Bruce Willis movies that any disability will simply evaporate in the face of big enough *cojones*. Now nobody—except maybe that Greenwich Village poet I used to know, who drove cross-country on state highways with her cat riding shotgun for company, killed cockroaches in our kitchen with her bare hands, and sent me postcards from Katmandu—had cojones like my mom. Having watched disability dissect my mom with surgical precision, and not having hiked around Mount Kailash or hand-killed any roaches recently, I suspected my cojones might not be up to laughing off a year's worth of hospitals. At the time I hadn't figured out that Mr. Willis has his injuries applied with Supracolor, possibly while lying in a gold-plated Barcalounger drinking wine coolers, and nothing could have terrified me more than the prospect of proving my cojones weren't bigger than the laws of physics.

It's also relevant to say that a pipe dream is an untestable hypothesis. Untestable hypotheses are just beliefs you make sure you can't check on, so you don't have to find out if they work. A good science course will teach you to avoid falling in love with ideas you can't try. A really good science course will teach you that, if you don't have a lot of confidence in your own ability, untestable hypotheses are as addictive as cigarettes. You can't prove they'll work, but you can't prove they won't, either. In other words, an attempt can fail, and a plan can go pieces, but a pipe dream stays perfect forever and ever. For example— "Someday I'll have all these stupid organs removed. Instantly, everyone will stop mistaking me for a woman, and my life will effortlessly become wonderful." I had a lot of good science courses, but I didn't take them personally.

Paul, on the other hand, took all his science courses personally. A true child of the space race, he scanned the news daily, waiting with bated breath for banner headlines announcing contact with peace-loving butt-brained aliens, antiaging pills, and the combined cure for cancer and five o'clock shadow. One day, bursting with excitement, he announced, "Wonderful news! I just found out about a new surgical breakthrough! Doctors have invented a surgery that does everything a hysterectomy would do for you, only it's much easier."

"Oh, what, only six months flat on your back?"

"No, it's an outpatient procedure. You can walk in and out in an hour."

"If you've got a million dollars in your pocket."

"No, not at all. It's very simple, and cheap, too."

"And invented by Dr. Boris Badenov, who performs them by telekinesis at the famous Russian Psychic Institute in Minsk."

"Oh, be *serious*. I thought you'd be pleased. It's not an experimental procedure or anything; it's called—hang on, I wrote it down—endometrial resection, and lots of doctors do it. I saw all about it on Sally Jessy Raphael."

"Sally Jessy Raphael? Don't you know what that does to your brain cell count?"

"I don't usually watch anymore, but I saw a little description in the TV Guide, and I figured I'd better check it out, in case there was anything that might help you."

Faced with this breakthrough, my pipe dreams and my nightmares took a stroll down my cerebrum, hand in hand. I took a long hard look at the mechanics of actually accomplishing what I wanted in real life—finding a surgeon, checking credentials, getting the money, inventing a con that would convince the surgeon to do what I wanted instead of landing me on my ass in a psychiatric hospital—and ran like hell. I took the radical step of deciding it would be impossible to find a reputable surgeon in Los Angeles, and probably wasn't worth it anyway—me and my cojones were just fine.

Undaunted, Paul consulted with the newly anointed Love of My Life, Dawn.

"Paul told me about this surgery thing."

"Yeah?"

"Are you really interested, or is this just one of Paul's brilliant schemes?"

"I'd do it in a minute, if I could."

"Even going to the hospital and all?"

"I wouldn't have to stay in the hospital. I did some research, and Paul's actually right; it's easy and safe, which is exactly what I wanted."

"I don't know that surgery's ever easy and safe."

"This isn't major surgery. It's taking these goddamn pills forever that's dangerous. I'm worried about that."

"So what's stopping you?"

Haltingly, I described my last attempt to contact a surgeon. The last time I'd looked into surgery, I was seventeen, shivering in the abject terror and equally abject gullibility of youth—that the cops were going to kick down my door and haul my ass back to Nebraska, that the counseling service had tapped my phone and was sending the men with the funny coats any minute now. The hospital I'd called for information had transferred me like a hot potato—once, twice, a dozen times. Finally I managed to quaver my question for the twelfth time: could a hysterectomy be performed as voluntary surgery, if I had the money? A harried-sounding woman of unknown qualifications choked once, breathed, "Jesus Christ," and hung up on me.

Dawn gave me a long look.

"Is this surgery really what you want?"

"Yeah, I mean, I'm fine, but . . . yeah."

"Okay. Paul and I can call the doctors."

"But there's no way to find a surgeon who's both experienced with the procedure and willing to do it as an elective surgery."

"That's what the phone book is for."

So I sat with my mouth open and watched Dawn and Paul politely call every surgeon in the greater Los Angeles area. On the second day, they found one who was both qualified and willing to do the surgery.

All that was left was the money and the con. A year later I had a union job in San Diego at thirteen dollars an hour and a plausible story to tell. I made an appointment and drove back to LA. The surgeon was tanned and fit and no older than I was, with an office in Westwood, a bright open smile, and a thick file of successful surgeries. We did exactly what doctor and patient should do, in my pipe dream: go over the procedure carefully, in detail, talk about risks and results and possible outcomes, sign a release form, arrange a day and a time, and pay. He told me the surgery probably wouldn't substitute for taking the offending organ out entirely, but I wasn't listening. Oh, and there was another little deviation from the pipe dream. I lied, and I lied, and I lied. I told him I was in line for collecting expeditions to the rainforests of Costa Rica, and a million miles from anywhere was not the place to suffer female complaints. It's possible that he believed me—he could verify my employment as a keeper at a major zoo—but I think it's likely that he didn't care. He was honest about the risks, and he was the first medical professional I'd talked to who thought what I did with my body was my own damn business. In other words, he acted like a surgeon instead of a psychiatrist. Which made the second lie a little painful.

The surgeon said, "You understand that you'll be sterile if you have this surgery? Have you ever thought about wanting children?"

"No, I've never wanted children."

"Are you absolutely sure? People sometimes want children later in life."

When Paul was twenty-one, he'd had, as he put it, his "tubes tied." Getting a vasectomy in Wisconsin involved taking a Greyhound to the only clinic in the only town in the state willing to sterilize someone young, healthy, and white. The same year my mother had opposed my plans for surgery so grimly because she was convinced my future self would want to bear children. In desperation, I gave the surgeon my best smile and said breezily, "I'm certain. Look, this is a little awkward, but children just aren't in my future. I don't have sex with men."

I watched his mind visibly settle to rest, pillowed on the word "lesbian."

Ten minutes later, we were on to the subject of surgical complications, and the words stared back at me from my paperwork: CURRENT MEDICATIONS.

The only item on my current list of medications was birth control pills. I knew they could be a surgical risk. I'd opened my mouth to ask about it, when I suddenly realized I had just talked myself into a corner.

"Would there be any complications from birth control pills?" I asked.

"Are you taking them?"

"Oh, no, not now. But I did take them in the past, and I was wondering . . ."

"How recently?" he asked, looking at me carefully. "It might matter." And, though he didn't say it, "Are you *sure* you don't want children?"

Danger, Will Robinson.

Now I had to lie or I had to trust him. He had a phone on his desk. His office was fourteen floors up in a huge one-stop medical complex. I thought about a floor full of taupe-haired mental health professionals. I thought about how fast my one shot at surgery would evaporate if I told the truth. One wrong answer and—Paff!

"Oh," I said casually, "I stopped taking them a long time ago." A little lie.

The last thing he asked me was if my family knew what I was doing. The last lie I told him was that I'd told my mother. He looked at me quizzically. "How does she feel about it?"

"Oh," I said airily, "she doesn't mind. Actually, she approves."

He looked surprised, but he didn't say anything. I was an adult, he was a surgeon, and family matters weren't his business.

That night I sat on the beach with Paul.

"So," he said, "how does it feel to finally be getting what you want?"

"I don't know. I mean, I'm really excited about it, but I feel sort of weird, too, about knowing the surgery won't even leave a scar. Not that I want scars, but . . ."

"But what?"

"Just that I'm going to come out looking exactly the same on the outside as before. Not that I give a damn about what I look like to anybody else. But I'll still look like this completely normal woman."

"You don't look much like a woman to me," said Paul encouragingly. "With your jacket on you look really good, and hardly anybody notices the breasts anyway. The guy behind the counter called you 'Sir' again today."

"I know, but they're still *there*."

"Well, you told me you were going to do the breast reduction next thing . . ."

"How the hell am I going to come up with a story to get the damn things off altogether? I mean, it'll be easy to get them small enough that if I dress right nobody will notice, but I don't want to fuck with clothes anymore; besides, it's not about what other people think I am, it's about, I don't know. Like your friends who do their religious ceremonies without any clothes on because they want to be naked before God."

Paul took my hand. "I know it's hard sometimes. But you've got this surgery—look at me, there's nothing yet for my hair. We'll figure out the breast thing later, or maybe by then they can do body sculpting in vats, like in this cyberpunk novel I read."

"Paul, I don't want to be fashion statement of the week. I'm going through all this shit because I'm different somehow. I am glad I'm doing this one first; it's more important than the breasts. I don't give a fuck

103

about what other people think. It just seems like I should end up different on the outside, too. Like there should be some kind of mark."

I scheduled the surgery for a four-day weekend and took the bus up to LA with Dawn and Paul, knowing I probably shouldn't try to drive. Not driving myself home was a hard weakness for my cojones to admit. I was being reasonable. Reasonable slid slowly toward terror doing a clever imitation of numb. Paul bought me Victorian adventure stories, promised to read to me during my recovery. A couple of days before the surgery, I quit taking the pills; I figured forty-eight hours would be enough time for the drug to clear my system. It would have been nice if I could have asked my surgeon. Oh, well.

Lacking the sense for prayer, I tried luck, negotiation: the stars were wrong, the offerings rejected, all vital signs negative—mayday, mayday. I didn't know that much terror wasn't business as usual, all forgotten except the terrible frozen ride to the hospital, endless as Los Angeles. The friends who drove me trusted me enough not to ask for details I didn't volunteer.

And everything still might have been fine except that nobody knew I had a tumor the size of a grapefruit in my abdomen.

Most microsurgeries, like the one I was scheduled for, are quick outpatient procedures done under gas anesthesia through incisions about an inch long. Gas anesthesia has a long history beginning with the use of ether, a blessing in the days when the only alternative was getting patients drunk and then holding them down. In large doses over time gas anesthetics can cause intoxication, dangerous levels of sedation, and long delays in regaining consciousness. For this reason they are now only used for short, simple surgeries, like the one I was supposed to have. Modern major surgery uses intravenous anesthetics, which are much safer over long periods of time. Unfortunately, gas and iv anesthetics do not mix; once you've started one, you have to stick with it.

My phone book surgeon turned out to be a national expert in microsurgical techniques. He was in the habit of sticking a fiber optic probe through his incisions to take a quick look around the body cavity and make sure everything was all right. This is how he found my grapefruit. It had been there a long time. The body stabilizes such a mass of tissue by webbing it tightly to various organs so that it doesn't roll around kicking stomach and kidneys like a soccer ball. If a tumor is cancerous, these webby adhesions may spread the cancer to various organs. It took my first surgeon nine and a half hours to remove the tumor and all its adhesions through two incisions an inch long, under gas anesthesia.

Surgeries over four hours in length have a greatly increased risk of complications, particularly thrombosis, the clotting of blood within the veins. After the surgery it took me two days to regain consciousness. Immobility and deep sedation after surgery greatly increase the chance of thrombosis. Estrogens, the active ingredients in birth control pills, also increase the risk of thrombosis. You can take your pick of causes.

Three days later someone drove me back to San Diego with a catheter bag strapped to my leg. Dawn and Paul fed me Jello and Victorian adventure while my surgeon negotiated a week's delay in my supervisor's sudden new plans to fire me. A week after I left the hospital, I went back to work.

Two weeks after I left the hospital, my surgeon called to say the tumor had been benign, not cancer at all. By that time the blood in my left femoral vein—the major vessel returning blood to the body from the leg and thigh—had begun first to slow, then to freeze tight. One day I drove to work and couldn't make it down the hill to the time clock. So I dragged myself to an urgent-care center, where the doctor on duty charged fifty-six dollars to agree with my theory that I'd sprained my hip somehow and give me large quantities of drugs. Three days later I was lying around watching my leg swell up with the detached fascination characteristic of a gram of hydrocodone and ten milligrams of Valium every four hours when my mother called.

"Hi," she said uncertainly. "Is everything all right?"

"Fine," I said airily. "I'm fine."

"Your voice sounds funny."

"No, really I'm fine. Everything's all right."

A few hours later she called me again.

"Hi," she said airily. "Does my voice sound funny?"

"A little," I said uncertainly. "Why?"

"I'm ten thousand feet over Utah, talking on an Airfone. Isn't technology wonderful?"

I dug the phone into my sternum and gestured frantically for Dawn and Paul.

"Uh, Mom, what are you doing over Utah?"

"Oh, I'm on my way to see you. I'll be there in an hour. Can somebody pick me up at the airport?"

My drug-addled brain couldn't work out the details of saving my own life, but it took me less than sixty minutes to construct a plausible deniability that would make Richard Nixon weep with envy. I told my mother I'd gone in for a fiber optic exam of some old digestive problems, they'd found the tumor and taken it out. I didn't want to tell her about the surgery until we knew the tumor wasn't cancer. Take that, Watergate conspirators.

My mother arrived at my apartment, took one look at me, and called an ambulance. I'd successfully protested to Dawn and Paul that I couldn't afford the ambulance fees, but I was silenced by the Power Field of Mother Defending Her Young.

"Hi, I'm Debbie, and I'll be your ultrasound technician." Debbie was a nice blond girl in a white lab coat. She covered my leg in Vaseline and began to stroke it lovingly with something that looked like a marital aid. She looked at me and her brow wrinkled. Uh, oh. Bad news.

"Hey, didn't I go to high school with you? Yeah, Debbie Johannsen, you remember me, tenth grade? What a coincidence!"

"Uh, yeah. Great. How's my leg?"

The marital aid began to produce high-pitched squeals and clicking noises. Apparently my leg was a highly radioactive mutant.

"Oh. It looks like you've got some, uh, little solid places."

"How little?"

"Well, they seem to start here behind the knee and go, um, all the way up into the groin." Debbie looked at me sadly. "Well, it was great to see you again. Good-bye."

I woke up in a hospital bed. A jolly doctor with a thick German accent approached.

"Now if at all you move, the clot material might break off and travel right to your brain. Then—Paff!—all over. Ha, ha! So now you lie very still, no moving."

"For how long?"

"Oh, a week or two. Now remember, no moving, none at all. Might make the bathroom hard, ha, ha! Now, no worrying, either, drives up the blood pressure, and—Paff! Bye-bye."

I was in another Terry Gilliam movie.

Family members appeared out of nowhere. They'd apparently been told about Paff.

"Mom, Dad, this is Dawn. Sorry I didn't mention it earlier."

"That's all right, honey, don't worry about it. Relax. Have some Jello."

A week out of the hospital for the second time, I took my cane and my union card and my brand-new pressure bandage, which looked exactly like one Victorian porn stocking minus garter belt, and went back to foil further attempts by my employers to keep me from making rent. Mom packed her bags, kissed me, and said, "Never, ever lie to your mother again."

"Okay," I said. Which was why, two years later, I would write her a letter to tell her I was having a sex-change operation.

In the meantime, I learned how to whimper, how to fall down on the floor, and how to let your loved ones help you not spray urine from your catheter bag on the nice tile at the mall. My little moment of Bruce Willis triumph was when after a month I could tie my own shoes. It would be a year before I could live without the cane, the stocking, and injections every eight hours. So much for the illusion that I was one badass High Plains Drifter, a closed system hermetically sealed from the outside world. So much for cojones.

On the one-year anniversary of my release from the hospital, I took a back road across the desert to a little lake, lay on my back among the tules, watched the terns circle above me, and figured I'd done my time in hell. Someday, when the memory of hospitals was good and faded, I'd go back for round two. Someday. For now it was enough that I'd done what I had to do and was alive and well. I'd paid through the nose for what I wanted, but now I had it, and I felt inordinately pleased with myself. From here on out, I wouldn't need anybody ever again, damn it. I was fine. The cojones were bouncing back nicely, thank you.

A year after that I found my surgeon had indeed been right, and the fix was temporary.

"Three headings define the vicious state of Samsara:
The misery of conditioned existence,
The misery of change and
The misery of misery."

Should we try to illustrate this triad of misery by similes, that of conditioned existence would be like an unripe fruit; that of change would resemble a meal of rice gruel mixed with poison; and the misery of misery would be like the growth of mold on fruit. Or again, the first is a general feeling of indifference, the second a feeling of pleasure, and the third of displeasure.

Gampopa, The Jewel Ornament of Liberation,
quoted in Pharmako/poeia, by DALE PENDELL

Still Life with Hormones

I'd had two hospital stays, a week of lying very quietly so as not to wake Death, and a year of rehabilitation. I'd done my best John Wayne, worked hard when I could barely stand. In return, my employer tried to fire me. I couldn't support my family. And the surgery didn't work. Birth control pills, the only medication I could get myself, might cause another blood clot, an event highly likely to wake my old friend this time; as I had learned in our brief acquaintance, Death doesn't sleep so soundly. The closet I'd backed myself into was airtight. The only options I had left were waiting for the air to run out or telling the truth.

"Paul," I said, "I need some help."

"Well," said Paul, "there's this wonderful new computer technology . . ."

In Portland, Oregon, the public library has a community service database. You can type in words, any words, like "tennis," or "Tourette's syndrome," and the computer will give you the location of all the tennis courts and classes in town or phone numbers for all the support services in the region for people with Tourette's syndrome. Paul, the eternal optimist, went to the library and typed in the word "transsexual." He came back with a printout listing contact numbers for five different organizations. There are only about half a dozen sexual-reassignment surgeons in the United States. The cities in which they practice become national centers for transsexual people. Unknown to us, Dawn, Paul, and I had just moved to one of them.

I called the number for something listed as an "inclusive group supporting transsexual, transgendered, intersexed, and cross-dressing people and their families and friends." A perfectly normal-sounding woman's voice answered the phone.

"Hello," I said. "Uh, um, I, um, I need some information. So, um, you're a transsexual, right?"

"No," she said. "Actually, my husband is a cross-dresser, but it's all right, we help all kinds of people."

I assured her that I wasn't a transsexual, either, but could they recommend a sympathetic doctor?

"Well," she said, "I've got a couple of names of people here in town. And while I'm at it, let me give you a couple of counselors who've been seen by some of our members, people they'd recommend, just in case you need to see someone."

"No, that's fine, I just need medical information," I said. "My problem is purely physical."

"All right," she said pleasantly. "But I'll give you the numbers anyway; sometimes it helps you get an appointment with the doctor if you've been referred by a counselor. And you don't need to be ashamed of yourself. That's really important, no matter who you are. It's not your fault. You see, men and women have completely different brains. I just read this wonderful book that tells all about it . . ."

"That's fine, thanks," I said. "I've just got a little medical problem, I've got to talk to a doctor, that's all. But thanks very much for the information. I really appreciate it."

I wrote down the number for the doctor and the number for the counselor, and then I sat in front of the phone with one in each hand until it was too dark to tell them apart.

Finally I called the counselor. If I told the doctor what I wanted, he might throw me out of his office and I'd lose my one shot at medical advice. If the counselor didn't like it, well, so I'd just blown a gasket on another mental health professional. No news there.

"So, how's life treating you?" said the voice of Suzanna Lansky, Master of Social Work.

I took a deep breath and then I told her about the surgery that didn't work, the blood clot that now made self-medication an opportunity for a little one-on-one with Death, and how I'd decided it was definitely really time to get some professional medical advice on the situation right now. And since I'd decided to stop lying to doctors, that would involve finding one whose gaskets wouldn't blow.

"Well," she said, "why don't you make an appointment with Dr. X and just tell him what you told me. Tell him I told you to make an appointment. He's very cool, and he's experienced with transsexual patients; he's not going to freak out. If he's got any problems treating you, you can come see me, and we'll work out getting you a doctor from there. Does that sound okay?"

"Okay," I said.

So I made the appointment, walked in to Dr. X, told him what I wanted, and gave him my complete medical history.

"Well," he said, "are you concerned about pregnancy?"

"Nope," I said.

"Having any pains or other problems you want to get rid of?"

"Just the basic one."

"Is there a particular illness you're worried about?"

"Nope."

"Well," he said, "there are several different ways to stop female hormone cycles. One is birth control pills, and I agree that they would be danger-ous for you at this point. There are some other female hormone options, though, like Depo-Provera, the birth control implant . . ."

We discussed these for a while. I explained that female hormones were really not at all what I was looking for.

"Well, another option is the hormone testosterone, and the third is a group of drugs called antiestrogens, which block the action of estrogen in the body."

Testosterone. I blinked slowly, once. As a naturalist, I knew it was the hormone responsible for the additional size, bone density, and muscle mass of male mammals. I knew that in cattle, the female twin of a bull is exposed to testosterone before birth, and as a result will be unusually large, active, sterile, and unable to give milk; farmers used to call them "freemartins." In spotted hyenas, naturally high levels of serum testos-terone create a species in which females outweigh males. Both sexes have a penis; in females, the scrotum is hollow and open in the rear to allow access to and from the birth canal. That testosterone is also a clear, straw-colored liquid that is pharmaceutically packaged in sterile five-milliliter bottles and can be safely injected into a human being was news to me.

"So," I said as casually as possible under the circumstances, "what's the difference between an antiestrogen and testosterone?"

"Antiestrogens work without major changes in your appearance. Basi-cally, fertility and hormone cycles stop, more or less as in menopause. The

111

downside of antiestrogens is they can have some potentially dangerous side effects."

"No side effects. I'm done with that."

"Testosterone has major side effects, too."

"Oh. Right. Cancers, and cirrhosis, like bodybuilders get." All the gyms I'd ever belonged to took note of the side effects of steroids, a hideous grab bag of potentially lethal conditions, as well as, say, just for instance, causing breast development and making your dick and balls shrivel up. So much for testosterone.

"Bodybuilders often take testosterone pills, or other steroids in combination, and in abnormally high doses. The risk factor there is extremely high. A low dose of injected pharmaceutical testosterone, not combined with other steroids, is relatively safe as medications go, as long as you have no history of liver problems. Basically, you need to have a blood test once or twice a year to make sure your liver is okay."

"But what about the, um, other problems guys who take steroids can get? Like, I don't know what a decent term for it would be; they call it, um, 'bitch tits.'"

"You mean benign breast development? Sometimes the steroid dosages these guys take are so high the testosterone begins to convert to estrogen. The two hormones are chemically very similar. If your levels of one get too high, the body spontaneously starts transforming it into the other. So these guys are trying to be macho by pumping so much male hormone into their systems that they start to feminize."

"So that only happens at, uh, really high doses?"

"At a higher dosage than a normal man would ever have in his system, even at seventeen or eighteen, when testosterone levels are highest. A higher dosage than you'd ever need for the effects you want. But testosterone has other side effects antiestrogens don't have. Serious side effects."

"Like what?" I said, bracing myself.

Dr. X said, "Deep voice, prominent Adam's apple, body hair, prominent muscles, increased sex drive, facial hair, enlarged genitalia."

I must have let out some kind of small sound, something like, Aha.

Dr. X cocked an eyebrow at me. "You could end up with a full beard. You might even go bald. Many of the effects, like genital enlargement and the changing of the voice, are irreversible. How would you feel about that?"

"Well," I said as casually as possible under the circumstances, "that would be okay."

"Are you sure?"

"It's not like a deep voice or a big dick is what I'd call a negative side effect. I, I mean, I'd, uh, I'd be very happy with most of those. Except for the bald part. I'd rather not go bald."

Dr. X smiled gently at me. The top of his head shone. "It could happen."

"I guess I could live with that."

"So do you want to try the testosterone?"

"Yeah," I said, as casually as possible under the circumstances.

He gave me a test to make sure my liver was healthy, then a month's supply of testosterone—long enough that I could see if I liked it, short enough that the effects would still be reversible if I did not.

I got my little vial of testosterone from Dr. X and took my prescription for syringes to a pharmacy nearby, in the mall. The mall pharmacist promptly asked me what I wanted with needles, and when I told him, promptly confiscated my prescription. So I called the support group, and the pleasant-sounding woman promptly gave me the number of a sympathetic pharmacy. The pharmacist there told me getting needles doesn't actually require a prescription. It does, however, require a sympathetic pharmacist.

A month later, Dr. X asked me how I was liking testosterone, and I told him, as casually as possible under the circumstances, that, short of cherubs removing the top of my head, entering puberty at age twenty-nine was the best fucking thing that had happened to me in my entire life.

On my medical chart under "Diagnosis" he wrote "Hypotestosterism," and told me to come back in another month. *Hypotestosterism.* Insufficient natural production of testosterone. Hallelujah. Somebody had finally figured out the name of my problem.

On my way out the nurse said, "I just wanted to let you know the whole staff is committed to being supportive of all the patients here."

"Thanks. I really appreciate that."

"Tell me if I'm being intrusive, okay? I wanted to say that I know what you're dealing with, maybe not much, but a little. I'm trying to lose weight, a lot of weight. It's a funny kind of balance. You've got to really want what you're going for, but at the same time you've got to find a way to not hate what you look like right now. It's hard. Sometimes I think that's the hardest part."

I looked at her. "No, it's not intrusive at all. Actually, it's the smartest thing anybody's said to me this year."

She blushed. "So if you need anything, you know, like if you want us to call you by a different name or anything, at any point, all you have to do is say so."

"Okay," I said, happy but a little puzzled. Why in the hell would I want them to call me by a different name?

Another month later Dr. X said, "So, how are things going?"

"Great, fabulous."

"Still liking the testosterone?"

"Oh, yeah."

"Okay, come back in three months."

Three months later he pulled up a chair and sat down across from me.

"From here on out, you need to realize that you're going to begin to show changes that aren't reversible, even if you stop taking the testosterone."

"I know. Hey, my bench press has doubled in five months. I'm growing out of the shoulders of all my coats."

"If testosterone is just something you wanted to try, this is really your last chance to stop and not show any permanent effects."

Ha! Soon, even if captured by mind control clones from the Planet of Taupe Hair, I'll be safe. I wait with bated breath.

"I'm not interested in just trying testosterone. It isn't curiosity. I just never knew this was an option for me. It's more than I ever thought I could have, not something I'm suddenly going to change my mind about."

Dr. X put his hands on his knees and looked at me quietly, almost sadly. "If you keep taking testosterone, the internal changes you're excited about are going to begin to show. For instance, you're going to start showing visible facial hair. You might want to give some thought to how you're going to deal with that."

Hey, I thought, I'll shave. Shaving's annoying, but I've never been big on the mountain man look.

Dr. X said, "Testosterone isn't going to get rid of all your breast tissue, for instance. Have you thought about whether or not you're interested in surgery?"

Surgery. Breasts. Oh, right. Sure, later on I'll find a plastic surgeon who does breast reductions, and see if I can tell some girly story to get all this shit off without making them suspicious . . . Oh. Wait. We're into this truth thing now.

"Well," I said slowly, "yeah. I mean, I guess you could say I've already had some surgery." I'd forgotten about what I looked like again. A little embarrassed, I said, "My plan was that I was going to see if I could get one of those plastic surgeons to just take them off."

Dr. X said, "I'm going to send you off to see Suzanna, the counselor you spoke with before. The two of you can talk about how to get you to where you want to be."

He refilled my prescription. This time under "Diagnosis" he wrote "Transsexual."

I stared at the paper for a long time, somehow obscurely disappointed. I had my meds, my biceps were bulging daily, and even the looming Mental Health Professional had already been established as someone who would not blow a gasket and send me off to a pink-and-blue boot camp in Utah. But still . . .

Hypotestosterism. Now there was a diagnosis a guy could live with.

A Wonderful Life

A riddle:
Something belongs to you alone
that you give away when you meet someone,
over and over and over again.

I didn't change my name until I was almost thirty. Like sex, like your face, like the small patch of skin at the base of the neck or the spine where people like to be tattooed, a name marks the space where private meets public. Your most personal possessions are the ones you only see in mirrors—"Hi, I'm Aaron, who are you?" That's why I didn't like the idea of changing my name; I clung to the fantasy that I could see myself just fine without a mirror, thank you.

For instance: there isn't any reason why the combination of sounds that made up my name should mean *woman*, rather than *man*, or *human being*. The sounds could mean *rock* in Swahili, for all I knew. So, was I a rock? Symbols (names, faces, sex, diagrams in books of organs—womb, vas deferens, triple burner—you've never seen) aren't real. My name didn't mean *woman*, because I'm not a woman; if other people thought it did, well, other people thought I was a *woman*, for God's sake. People were idiots. They watched Gillette ads and were deeply moved by the major emotional value of shaving. Their systems of classification included Jimmy Stewart movies, Norman Rockwell paintings, and Precious Moments figurines.

When I changed my name, the first person I told was my cousin, the clown. The second person I told was my barber.

"What happened to Sarah?" my barber asked.

My barber's name was Jim. He was an old queer out of San Diego. I didn't know what to tell him. All my plans had involved never telling anything important to anyone.

"Sarah's gone," I said after a while.

"Gone? Gone where?" he asked.

What I always want to say is "She was never here at all."

I said to Jim, "I don't know. 'Sarah' is just gone."

What I finally changed was the public domain. It's other people's worlds you're messing with. They might care. You have to request their cooperation. Ask for help with mirrors. You'll notice that you look quite different in different lights. In certain lights, in fact, you'll look exactly like an idiot.

In the state where I live, people who want to change their legal names have to post a form on the bulletin board in the county courthouse for two weeks. On the form you have to tell everyone the name they used to call you and the name you want them to call you now. From that information, any random person in town can recognize you. You want them to recognize you. I want you to recognize me. So much for detachment; the whole world will know who in the hell you think you are. Of course, if you want other people to recognize you, you might want to give them a clue who you think you are. You can't blame them for not knowing if you don't bother to tell them. It took me the better part of thirty years to figure this out.

In certain lights, in fact, you'll look exactly like an idiot.

The bulletin board in the county courthouse was covered with names. I had no idea so many people changed their names. When I held up my official notarized form, it was an impressive declaration of individuality, or freakishness, or something. Pinned up with a hundred others, it was anonymous. From a distance, they look a lot like ballots.

Results of unscientific bulletin-board survey of people who change their names. The categories are:

1. Young black men: Thomas James to TeJay, Washington to Muhammad.
2. Divorced women: retrieval of maiden name.
3. Transsexuals: Dennis to Denise, Tracy (female) to Tracy (male), fifteen dollars extra for listing change of gender.
4. Miscellaneous others: change to last name of adopted family, official New Age new name, change to avoid former perpetrators

or victims, change because former name was just too stupid. John Smith to Hafiz StarCrystal Chi'en Lung, Hafiz StarCrystal Chi'en Lung to Jane Smith.

5. New category, exhausted Muslim men, heads down: Mufad (Bosnian) to Marty, Abdulreza (Iranian) to Al, Muhammad (American) to Washington.

Life, liberty, and the pursuit of happiness. Courthouse basement, window two.

My name was the first thing that changed. Surgery is easy compared to posting your convictions, asking to be recognized. The hardest day comes when you first decide to choose and speak your name.

I'd just told Jim my name was Aaron. When I was a kid my mother told me Aaron would have been my name "if you'd been a boy." But neither name my mother gave me seemed to be mine now. If *Sarah* had to go because it was a name for the girl I never was, *Aaron* was a name for the boy I never was. So what was *my* name?

For a couple of months I had one name at home and a different name at work. Work had been advertised as a science museum. The visiting men all looked like Jimmy Stewart. The women looked like Doris Day or Archie Bunker's wife, Edith. We were instructed to "focus on customer service; avoid too much education." Every morning I'd get up and check my face in the mirror, trying to figure out if I'd become too much education. Finally I just decided to shave every day. I stood in front of the mirror with a razor in one hand and a brush in the other at six o'clock one Monday morning, wondering idiotically how much lather to use and whether it was really impossible to cut your throat by accident with a safety razor and, if you did, whether the paramedics would be laughing too hard to haul the body out. I stood there and waited. I waited until I realized I was waiting for an older man to come in and put one hand on my shoulder and not laugh at me and gently show me how. Then I told myself that this was not a fucking Gillette ad and I shaved and went to work.

Jim didn't push for an answer. When I went back for my next haircut, my friends had told him why I'd changed my name. He laughed like the world was a brand-new toy and told me that from now on, he'd have to give me a proper haircut. Jim opened a drawer and brought out a straight razor.

"I'll give you my haircut, like me. When you're short, you want to stand up tall, on top."

While he cut my hair he asked me questions. "You're not having one of those artificial-dick surgeries, are you? I hear those are real dangerous. You've got to take care of your health. Hey, its not the size that counts, believe me." He grinned and rested his hand on my shoulder. "You've got big shoulders now. You lifting weights? Yeah, you're going to look great. You'll be turning heads all over town."

He cut my hair like I was the star of a Hollywood movie, clipping a little, flourishing the scissors, stepping back, admiring the effect. When he was done, he picked up the razor in one hand and the lather in the other and faced me with his palms out, like a magician proving there was nothing up his sleeves. He lathered my face and shaved me gently, flipping off the extra lather with an expert limp-wrist gesture, touching up my sideburns, laughing in delight, giving me grooming tips and aftershave and telling me to keep it clean-cut and never, ever grow a goatee.

Jim wore the straight-appearing look. I told him he was too conservative. He showed me the hammer he kept in the window to use on the bashers and the Nazis. "Sometimes I feel like using it on those old guys who come in here, talking about how we ought to round up all the freaks and make a separate country," he said.

Jim hung out with a friend who had a woman's hips and an old boy's face, a leather jacket and a beret. "Hey, what do you think they thought of her?" he said. "I grew up in the ghetto. What do you think they thought of us back then?" He muttered about conservative. He told me old queer stories. When the crowds of old gray men who hang out in barbershops came in, he'd play straight to them, just a small-town Norman Rockwell barber man. He could play straight; he didn't have a girl's name. But he never touched up their sideburns with the straight razor.

After a while he started arguing with the old barbershop men. They'd say, "God, there's more freaks in the neighborhood every day. Somebody ought to do something about them. Hey, gimme a shave, too." He'd laugh and say, "Hey, get your *wife* to do it."

One day he just moved downtown. "I didn't give all those assholes my new address. They can stay home and listen to Rush Limbaugh. Down here is a better class of people," he said. We'd talk in his new shop, an empty room on the fourteenth floor of an office building, with a window on the air shaft. Downtown, everybody else was tall and pale and wore a suit and everything had brass trim. Downtown was too good a class of people to be seen with him.

His gold chain glinted in his chest hair, gray. He scuffed his flip-flops on the marble floor. "I hate being cooped up in here all the time," he said.

I called him up before the Pride Parade, but there was nobody left to answer the phone. He took too many pills one night for pain. Jim's gone.

Everything Jim did for me was as self-conscious and symbolic as a Jimmy Stewart movie or a Gillette ad. I'm not one for being deeply moved by the major emotional value of shaving. Jim's lips dropped laughs, dropped beads, fag jokes, wore a mustache, said "butch"; he wore his iron-gray hair cropped short. He was a very strong person, not like a lot of them, he said. He's dead. None of this story means anything, except what you decide it means. I remember exactly the way it feels when a razor moves over your skin for the first time and leaves its particular cold stinging. I remember Jim grinning and flaunting his razor from the wrists, touching up my edges like an impresario. The makeup artist for the beauty queen. Jim was an old queer from where the bars eat people and nothing is sure but sleeping on the beach is free, growing up watching Jimmy Stewart movies, boy meets girl, seeing Norman Rockwell covers on all the magazines. He knew all about plausible deniability, amazing suspensions of disbelief. He shaved my face and winked at me; what we knew was a family secret.

Today I watch the same old gray barbershop men go home alive. I used to imagine them seeing their children there, forming a touching Norman Rockwell scene, husbands and wives and children and the little grandchildren all together, and somebody's cooking supper. Momma's in the kitchen, cooking up something sweet for the next generation. It's a heartwarming Jimmy Stewart picture, with no room for freaks like Jim and me. I used to imagine everybody else this way: old men in barbershops, my own family. It's a picture of their world I made. I don't really know what they see when they go home. Jim is dead, and they're alive, and so am I.

Imagine each life matters, each loss a small important contraction, like a scar. Somehow, I lived for years thinking you could believe this way and be deeply moved by Gillette ads, or laugh at Gillette ads and common humanity and not be the kind of guy who jumped off bridges when things got tough. In other words, I thought the only lives that counted were the ones in Norman Rockwell pictures and Jimmy Stewart movies. But the Norman Rockwell pictures and the Jimmy Stewart movies lied. It didn't occur to me they lied about all our lives, not just mine. So all the names and rituals, the ways we try to recognize each other, were equally ridiculous, and all the people who believed in them were equal fools.

That was what I used to tell myself, before I changed my name.

I light a candle for Jim every year.

The Sex Change

The first person I saw go through a sex change was my cousin Jeff. He went through the process as something of a test case. I felt sure his line of work would give him a natural sympathy for my situation. My cousin Jeff is a clown.

Jeff's transition happened more or less by accident; he'd come to town to give a performance. At the time I had just changed my name, and sat spellbound in the audience with several friends, watching him negotiate an endless series of dangerous accidents and near disasters. Jeff juggled knives. One could go flying. He tossed heavy objects about. He could do himself an injury. He intercepted acrobats, whose bodies hurtled toward his at unseemly speeds, like so many animate spears. The dangers of impact. The show ended with him pressed into the seat of a tiny bicycle, pedaling furiously, the weight of the entire company supported on his back. His painted smile never wavered.

Then we went out for coffee and a sex-change operation.

On my way to meet him, I decided Jeff's delicate constitution couldn't possibly support my existence. So I instructed my friends to call me by the woman's name Jeff knew, the pronoun "she." My friends had just spent the past six weeks in a valiant effort to abandon this name and pronoun. One of them had begun accidentally switching pronouns on everyone she knew; many amusing scenes had followed. Coffee with Jeff was a slightly strained experience. I tried to make small talk, but words had suddenly become dangerous.

"So," I said, "isn't what you're doing, um, awfully *dangerous*?"

"Well, not really, as long as you know your limits, keep yourself in good shape, and stay aware of what you're doing." Jeff noticed his reassurance had failed to lighten the mood. He smiled and leaned in conspiratorially. "But," he whispered, "I do have . . . a unicep."

"A unicep?"

Since we were in the Pacific Northwest, our coffee was taken in a bookstore. As Jeff leaned forward, a troupe of Make Your Own Victorian Ladies' Paper Dolls appeared over his left shoulder.

"My top man came down on me wrong once," he murmured shyly. It's kind of like," he whispered, ". . . well, you know that muscle in your upper arm . . ."

"My bicep?"

"Exactly. It's kind of like that, only . . ."

Jeff reared back and pulled up his shirt, exposing the arm. His india-rubber face stretched into a cartoon grin, and he made a muscle. The arm bulged straight up, round as a ball, a macho parody. *I'm Popeye the Sailor Man,* Jeff sang reedily, *"Popeye the Sailor Man. I'm Popeye the Sailor, I'm Popeye the Sailor, I yam what I yam what I yam."*

"Jeff," I said, "I gotta tell you something."

"You're what?"

"I'm changing my name to Aaron." This was not going at all well. Jeff's face had gone slack. It wasn't a *horrified expression,* a cartoon slack, but a real slack—pale, expressionless. His face wasn't used to it.

"You can't do that." If Jeff couldn't handle it, I thought, nobody could. Oh, boy. The rest of my life was going to be bad. I braced myself.

"Jeff, I already did it."

"But you *can't* do . . . no, what I mean is, *you* can't do that."

"Why not?" Okay, I'll tell him about the surgery, the hormones. I'll reassure him; my appearance is going to change.

"It's okay for somebody else to have a name like that, but *you* . . ." He trailed off. The problem was too obvious even to mention.

We all sat for a minute in silence, heads down. We must have looked like a funeral party. Finally Jeff couldn't stand it any longer. He looked up at me and exploded, "You can't change your name to Erin. You're not Irish, you're Jewish!"

When I assume I know what's going on, I often find I'm fooling myself. Being transsexual puts me on the front burner of a debate, one active in both the most abstract of intellectual literature and the most secret places of the heart. Catherine Millot analyses transsexuality with semiotic theory and propositional logic. My mother sometimes weeps and rages. Gender-bending, queer magazines tell me, is in. Am I supposed to have more surgery when it goes out for the fall line? And how come gender studies and women's studies is the same thing? How come women write books analyzing male gender roles but get mad when men analyze female gender roles? I dunno. I could name stories in which I appear as heroic spy in enemy territory, traitor to the feminist cause, hot-shit dyke bait, postmodern deconstructionist icon. The show's offensive, it's exciting, it flatters my sense of self-importance. I thrill, I laugh, I cry. But I don't get it. I feel the power of what my experience might mean to other people secondhand, through the funhouse mirror of other people's hopes and fears. Most of the time, until they hit me, I don't have a clue what they are.

"No, Jeff, not Erin, A-a-r-o-n. Two a's. Like Papa Aaron, my mother's grandfather, remember?"

"Oh, God, you had me worried there for a minute. I thought you'd run off and joined some kind of Aryan cult . . ."

"Oh, no, not at all. Nothing like that."

"Good. Well . . ." Jeff looked me over carefully. "Two a's, right?" He drew them in the air, just to be sure. "A-a-r-o-n. Like . . . "

"Yeah. Like that."

"Ah. Pronouns, too?"

"Yep."

"Uh-huh. I live in San Francisco. I know about this. So you're . . . "

"Um-hum."

"Surgery and all that?"

"Um-hum."

"Ahh."

Jeff sat very still for a few minutes. I breathed deeply a couple of times and managed a look up at him. His face had gone quiet. Not slack, like before, not the elastic song-and-dance of expression his flexible features usually wore, but quiet. I had never seen him look like that. Under the mask of his face something flickered, made small ripples across the surface, fierce life beneath still water. In that strange unguarded moment, I

saw that what was moving beneath my cousin's suddenly unfamiliar features was his picture of me. He was having a sex-change operation. A little
late, I realized his makeup and rubber nose were as scant a protection as
my own bravado. I knew then, as I've known every time it's happened
since, that the operation must be frightening. Some sex-change operations
take months, even years. Some are dangerous. I know now they must be
terribly painful. And the only part in the operation I can take is to advise
the surgeons: spare nothing a thorough examination. Practice, practice,
practice. Proceed with confidence, with love, with care.

"Well," Jeff said finally, "I like it a whole lot better than the other
option."

I take injections of testosterone solution, which replace the hormones
my own testicles do not produce. My testicles are made of silicone, like
my mother's breast implant and my cousin's clown nose. My surgeon
put them into my scrotum, which he sewed up when he took a 38-C cup
worth of fatty tissue off my chest. I've had a lot of plastic surgery. What
I haven't had, really, is a sex-change operation. Over the years, I've put a
lot of friends and relatives, as well as not a few strangers, through the operation that changes me from a woman to a man. People who have met
me since my surgery occasionally put themselves through a reverse sex-
change operation, deciding I'm a woman instead of a man when they find
out about the surgery I've had. That's a process I'm not fond of, but what
can I say? The figure in another person's mind may wear your face, but
it will forever, inseparably, belong to them. Each of us has to create the
world we live in for ourselves. However much we may want to intervene,
to help a loved one, or to change an image we can't stand, we have neither
the right nor the power to stick our fingers through the skull and shape
that other mind. The operation is their decision.

This particular decision—whether to convert myself from a woman
into a man—is one I've never had to face. Like most people, I think, I find
the idea uncomfortable, and more than a little suspicious from a feminist
standpoint. The reason I didn't have to make this kind of choice was that,
in the world of my own consciousness, I never was a woman in the first
place. And, for better or for worse, our own truths are the only truths we
ever know.

. . .

We take our shape, it is true, within and against that cage of
reality bequeathed us at our birth; yet it is precisely through
our dependence on this reality that we are most endlessly
betrayed. | JAMES BALDWIN, Everybody's Protest Novel

The ancient Greeks told stories about a prophet named Tiresias, who had
been both a woman and a man. As a result of this peculiar experience, he
became more famous than Dr. Ruth. Eventually, his fame reached the ears
of the gods, who were not immune to marital difficulties. Zeus and Hera,
the gods' king and queen, called him in to judge a dispute over whether
men or women had a better time at sex. Tiresias answered in favor of
women. Hera, enraged, struck him blind.

A couple of thousand years later, men ask me what it's like to be a
woman, and women want to know what it's like to be a man. Hey, I'm not
Tiresias, I just play him on *Jerry Springer*. If I could have been a woman,
I would have been. But I'm not. This curious little fact finally made me
two different things—a transsexual, and a man. So I've only got half an
answer. And that's just enough to make me aware of my power to offend
the ruling goddesses and gods of our own era.

As a transsexual, I've spent time in the fascinating world of gender psychiatry, male and female hormones, sex-reassignment surgery, and the
equally fascinating netherworld of finance and politics behind them. My
perspective is influenced by my own experiences, by my training as a biologist and historian of science, and by my career, since my surgery, in
theatre. In other words, I can draw conclusions about the social uses of
an insanity diagnosis, describe the physical effects of testosterone, tell how
the nursing staff at the hospital where I had surgery reacted to me, or do
a striptease to "Frank's Wild Years," but I can't explain my gender. I seem
better equipped to mirror gender for others—I can see how they reacted
to me when they thought I was a woman and how they react to me now
they think I am a man.

I do know what it's like to live as a man. As a man in the world—that is
to say, as someone with a social existence, which in our society requires
gender before age or class or even race—I am caught as much as any other man or woman in the myths of brotherhood and sisterhood, women

and men. Demeter and Persephone, Gilgamesh and Enkidu, Frieda Kahlo, Tupac Shakur, Arnold Schwarzenegger. They have in turn changed me. Much of what it's like to be a man is in my struggle with these myths, their beauty and their bullshit. Because, as men in the world, we have to choose ways to love both women and other men. We are asked to live within the circle of what men do and are. And the smaller that circle gets, the more of our energy is wasted in rebellion or conformity.

I can tell what its like to love as a man, and to be treated (as well as the circumstances of one man's appearance and culture can tell) the way men are treated. Since I've also seen how the same person is loved as a woman, and treated as women are, in the same places by the same people, I know more about the differences than most men. The differences are sharp. They may not be what you expect.

And I know something else. I know what it's like to have lived as a not-man and a not-woman, also as not-straight, not-lesbian, not-gay, not-minority, not-majority—in other words, to have lived imprisoned in an isolation created by the very categories that are supposed to shelter and support us all. If poor people can be described as "have-nots," I stand as one of an invisible, unnamed, and uncounted group, the "am-nots." This "minority" may be one to which all of us, in our most secret selves, belong. Perhaps its time for us all to come out.

Are these gendered issues? The caution I would like to offer is that life doesn't separate so neatly into boxes. Isolation has been the worst danger for me, as a human being and a man. Beyond the silences between people born from hatred, ignorance, or fear, lies another, deeper silence. It is the silence that equals death, born of the conviction that there's nobody else out there to hear. This lie (for I maintain that in every human circumstance this silence is a lie) can sever the slender umbilical thread that connects our lives together. Though I've survived in a maze of elaborate lies, this denial of ourselves in each other is the lie I have found most lethal and most difficult to fight. The lifeline that saves me in my darkest hours has always been nothing more or less than another voice in which I can hear my own.

He is not, after all, merely a member of a Society or a Group
or a deplorable conundrum to be explained by Science. He is—

and how old-fashioned the words sound!—something more than that, something resolutely indefinable, unpredictable. In overlooking, denying, evading his complexity—which is nothing more than the disquieting complexity of ourselves—we are diminished and we perish; only within this web of ambiguity, paradox, this hunger, danger, darkness, can we find at once ourselves and the power that will free us from ourselves. | JAMES BALDWIN, Notes of a Native Son

Surgery II

I wrote my mother a letter to tell her I was going to have a sex-change operation. The letter took up the better part of a dirty yellow steno pad I'd scrounged up while I waited for a tow truck by the side of a state highway. I sat on the edge of a cliff and wrote seventeen pages of why I'd want to do something to myself that seemed so horrible. I told her I'd understand if she didn't want to talk to me for a while. I told her she could ask me anything, though, anything she wanted.

She didn't ask me why a nice girl like me would want to do something so horrible to herself. Not once. She didn't ask me why I thought I wasn't a woman. She believed me when I told her I wasn't a woman. This was the one response I was not prepared to get from anyone.

My mother asked me three questions.

She said, "Do you have a good doctor?"

She said, "What's going to happen next?"

And she said, "What does it all mean?"

What does it all mean? Umm . . .

My mother on the phone, telling me she has cancer. "I can handle the diagnosis. I can go to the doctor. I can take the tests and fill out the paperwork and go to the hospital. But I can't figure out what it *means*." She's crying, tinny, pressed against my ear, a thousand miles away. "What does it mean? You're smart. You're a biologist. Just tell me what it *means*."

I said, "It's not your fault. You didn't do anything. It doesn't mean anything. It doesn't mean anything at all."

I said it over and over and she just kept crying. So I went to the library and copied statistics and survival rates and information on random mutations and oncoviruses and highlighted the most important passages and sent the whole thing to her. She called and said thank you and I said 94 percent survival rate and she tried hard not to cry and said she still wasn't sure what that meant.

A couple of weeks later I strapped a six-foot stalk of brussels sprouts into a cardboard box and mailed it to her, express. She called back and said thank you and she wasn't crying anymore. She told me now she saw how things lived and grew and she understood the story.

Some things that happen to people don't make any sense. We've got to make them make some kind of sense; any kind will do. Any story to explain:

Once upon a time when I was very young, my father's second wife Peggy, who is an artist, brought us home a magic book. And this book was full of riddles, and the riddles were the answers to all kinds of questions you might never know how to ask. In the book Peggy brought us, there was a picture of a young boy and his father, standing on the deck of a ship. The boy told a story, which was another picture of a young boy and his father, standing on the deck of a ship, telling another story, which was another picture, of the boy and the man. And so on, forever. The boy said:

"It was a dark and stormy night. We were sitting on the deck. The ship was sinking. The captain said, 'Tell me a story, my son,' so I began, 'It was a dark and stormy night. We were sitting on the deck. The ship was sinking. The captain said, "Tell me a story, my son," so I began . . .'"

FIRST STORY

The Harry Benjamin International Gender Dysphoria Association, *The Standards of Care for Gender Identity Disorders*, 5th version

"The major purpose of the Standards of Care (SOC) is to articulate this international organization's professional consensus about the psychiatric, psychologic, medical and surgical management of gender identity disorders. Professionals may use this document to understand the parameters within which they may offer assistance to those with these problems."

"**The Gender Identity Disorders are Mental Disorders.** To qualify as a mental disorder, any behavior pattern must result in a significant adaptive disadvantage to the person and cause personal mental suffering." [Whether every such behavior pattern would qualify as a mental disorder is not discussed in the Standards of Care.]

"Patients with GID [Gender Identity Disorder] . . . were to be sub-classified according to the sex of attraction: attracted to males; attracted to females; attracted to both; attracted to neither."

"The purpose of the [classifications] is to organize and guide treatment and research. . . . It has not been sufficiently studied, for instance, whether sexual attraction patterns predict whether or not a patient will be a mentally healthier person in five years with or without [legal access to medical treatment]."

"Many persons, including medical professionals, object on ethical grounds to surgery for GID. In ordinary surgical practice, pathological tissues are removed in order to restore disturbed functions or corrections are made to disfiguring body features to improve the patient's self-image. These specific conditions are not present when surgery is performed for gender identity disorders."

"**Conditions under which Surgery May Occur.** Surgical treatment for a person with a gender identity disorder is not merely another elective procedure. Typical elective procedures only involve a private mutually consenting contract between a suffering person and a technically competent surgeon. Surgeries for GID are to be undertaken only after a comprehensive evaluation by a qualified mental health professional."

"V. The Mental Health Professional's Documentation Letters for Hormones or Surgery Should Succinctly Specify:

A. The patient's general identifying characteristics

B. The initial and evolving gender, sexual, and other psychiatric diagnoses

C. The duration of their professional relationship including the type of psychotherapy or evaluation the patient underwent

D. The eligibility criteria that have been met and the MHP [mental health professional]'s rationale for hormones or surgery

    E. The patient's ability to follow the Standards of Care to date and the likelihood of future compliance

    F. Whether the author of the report is part of a gender team or is working without benefit of an organized team approach

    G. The offer of receiving a phone call to verify that the documentation letter is authentic

VI. One Letter is Required for Instituting Hormone Treatment; Two Letters are Required for Surgery

    A. Two separate letters of recommendation from mental health professionals who work alone without colleagues experienced with gender identity disorders are required for surgery and

        1. If the first letter is from a person with a master's degree, the second letter should be from a psychiatrist or a clinical psychologist—those who can be expected to adequately evaluate co-morbid psychiatric conditions."

"XII. Requirements for Genital Reconstructive and Breast Surgery

    A. Six eligibility criteria for various surgeries exist. . . .

        1. legal age of majority in the patient's nation

        2. 12 months of continuous hormonal therapy for those without a medical contraindication

        3. 12 months of successful continuous full time real-life experience

        4. while psychotherapy is not an absolute requirement for surgery for adults, regular sessions may be required by the mental health professional throughout the real life experience at a minimum frequency determined by the mental health professional.

        5. knowledge of the cost, required lengths of hospitalizations, likely complications, and post surgical rehabilitation requirements of various surgical approaches.

        6. awareness of different competent surgeons

    B. Two readiness criteria exist

        1. demonstrable progress in consolidating the new gender identity

        2. demonstrable progress in dealing with work, family, and

interpersonal issues resulting in a significantly better or at least a stable state of mental health."

"Options for Gender Adaptation
Processes
2. acceptance of the need to maintain a job ... or not to distress a family member as currently having a higher priority than the personal wish for constant cross-gender expression."

"XIII. Surgery
B. Genital and Breast Surgery for the Female to Male Patient.
1. Surgical procedures may include mastectomy, hysterectomy, salpingo-oopharectomy, vaginectomy, metoidoplasty, scrotoplasty, urethroplasty, and phalloplasty.
2. If the objectives of phalloplasty are a neophallus [penis] of good appearance, standing micturition [pissing], and/or coital ability [meaning either a penis that can fuck a vagina, or one that has functional nerves and allows you to enjoy sex; the ethical standards for surgery don't distinguish between the two], the patient should be clearly informed that there are both several separate stages of surgery and frequent technical difficulties which require additional operations.
3. Reduction mammaplasty [breast reduction surgery] may be necessary as an early procedure for some large breasted individuals to make the real life experience feasible."

I. EPIDEMIOLOGICAL CONSIDERATIONS

Prevalence ... The earliest estimates of prevalence for adults were stated as 1 in 37,000 males [transsexual women] and 1 in 107,000 females [transsexual men]. The most recent information ... is 1 in 11,900 males and 1 in 30,400 females. Four observations, not yet firmly supported by systematic study, increase the likelihood of a higher prevalence:
1) unrecognized gender problems are occasionally diagnosed when patients are seen with anxiety, depression, conduct

disorder, substance abuse, dissociative identity disorders, borderline personality disorder, other sexual disorders and intersexed conditions;

2) some nonpatient male transvestites, female impersonators, and male and female homosexuals may have a form of gender identity disorder;

3) the intensity of some persons' gender identity disorders fluctuates below and above a clinical threshold;

4) gender variant behavior among female-bodied individuals tends to be relatively invisible to the culture, particularly to mental health professionals and scientists."

ANOTHER VOICE

"I do not believe female transsexuals [transsexual men] should be divided into primary [allowed to have medical treatment] and secondary [not allowed to have medical treatment] groups but rather that these very masculine females are the far end of a continuum of butch homosexuality."

DR. ROBERT STOLLER, *Presentations of Gender* (Yale University Press, 1985)

Translating this material into English is rather difficult. According to Robert Stoller, an up-to-date accepted medical authority on transsexuality at the time I transitioned, transsexual men do not exist. And butch lesbians should not have access to hormones or surgery. The standards of care were designed as a kinder, gentler alternative to the ministrations of doctors like Stoller. As far as I can tell, according to the standards of care in 1996 when I transitioned, the correct and ethical treatment of me would have been as follows: On my contacting Dr. X, he should have refused to see me or speak to me, other than to refer me to a mental health specialist. Ideally, I should not have been referred to Suzanna Lansky at all, but rather sent to a research program at a university hospital where I could be studied as my psychiatric treatment progressed. However, Suzanna Lansky would have been allowed to see me instead.

Her job would have been to keep me in analysis for the longest time she could ethically allow, in order to observe me and test for the more serious illnesses—schizophrenia, drug addiction, paranoia—which, since homosexuality is no longer considered a mental illness, are considered the frequent causes of transsexualism. If she found any evidence of addiction or psychosis, her job was to ensure that I was psychiatrically evaluated and medicated as necessary to keep my illness under control. At some point in this process, she would decide if and when I was ready for my Real Life Test. At her direction and under her control, I would attempt to live for a year as a man in such a way that no one in my work environment or my personal life would believe I was actually female. This is called the Real Life Experience. Before and during this Real Life Experience, I would not be allowed access to anything that might cause my body to become physically more masculine.

Since, in my case, my breasts were so big that they could not be hidden, she would give me permission to have breast reduction surgery. In no case would I be allowed to have the breasts *removed*, only made small enough that I could conceal them by binding them tightly with elastic for a year.

If, after a year of this (in addition to the time necessary for breast reduction surgery and recovery), anyone significant in my life did not accept me as a man, or if, at any point, I had given up on the attempt, I could be judged to have failed the Real Life Experience. My therapist would then decide whether I would be allowed to try again, or whether I would simply be classified as not transsexual and refused further treatment.

If and when I passed the Real Life Experience, I would be allowed to see Dr. X, who would be allowed to prescribe me hormones. I would have to be on hormones for a minimum of one year before I would be considered for approval for surgery.

I would then be referred to a psychiatrist who specialized in the analysis of transsexuals, preferably at a university gender clinic where I could be studied. I would remain in analysis with this psychiatrist for as long as the psychiatrist felt was necessary, preferably longer if I were not being studied at such a clinic. At the discretion of this psychiatrist, I would be certified eligible, or not eligible, for surgery. What types of surgery I would be allowed and when would also be at the discretion of this psychiatrist. My original therapist would have been allowed to certify me as ready for any nongenital surgery, without the additional approval of a psychiatrist.

However, according to the standards of care at the time, there was some confusion as to whether breasts were genitals. All female reproductive organs were definitely genitals. Any surgery that might cause sterility, being genital surgery, would have to be independently approved by both mental health professionals, along with any genital surgery that was actually on the genitals.

If, and whenever, both mental health professionals had diagnosed me with Gender Identity Disorder and certified I was eligible for surgery, I would be allowed to visit a surgeon. The surgeon and I would be allowed to discuss only those procedures for which I had been approved. If the surgeon also approved, I could schedule these surgeries. My surgeon generally scheduled his surgeries a year in advance, so a year after the entire process was complete, I would be ready for surgery.

Since both extensive breast binding and the scars from breast reduction surgery make successful chest reconstruction difficult, part of my mental health therapy would include making sure I understood that my surgery might have poor cosmetic results.

At the time of my surgery, transsexuals were specifically excluded from the decision-making body that determined the standards of care for transsexuals. As the result of years of diplomatic and political maneuvering, which involved transsexual mental health professionals achieving positions of authority by hiding their transsexual status, the standards of care were revised. Under the revised standards, if a trans person has been using hormones without medical help, a doctor is now allowed to give them medical advice and access to legal and safe medication. Under the revised standards, if a trans person tells a counselor that they have previously risked death and disability trying to change their bodies without medical help, the counselor is now allowed to refer them to a competent doctor. In 1996, the doctor and counselor who saved my life by giving me immediate access to medical care could have been fired from their jobs, lost their professional licenses, and been barred from seeing transsexual people for the rest of their careers. In writing these essays, I realized that reporting they saved my life might injure their professional reputations, and I chose not to use their real names.

SECOND STORY

One day in junior high school I was walking down the stairs to get some aspirin from the nurse's office for a sudden headache when I suddenly realized that the arm on the banister didn't belong to me. It was a perfectly acceptable arm, a right arm, accompanying my progress toward the office. It just wasn't mine. When I tried urgently to explain this fact to the nurse, I was met with a blank stare I wouldn't learn to recognize for years. She asked if I meant that my arm was paralyzed. No, I answered, I could move it just fine. Did it hurt? No. Did I mean I couldn't feel it? I prodded the alien limb gingerly. There was an appropriate sensation in the vicinity. No, I could feel it. I also wasn't stupid; I was perfectly aware that it looked much like my left arm and was obviously attached to my right shoulder. But it wasn't *my arm*. The nurse decided I was incoherent. Since I was also grabbing the left side of my head and vomiting uncontrollably by now, I ended up in the hospital rather than at a psychiatrist's office. When the pain went away, my arm came back. Years later I read an essay by Oliver Sacks in which he describes exactly this experience of an alien limb as a characteristic symptom of nerve damage. Apparently, the neurological chaos of migraine can trigger the sensation as well.

I have vague, unpleasant memories that relate to the observation of a perfectly normal female body undergoing a perfectly ordinary transition to adulthood. There was, for instance, no detectable nerve damage of any kind in the breast tissue that began to appear more and more frequently within the close range of my vision. There was no traumatic accident or illness associated with the body's growth that would reconcile my experience with the syndrome described by Sacks. It was a perfectly good body, healthy and, I'm told, quite attractive. It just wasn't *mine*. I could deal with parts of it in isolation, recognizing a shoulder, an elbow, my hands and feet. I could take up weightlifting or go swimming and recognize that the body improved in both appearance and comfort as a result. I wasn't stupid; I recognized that this body was attached to me. However, I couldn't, for instance, see myself in mirrors. There was a vague, moving outline that I always noticed. If I stood still, the image tended to disintegrate into unrelated fragments, as with one of those trick photographs which, if you can't find the hidden image, leave you with a headache, wondering—is it properly focused? Damaged? Upside down? I couldn't recognize myself in photographs. This problem does not tend to make you a snappy dresser. I used to shop for clothes by asking a companion for the name of a media character that the article in question made me resemble. My companions quickly learned that "Winona Ryder" was not an answer that would earn them my undying love.

Sacks described a patient who had lost ownership of his injured leg. The presence of a detached limb in his bed horrified him so much that he repeatedly tried to throw it away, with disastrous results. Many transsexuals try to remove the foreign body parts themselves, if surgery is not available. In my own case, I followed time-honored scientific procedure. You take your two conflicting specimens, choose the one that you think you have the best hope of understanding, and put the other one out of your mind, in a drawer in the corner. Eventually, some brave soul would open the drawer and attempt to reconcile or name the contents. In the old days, the drawer in the corner was always labeled *Vermes*: Worms.

Sacks became interested in the problem of lost body parts only after he experienced it himself as the result of an accident. Unlike transsexuality, the loss of ownership of an arm or a leg is a common condition. Until that time, however, like his own doctors, he just didn't believe the problem was real. The problem is invisible, so it doesn't make sense, so it must not be really happening. The drawer in the corner of Western medicine is labeled *Psychiatry*.

In seventeen pages, this is what I tried to tell my mother:

Actually, there's no such thing as a sex-change operation. There are a lot of different operations. For instance, the surgeries I decided to have were originally invented for infantrymen whose testicles had been destroyed by land mines (scrotoplasty), for women with cancer of the reproductive organs (salpingo-oopharectomy), for intersexed children operated on to make their genitals look "normal" (genitoplasty), and for men who grew breasts at puberty, a condition called—if you are not transsexual—gynecomastia (double mastectomy as chest reconstruction). These surgeries are still performed on those categories of people, but in those cases, people don't tell Mom and Dad that what they're getting is "a sex-change operation."

If you need surgery and you're not transsexual, one of two things can happen to you. You can look at the state of your own body and decide surgery is something you need to change the way your body looks, for personal reasons. Then you choose the surgery you want and pay for it on your own. Cosmetic plastic surgeons usually perform this kind of surgery. Insurance companies classify this kind of surgery as "unnecessary, voluntary, and cosmetic."

The other thing that can happen is a surgeon can look at the state of your body and decide surgery is something you need to change the way your body works, to improve your health. The surgeon usually chooses which surgery to perform, and insurance companies will usually pay for it. Plastic surgeons don't usually perform these kinds of surgery; they're done by various surgical specialists. Insurance companies classify these kinds of surgery as "necessary, not voluntary, and noncosmetic."

There is a third category of surgery, rarely discussed. Occasionally, children are born with accidents of development—a small tail, a horn, extra or fused fingers, arms, or legs, ears or eyes set at different heights. These odd features cause no physical harm in themselves, though in the past such people were often murdered because of them. Sometimes a victim of disease, accident, or war may be left with damage that causes no functional loss—a woman who loses one breast to cancer, a man whose testosterone comes from a bottle rather than from the testicles lost to a land mine. Surgeries to create a "normal appearance" in these cases are called *reconstructive*, as distinct from *cosmetic*, plastic surgery. Of course, in the case of reconstructive surgery for accidents of birth—removing a tail or the sex organ of an intersexed child assigned as female, for instance—reconstructive surgery does not, in fact, reconstruct anything that was lost. It creates new forms for the person's body. My primary surgeon was a reconstructive plastic surgeon.

Land mines and chemical weapons were first widely used in World War I and caused many injuries to the hands, face, and genitals. Reconstructive plastic surgery, at that time, was rarely performed. After some debate, the German government decided to keep certain men—those whose appearance had become so frightening as to be considered bad for the nation's morale—confined to secret sanatoriums for the remainder of their lives. The public and the men's friends and families were told they were dead.

Their existence was revealed only by a photographer who managed to smuggle a camera inside.

Reconstructive plastic surgery is now widely available and performed by respected surgical specialists. For instance, though the balls made by scrotoplasty are nonfunctional and created by a reconstructive plastic surgeon, if you are an infantryman who stepped on a land mine or an intersexed child assigned to be male, insurance companies generally consider these surgeries "necessary, not voluntary, and noncosmetic."

Before I had surgery I spent a lot of time talking with transsexuals: half a dozen women and a couple of men. All of them said they'd tried to commit suicide when they didn't have enough money to pay for surgery. Sex-change surgeries cost a lot of money. Insurance companies never pay for them because, as plastic surgeries, they're considered "unnecessary, voluntary, and cosmetic."

I had to explain to my family that in a "sex-change operation," some surgeries change how your body works. One of the surgeries I wouldn't have, for instance, extends the urinary tract from the base of the penis to the tip. These surgeries are performed by various surgical specialists; urologists work on the urinary tract and remove male reproductive organs, gynecologists remove female reproductive organs. None of these surgeons are plastic surgeons, and none are considered "sex-change doctors."

Some surgeries reshape masculine surface anatomical features into feminine ones and are used by transsexual women. Some of them reshape feminine surface features into masculine ones and are used by transsexual men. These operations change how your body looks and are performed by plastic surgeons. The interior of the body is invisible. Sex chromosomes, ovaries, testes, uterus, prostate, fertility—all are invisible. The surgeons who changed the functional, biologic sex of the inside of my body are not considered sex-change surgeons. In fact, the most profound biologic sex change is caused not by surgery but by hormones. All the surgical work that defines me visually and legally as a man is on the surface. My "sex-change doctor" is a plastic surgeon. At the time of my surgery his office was shared with a reconstructive plastic surgeon who specialized in work on birth defects of the hands and a reconstructive plastic surgeon who worked on patients with very unusual faces.

I had to explain to my parents that I was having plastic surgery, but I wasn't having plastic surgery. Two mental health professionals would diagnose my life, as a physician might diagnose my body, then would choose whether I would be allowed to speak with a surgeon.

Before I had surgery I went through a series of mental health counseling sessions and a psychiatric evaluation and was diagnosed as the victim of a major mental illness. One definition of this mental illness is that I expressed a desire for hormones and surgery. For ten years I expressed a desire for and received hormones (birth control pills) and had surgery that changed the way my body worked. I faced the diagnosis of mental illness only when I began to find ways to change the way my body *looked*.

According to the rules of the evaluating psychiatrist's job, if he had decided that I was mentally healthy, I would not have been allowed to have surgery, because a mentally healthy person wouldn't want what I wanted. I made it clear to him that I wanted surgery. He diagnosed me as mentally ill. I thanked him.

As long as I had lied to doctors, had surgery under false pretenses, and treated myself with hormones without concern for recommended dosages or risks, I was considered competent to make medical decisions for myself. The moment at which I decided to take responsibility for my own health and to cooperate fully and truthfully with my physicians in dealing responsibly with my treatment, my diagnosis became mental illness. Diagnosed as mentally ill, I became legally incompetent to decide on treatment options for myself. I went through this process voluntarily, more or less; like all transsexuals, I had to be declared mentally incompetent to make surgical decisions for myself before a competent and experienced surgeon was willing to perform surgery on me.

The problem isn't with the surgeries I wanted; you don't need a psychiatrist to allow you to have a chest reconstruction, a scrotoplasty, or a salpingo-oophorectomy, even if the existing tissues aren't diseased, as long as you're not transsexual.

The mental illness isn't defined by wanting to change a body that's already normal; you don't need a psychiatrist to decide your facial bones are a disfiguring feature in order to have a nose job. Nontranssexuals regularly have their nonpathological breasts and penises enlarged without psychiatric approval. Breast reduction is also available and considered normal. Wanting a smaller *penis*, however, seems to be in a different category.

The problem isn't about changing gender. All over the world, intersexed children routinely have their sex organs surgically altered without their consent. This is done because some psychiatrists believe these children will have a different gender identity if they are operated on than if they are not. These surgeries have much more important functional effects than mine; though my sex organs cannot give me children, they can give me pleasure. The surgeons who remove the penises and clitorises of intersexed children do not need permission, either from the child whose body will be affected or from a psychiatrist who has made a personal evaluation of what would be best for each child's mental health.

The mental illness isn't even mental. I never billed my insurance company for any care I've had since my diagnosis; I was told any care tied to a GID diagnosis will automatically be excluded from coverage by any policy issued by any insurance company in the United States. However, years after my surgery, my doctor's office accidentally sent a bill to my insurance company. The bill for the blood test I have once a year to check my liver function was returned to me with a statement that read, "Your insurance policy provides no coverage for mental health care."

I wish I could offer a definition of the word "transsexual" more meaningful than "someone who wants 'sex-change surgery.'" As far as I can tell, it has to do with whether what you want for yourself is the same as what someone else would want for you. Wanting what a "normal" person wouldn't want is considered evidence of mental illness. Surgery is then the physical treatment for what is considered a *nonphysical disease*: a mental illness in a healthy brain, a sickness of inappropriate desire. I become my own incubus. Technically speaking, of course.

Therefore, only transsexuals are excluded from legal and financial protection because our treatment is physical, "unnecessary, voluntary, and cosmetic." However, we can't control the fate of our own bodies because our treatment is mental, "necessary, not voluntary, and noncosmetic."

Though the standards of care for transsexual people have been revised, the basic definition of transsexuality has not changed. In modern times, AIDS, gout, and diabetic obesity have been reclassified from moral deviance to physical illness. Intersexuality has been reclassified from moral deviance to congenital physical problem. Left-handedness has been reclassified from congenital physical problem to normal human variation.

Homosexuality has been reclassified from moral deviance to mental illness to normal human variation. Epilepsy and Tourette's syndrome have been reclassified from moral deviance to mental illness to physical illness whose symptoms involve thought and behavior (and whose treatment, incidentally, can be covered by insurance). Transsexuality remains classified as a mental illness, treated as a physical illness, and morally judged in the worm drawer with those other illnesses of inappropriate desire, the sexual perversions.

It took most of seventeen pages just to explain the procedure I would go through to my mom. She still didn't ask me why I wanted to do this horrible thing to myself. There were times when I wondered, though my idea of the horrible thing I was doing had nothing to do with the surgery.

The two mental health professionals who evaluated me gave me permission for the surgeries I wanted. Just as important, they and my doctor also chose for me a new name—transsexual. With my new name came a new language to describe how I felt, what I wanted, and why. Using that new language was my choice. It gave me words to describe the indescribable, explain the inexplicable, to say what I had no words for. They weren't the right words, but they were something. So I told my mother I was a transsexual, and I was having a sex-change operation.

One definition is, perhaps, *the place where boundaries break down.*

THIRD STORY

After a year of testosterone therapy, I was shaving every couple of days, my upper-body strength had doubled, I'd lost twenty pounds of fatty tissue from the hips and breasts, my shoes were a size larger, I'd grown out of the shoulders of all my jackets, and I was singing baritone. I went back to Nebraska the year after Brandon Teena died, sat with my dad in his sport-utility vehicle, and tried to explain about sex-change surgery.

He said, "Some of these books you gave me . . . I'm pretty uncomfortable with the politics. They're so crusading."

"I'm not on a crusade. I'm just not going to hide anymore."

"But you don't have to be so, well . . . are you sure you want to go ahead with this surgery thing so soon? This is the rest of your life you're talking about. I know you've always said you don't care what people think, but as you get older . . . honey, you start to care about community, about being comfortable in a place, about other people being comfortable with you. You start to care about other people . . ."

"Dad . . ."

"All I'm saying is, you could be more discreet, maybe just wait a little longer."

"Dad," I said, "I'm not going to be ashamed of myself. I know it would be more convenient if I hadn't changed my name until after my surgery, I know I still don't look completely . . . I know doing a lot of things differently would be more convenient for other people . . ."

He slewed around to stare at me. Between the lofty professorial brow and the noble tweed beard was my dad, his face grim with fear. "I'm not talking about convenience, damn it! High-mindedness is all well and good, but I'm talking about your safety. I just don't, you know there's been some trouble in the state recently over this . . ."

He turned to stare intently at the speedometer. "I just don't want you to get hurt."

"Dad," I said, as gently as I could, "I do care. I want to be honest with people. And it's too late for me to hide, even if I wanted to. I've already been through a lot of changes this past year, physical changes . . ."

"But that's just it," he exploded. "I haven't noticed any difference in your appearance at all. You still look exactly like you used to!"

When I was diagnosed as transsexual, I had never seen a postoperative transsexual man, even in a photograph. I was a specialist in social issues in human biology, a biology teacher, widely traveled and active in queer politics in major cities and liberal college towns. I had no idea whether surgery would leave me looking like a man, like a disfigured woman, or like a person who had been disfigured until their sex organs were erased. Was surgery the punch line of a very expensive cheap joke? A consultation of the scientific literature on the subject yielded no images whatever—but, from the leading psychiatric expert on sex-change surgery, this quote:

> Guppies can change sex; humans cannot.
> STOLLER, *Presentations of Gender*

Queer literature, medical literature, and psychiatric literature all agreed: I always was a woman, and if I had surgery, I'd still be a woman.

All I knew was that I'd rather go through life as a man everybody thought was a woman than as a mutilated man everybody thought was a woman pretending to be a man. I suppose that this is why the Harry Benjamin Standards of Care require transsexual people learn to face this issue through the "Real Life Experience." It's good to find out how you deal with the fact that people may never see you as you want to be seen. For instance, people never saw me as a man until I took testosterone and had sex-reassignment surgery.

When I was diagnosed as transsexual, photographs of people who had sex-reassignment surgery were available only through the surgeons who performed sex-reassignment surgery. According to the standards of care, I couldn't talk to such a surgeon until I'd convinced a mental health professional that I *wanted* sex-reassignment surgery and they decided to allow me to have it.

But a mental health professional can either diagnose you as mentally ill or not. So if they didn't diagnose me, I wouldn't even be able to see what people who had surgery looked like. If they did, I figured my best news would be that electroshock therapy was passé. The worst news would be that I'd pay my entire income for a psychiatrist to try behavior modification and mandatory drag on the theory that, eventually, clothes would make the woman. What condition would I be in after a year of pastel pink minidresses and nausea induction treatments?

From these tender thoughts I was saved by the ministrations of Suzanna Lansky, Master of Social Work. I walked into her office and was met by a middle-aged woman wearing large bead necklaces, the distinctive field mark of a hippie social scientist.

"Have you ever been in trouble with the authorities?" she said.

"No," I said.

"History of violence? Arrest record?"

"No!" I said, outraged.

"What's your work history?"

"I've been doing science education down at the museum for the past year. Before that, I was a zookeeper at the San Diego Wild Animal Park."

"Has anyone ever filed a restraining order against you, anything like that?"

"Of course not."

"Suicide attempts?"

"None, thank you very much."

"Ever been in a locked ward?"

"NO! Listen, I came here in good faith. Now what the hell is this all about?"

"Look, my other job is working for the courts, deciding who gets involuntarily committed to mental institutions. If you're not a danger to yourself or others, you can pretty much decide what you want to do with yourself. That's all it's about, dear. That's the only thing that matters to me. I'll have to check your records, but you look okay to me. Now, are you just here for your letter, or do you want counseling?"

"Uh, I'm after the letter, thanks," I said, considerably taken aback.

"Okay," she said. "It's not like these are mutually exclusive categories, by the way. You can come to me for your letter and for counseling, too, if you want. You're going through some tough times here in the system. Sometimes it helps people just to have somebody you can talk to about it. Okay?"

"Okay."

"Good. Now, here's the deal for the letter. You come see me three times, I'll charge you a hundred bucks, and if nothing particular comes up that either of us feels you need to get worked out before you head for surgery, I'll send you off after the third session with letters for the surgeon and the DMV. Fair enough?"

"Fair enough," I said, settling back. "The only thing is, I don't have a lot of cash."

"Listen, hon, the surgeon and the psychiatrist are going to charge a lot more than a hundred bucks. Do you have the finances set up?"

"I've got a price list from the surgeon and the money all set out. I'm just trying to save everything I can . . ."

Suzanna Lansky looked at me severely. "I'm going to level with you. I only charge what I need to make my rent. If you're hurting, or you can't afford surgery right now, we can definitely work something out so you can have information, meet TS guys, get references, support, and come

146

see me. But if you're getting ready for surgery, you need to know that everybody in this business is making money. The surgeon's going to make anywhere from about $5,000 up to $100,000. The psychiatrist you'll have to see charges $150 an hour. In this system, everybody gets their cut. Mine is a very small cut. But if the surgeon is getting his cut and the psychiatrist is getting his, then I don't deserve less from you than what I'm asking."

"I see your point," I said. "I've got the money."

"So what do you feel like talking about?"

I had discovered the real danger wasn't a mental institution, and it wasn't a therapist hell-bent on the urban renewal of my mind. The real danger in my situation was hope. You can escape from a mental institution, but you can't escape from hope. It seemed like a hell of an incurable mental condition to get as a joke.

Mercifully, the first generally available photos of transsexual men were published at about this time. They looked startlingly unlike women who'd had their entire bodies caught in mechanical rice pickers. The bodies of postsurgical transsexual men are not those of defective women. Some observers might see our bodies, with their scars and anomalous penises, as mutilated, but even in this reading my body would be seen to be the mutilated body of a man. These are dangerous images.

Shortly thereafter the surgeon's staff decided that since I now had one letter from a mental health professional certifying I was transsexual but not actively psychotic, I could come down and have an exam and a chat with Dr. Meltzer. And, oh, yes, I could schedule surgery. Just chest surgery, you understand, until that second letter arrives. But it's a good idea to schedule these things early, the doctor's usually booked about a year in advance.

So, firmly penciled in for thirteen months into my surgeon's future, I stopped by to pay him a visit.

Dr. Meltzer looked rather like Jerry Lee Lewis's other cousin, the respectable one who'd avoided rock and roll and religion and gone on to medical school. He'd emerged with a wardrobe of custom-tailored suits, a degree in reconstructive plastic surgery on his office wall, and a favorite phrase. He used my name and the correct pronouns, clipped hordes of surgical slides of "my guys" onto a light box with the air of a man passing out wallet photos of his kids' school ballet performance, and responded to my blizzard of questions on life-threatening complications with a twinkling and practiced smile. "Hey," he said, over and over, "it's just skin."

For the serious stuff, he sent me on a round of preliminary appointments that closely resembled clowns emerging from a Volkswagen—hematologists, anesthesiologists, hospital scheduling staff. Everyone was professional, pleasant, honest, and informative. Along the way I got to discover that anesthesia was my only significant risk, except that I had one gonad bigger than it should be.

"It's probably just not atrophied from the testosterone," one of the doctors said. "That sometimes happens; nothing to worry about. The chances of a tumor, with your age and history, are very small. It's not worth doing a biopsy as long as we're going to go ahead right away and get it out."

So I also had the pleasure of meeting a gynecologist named Paul Kirk.

"Now, don't worry," whispered Paul Kirk's nurse. "He's very good. He's just got a kind of, um, strange manner with some of his patients."

We began with a physical exam, conducted in total silence. The only time he spoke was to tell me he could let his nurse watch, if I'd be more comfortable with a woman in the room. I declined to make him the same offer concerning his next prostate exam.

"Hello," I said instead. "I'm here for a pre-op consultation. I need to go through the biological consequences of the various gyn surgeries with you and find out exactly what my options are."

"Hmmf," said Paul Kirk. I waited for several minutes. He did not look up.

"One of my concerns is with what kind of medical care would be needed for any organs left, and whether diagnostic access would be physically possible," I said.

"You can't just sew it all shut, you know," said Paul Kirk.

"Yes, I'm aware I do not have that surgical option," I said pleasantly. "Which is why I need to understand, in exact anatomical detail, what options we are talking about."

"Talk to Meltzer," said Paul Kirk.

"I have, and he sent me to you."

By now he had been staring at the same single sheet of paper for the past twenty minutes. I asked him a few more questions. He repeated his previous comments. I told him I was a biologist; he could use technical terminology.

The room filled up with an uncomfortable silence. I suddenly realized this was the uncomfortable silence of a man convinced I was lying. Shortly afterward I realized I'd been trying to have a technical discussion for the last twenty minutes with a man who would not make eye contact with me.

"Perhaps," I said finally, "we could start with the relationship between exterior and internal anatomy. You could just draw a picture."

He seized a pen and began to draw a diagram of normal female anatomy. As he drew he explained once more the reasons why I couldn't just have it all sewn up. As he spoke he went over the lines of his drawing again and again and again.

It did not take me longer to wring the most critical required information from the lips of Dr. Kirk than, say, a fourteen-round grudge match with a bear.

Later I discovered he had canceled his participation in my surgery at the last moment. I assume somebody up there was looking out for me.

Much later I learned Dr. Kirk has been a consistent presence for the past twenty years in the committees that plan public insurance coverage in the state where I live. Several years after my surgery, these medical advisors were asked to recommend whether any sex-change surgeries should be covered by public insurance. The medical advisory committee advised against coverage, citing the following reasons:

There is no good evidence that transsexualism causes other psychiatric disorders. In fact there is good evidence that the opposite is the case . . . medical evidence on sex reassignment surgery was plagued by a number of important failings. . . . [For instance, many] of the studies use self-reporting of people who have undergone sex reassignment surgery as the end point of judging success or failure.

Report of the Oregon Health Services Commission, 25 February 1999

Apparently, the fact that I am transsexual proves I am not qualified to judge whether my surgery, or my life since, has been a success. But if I am not, who is?

"Hey," Dr. Meltzer's receptionist said, "great news. We've got an appointment for surgery that just opened up next month."

"For the chest?" I said.

"Weell . . . I can tuck you in here with some extra time," she said, smiling brightly, "just in case that second letter comes along."

I called the psychiatrist from a pay phone in the lobby.

"Weell," said another receptionist helpfully, "the doctor is usually booked solid about six weeks in advance . . ."

"Today. Tomorrow. Next week. I can be there in fifteen minutes," I said.

"Weeelll . . ."

I breathed deeply and explained the situation slowly and clearly in an absolutely perfectly sane tone of voice.

"Next month," the receptionist said, and gave me an appointment a week and a half before my surgery date. I had a week and a half to convince Dr. Y, psychiatrist, that I suffered from an extreme, uncontrollable form of the appropriate psychiatric disorder and was also simultaneously, absolutely, perfectly sane. No problem. Moses talked to God, right?

Tucked behind a fifteen-foot walnut father-figure desk, Y was the pale gray color of a fancy mouse and looked bored. He asked me if I played with dolls or trucks as a child. I told him I was into museum specimens.

He asked, "How long have you been engaged in your Real Life Experience?"

"All my life," I said.

"Ah," he said. "Well, how long have you been cross-dressing?"

"I've dressed like this since I was three years old. Nobody ever noticed."

"Adolescent romantic experiences?"

"Didn't have any. Everybody thought I was a lesbian. Never could figure out why."

He said, "Have you ever loved a man?"

Before the appointment I had spent several hours fervently praying I would not be asked this question. A psychiatric evaluation by a total stranger who wants to know if you prefer pink to blue is not a wonderful place to come out as a gay man, even under the best of circumstances. I suppose the best of circumstances might be your sexual orientation not being listed in the Diagnostic Manual of Mental Disorders. I had decided I would never lie to a doctor again. I sat quietly for several minutes.

The psychiatrist gave a small, delicate cough. "Have you ever loved a man *as a woman*?" he said.

"No," I said. We moved on.

At the end of the session I said, "I'm going to leave you with a printed copy of my personal history. I wrote it up because I'm scheduled for surgery in a week and a half, if I miss that date the next one's not for a year, and I've got an enlarged gonad the doctors are a little worried about. They're a little worried about cancer. I told you about my medical history and my surgical concerns. If you're satisfied with my mental health, and my history seems congruent, it would be really important for my physical health if you would allow me to get surgery."

"No one is going to force you to do anything that could be dangerous to your health. Normally, breast-binding is part of the Real Life Experience . . ."

"They've been too big to bind since I was twelve."

"You can always have breast reduction surgery now, so you can bind them, then come back for approval to have them removed altogether in a year or two."

"My surgeon says breast reduction scars create problems for chest reconstruction later. And this is the bottom line: the more times I have surgical anesthesia, the higher the risk I'll have another blood clot and die."

"You seem to have met the qualifications for Real Life Experience. You may be ready for chest reconstruction surgery."

"I already have approval for chest reconstruction surgery. I want to have everything done at once; it was the consensus of an anesthesiologist, two surgeons, and a hematologist as to the safest way to treat a patient who's had a blood clot. I may have cancer. I have a surgeon ready to operate next week. But he needs your approval."

"You can go in for a biopsy instead. After that, if there's a medical problem, you can have the one ovary removed. Since that would be an actual, real need, it wouldn't require my permission. Then, after I'm sure you have a proper mental adjustment, you can go back for another operation to have the other one removed under the GID diagnosis. No one's going to do anything that would risk your health."

I stared at him. Apparently he wasn't concerned that dying might risk my health.

"We can't rush things here," he said. "You've obviously got some kind of gender dysphoria, but if I just wrote you a letter, there are professional considerations, I'd be leaving myself open to . . . " He stopped. I stared at him with what I am sure must have been some kind of facial expression. Then he said, "See if the receptionist has an appointment for next week."

She did. A week later I paid him another $150, and he wrote a letter certifying me as mentally ill: diagnosis—Gender Identity Disorder.

A year after I first decided to go through the whole process, I was actually allowed to have surgery. When everyone is on your side, none of the mental health professionals is troubled, everyone's secretarial staff has been personally trained by God, and everything goes as smoothly as the regulations can possibly allow, it takes about a year to get surgery. In the meantime, the technical literature offered cheerful Freudian analyses of why a nice girl like me would want to do this horrible thing to herself. All the literature said I hated myself—in other words, hated women.

I called my mom. I said, "Is there anything you want to ask me?" She said, "When's your surgery? I want to make my airline reservations." I said, "Are you mad at me about anything?" She said, "If you knew how important this change was to me, why the hell didn't you write your letter to me on better quality paper?"

The day before surgery, this is what my surgeon did:

He met me in his office at ten o'clock at night, as dapper and cheerful in a tweed Armani suit as a new-minted Victorian Explorer. With a blue indelible marker he drew a series of arcs and dotted lines across my body. Then he closed one eye, squinted carefully, and drew a black X on each side of my chest, where, tomorrow afternoon, my nipples would be. My skin looked like a treasure map. "This is the part," he said, "that I like to do in advance. It's a little tricky, finding the exact place where they belong."

While he was looking for exactly where to put the lines, he stared at my body for a long time. I stared that way at a woman on the bus once. I was doing a portrait of Richard Francis Burton at the time. I'd gotten on the bus to go to the library to find pictures of his nose, but his nose was already on the bus. The woman it was attached to saw me staring and crossed herself; I think she thought I was a molester. The stare is a kind of abstracted, intense gaze that makes a lot of people feel uncomfortable sitting for artists or dealing with surgeons—they're looking at your body but not seeing you.

When my surgeon stared at me the same way that night, I realized he was looking at my body today and seeing me tomorrow.

Afterward he said, "Let me show you a great trick. You'll love it. I'll show you how you're going to look." We went over to the mirror. He folded a small towel and held it up in front of my body, along the path of one of the lines he'd drawn. Above it, the cut lines of my pecs reflected in the mirror. Below it, the hanging skin of the remaining breasts was hidden. "What do you think?" he asked.

What I didn't say was that I knew all about that trick already, only when I did it I didn't need a towel.

The day before surgery, this is what the hospital did:

The receptionist informed me that I was scheduled for surgery at 8:30 a.m. She said, "Arrive a little early, and remember to bring your check for the full fee. You won't be allowed to enter the building until we've cleared your check and have the money."

The day before surgery, this is what my mother did:

She called me on the phone to wish me luck. She told me not to be afraid. She told me she loved me. Then she said, "You should do something before the surgery, some kind of little ritual. Here's what I did. You say good-bye to your breasts, and thank them. Before I had my cancer surgery, I thanked mine for nursing you and your brother. Of course, you never had children, never wanted children, so you wouldn't do that. I thanked mine for being beautiful. I know you never liked your breasts, never thought they were beautiful, so maybe you wouldn't want to do that . . . I thanked mine for being good to me, for being part of my body, a beautiful woman's body, part of myself . . . um, I guess that would be yourself as a woman . . . umm. . . ."

When she used to talk this way to me, I used to get angry. Now I just wait. All of a sudden the words I'm trying not to listen to stop.

After a minute she says quietly, "Oh."

"I just got it," she says. "Oh, honey, I finally got it. They haven't been good to you, have they?"

She sees me. She *sees* me! I wave.

"Oh, boy," she says. "Congratulations. I'm sorry it's taken me so long. I bet you're sure glad to have them off."

The day before my surgery, this is what I did:

I took myself to a low hill on the edge of the city to make a song. Here, the hill called Powell Butte is the only place for miles lifted a little closer to the sun. This song was made with a rattle wound with flicker feathers, out of the flight of small birds, crows, and the wind and the sun that lend direction, so that, on top of Powell Butte, when two roads cross you can tell which one leads toward the mountains, and which one wanders to the sea.

On top of Powell Butte, the park service drove a burst of railroad ties into the earth. They spray in all directions, making a compass whose points are marked with mountains. The park service has provided the mountains with brass name tags: Adams, Hood, Jefferson, St. Helens. Other people mark the same mountains with different names; the one marked as St. Helens was the most beautiful of her sisters once, and the most vain. She claimed for herself their one mirror, and for centuries she carried it as a quartz-clear volcanic lake far up one flank. From the top of Powell Butte you can see the mountain, still beautiful, rising up out of the hazy air. Her profile isn't what it once was, but it is a long, long way from the story in a book I read once, about someone who survived a disease no one survives. In that story, if you're left looking different from other people, you spend the next twenty years in small rooms in hospitals, over and over, hoping for this time, maybe, a normal face, a normal life. The surgeries I chose left me looking different from other people. Not on the street but in private, in front of friends, lovers, in front of the mirror. There are other surgeries, ones that promise you'll look normal, be normal; if you just have enough surgery, nobody will ever know you were ever different. These surgeries remove large quantities of flesh from one part of the body and replace it somewhere else. They don't always work; often, the flesh rejects a new form so unlike the old, and the sites, both old and new, are left damaged.

Surgery II

Memory is physical; it can be excised, reshaped, grafted. The danger is that if you allow too large a piece to be removed, enough might not be left to sustain you. The procedure works well for some people. They pay the costs, perhaps gain some advantages I do not have. It isn't what I'd choose.

So, make another story instead, in the sun on top of Powell Butte, where the crows are always watching. Small birds make fussy gleaning noises in a thicket not far from three firs alone on a ridge, rising into the sky. We're all making stories out of each other. We can't help it. For instance, there's a story about the Sun Dance, where Lakota men would be lifted into the air on thongs cut through each breast. They say the men who danced the Sun Dance were much loved, because they danced to make the nature of the sacrifice visible to everyone: to lose something, and, by your losses, to be made whole. People knew the value of what these men had done; to make a point of the worth of their word, they would display their scars. Suspended by the skin they had chosen to sacrifice, they had danced until the flesh came free to release them. Before the dance, a man would sing:

> *I will live*
> *I have said it*

Freaks

The first thing I remember when I woke up after the operation was an attendant asking me urgently, "Where do you hurt?" I gave him the answer that was excruciatingly obvious at the moment; I told him my balls hurt like hell. He looked quickly away and then asked if there was anywhere else I might be hurting. It suddenly occurred to me that *he didn't believe me*. It wasn't my pain he didn't believe in, it was my balls. He knew they were there, of course, in *theory*, but they weren't going down too smoothly in what we like to call *real life*. So I'm lying on a hospital gurney in excruciating pain, thinking we have a little dysphoria problem here, a little trouble dealing with reality. Only this time the other person is the one with the little fucking problem dealing with reality. The miracle of surgery is the way the surgeon can take your mental disorder and graft it onto other people.

The attendant was attempting to reject the transplant. Under the surreal light of the recovery room I kept thinking, clap your hands if you believe in fairies, everybody.

Later that night we got to duke it out with the immune system of the hospital staff. Some cells ignore the intruder, while others refuse assistance to the foreign body in their system. In the morning the discharge nurse neglected to provide necessary postoperative care instructions and devices, tried several times to forget prescriptions for painkillers and antibiotics, and giggled hysterically through the entire process. As a result I nearly ended up with a collapsed lung. Since one of the things refused to me during that first night was painkillers, we'd been too tired by morning to fight about everything I needed. The transplant thrived, nevertheless.

When we got home I discovered that my surgeon had equipped me with a jockstrap printed with the Stars and Stripes. Jack Armstrong, the All-American Boy.

In my dream just before the surgery I looked into a mirror in a hotel room on my way back to LA. I'd walked the whole way, effortlessly, through the ruins of a civilization destroyed by the irresistible sea. I was tall and blond.

When I started sprouting thick black hair in unlikely places I realized I'd seriously thought having a sex change meant I was going to get a whole new body. I had mine all picked out; I found it in the ads in the back of the *Advocate*. Baldness and knuckle hair and a pattern of beard growth that consistently caused strangers to stop me on the street with the assumption that I have special knowledge of farming with a horse-drawn plow had not been on my list. You do not get a whole new body. The body that you get is yours.

My cousin Jeff is the kind of acrobat who carries ten people on his shoulders while riding a bicycle; imagine this act captured on scratchy black-and-white film from the vaudeville era. I seem to have become my cousin's action figure.

Realistically, what do I look like in the mirror? What I look like in the mirror is no Greek statue but a Roman copy: a little thin in the limbs, a bit thick in the middle for perfect symmetry, a bit awkward, but handsome, workmanlike. Most of the Greek statues you see in books and museums are really Roman copies. We are serviceable renderings of a lost ideal.

Of course, there are also the big scars across my chest, the tight balls, the little dick that lies comfortably in the fold between my testicles. That, too.

The type of genital surgery I had is called metoidoplasty. Unlike phalloplasty, the construction of a penis from whatever other body parts the surgeon has determined you can spare, metoidoplasty actually wasn't developed for men who'd had their dicks shot off in the war. Like my back hair, it operates on the assumption that you have an inheritance to begin with, like it or not. It is a modification of your existing sex organs; the one you get is yours. I decided on metoidoplasty after seeing a photograph of the finished procedure. A photograph of the finished procedure is what you call a porn shot of a transsexual. Like most men, the gentleman in question was a size queen, and he made damn sure he was at full extension before his groin, thighs, and one highly suggestive hand were preserved for posterity. If you've seen car ads in which a man presses his nose to the dealership window, slack-jawed with lust, and murmurs, "I want one of *those*," let me assure you that, on the scale of desire, new cars are overrated.

In other words, I thought the picture was erotic.

A friend and I once saw a film clip of a vaudeville act. On the scratched old black-and-white stock, a buff, barrel-bellied man dressed as Rudolph Valentino drank kerosene and breathed fire while I watched, spellbound. The next night, at a party, I listened to my friend describe the act of the *regurgitator*, with disgust, as *throwing up stuff*. Throwing up stuff is, after all, what he did. Beauty is in the eye of the beholder.

Periodically I see artwork depicting *hermaphrodites*; abstract pillars filling a room, with one bullet-bra point low down and two high up. Movies with names like *Tits and a Dick*. A transsexual man named David Harrison wrote that he'd planned to appear in a porn film once, but the producers canceled it—no possible source of erotic appeal. The sex organs of men remind me of clusters of ripe fruit, soft and pendulous as French plums. In the mirror of my better moments, I am reminded that the tiny hands of bananas sold in gourmet stores have their own delicate charms.

Realistically, you might find something like my body in the photographs of Joel-Peter Witkin. It would fit nicely between dwarfs and cancer victims, posed in sepia against the velvet drapes, illuminated by something with fringe, some dried fruit, memento mori. In interviews the photographer stresses his sympathy for his subjects. I do not see him standing among the other freaks in his pictures. I do see a lot of his style these days. The last time this gothic act was popular was the colonial era, the vaudeville era, and the style was called Orientalism.

At the party three of us sat around a book of photographs by Edweard Muybridge. He was a photographer of the vaudeville era who invented a procedure for taking pictures of moving creatures in rapid succession. Against a black background ruled with regular white lines for measurement, Muybridge photographed galloping horses, leaping cats, flying vultures, and hundreds of people, mostly in the nude. *Woman walking, carrying bucket. Hod carrier climbing ladder. Woman with hand to mouth, walking down incline. Man throwing seventy-five-pound boulder. Paralytic child walking on all fours*. Laid across the page, the picture sequences resemble strips of film from an old movie.

We sat around the book, admiring the curve of the hod carrier's back, smiling at the languid air of a woman smoking a cigarette, watching her naked companion in a chair, laughing at the runner in his jockstrap and modest little tasseled cap. My friends remembered a sequence of a legless boy climbing down from a chair. They pointed at the particular frames that had inspired them with horror. The moment at which he lifts his right hand. The moment at which he reaches forward, the strong muscles in his shoulders outlined against the light. I am looking at the frames, the shudders of my friends, the abstract shapes dissolving into light. The moment I remember is the moment when the paralytic child, trotting on her hands and feet across the sea of shutters, has turned to face the cameras. She is grinning with delight.

Because most of his models posed nude or nearly nude, Muybridge was accused by his contemporaries of being a pornographer. Because the men typically wore jockstraps, while the women wore nothing at all, he was said to be exploiting women. His response to the critics was his body itself. On the frontispiece of his photo collections, a tall, stooped old man with a shock of white hair and an incredible beard rises from a packing crate as if to welcome visitors, his face still in shadow. He strides purposefully toward the lights and cameras, arms swinging ("The normal stride of a biped consists of two uniformly executed steps. Shakespeare recognizes this fact in *The Merchant of Venice*, act iii, sc. 4: "'I'll . . . turn two mincing steps / Into a manly stride'" [Edweard Muybridge, *Animals in Motion*]), his freakish, impossibly pendulous testicles dangling in the air against the grid of measurement.

Testosterone

As Adrienne Rich explained at the New York Lesbian Pride Rally of 1977, feminists must build their own women-centered, women-loving culture and identity, rejecting the violent, self-destructive world of men. | LYNNE SEGAL, Straight Sex

When I started taking testosterone, my skin felt all the time as if a strong breeze were running across it; that strange electric sensation you feel when you are about to be touched. All the time. I started buying jeans a size larger in an effort to keep the high wind at the crotch from making off with me entirely. The only question people usually ask me about testosterone is whether it makes me feel some urge to kill.

Testosterone makes you hungry. Desperately, ravenously hungry. I spent the first couple of months eating more or less constantly, remembering my brother as a teenager showing up in the middle of the night to empty the refrigerator. He used to drive me crazy enough to wrap Pop-Tarts in plastic and shove them down into bags of cat food to keep them away from him long enough so I could have one. I never saw this experience from his point of view before. For about six months I would have eaten the neighborhood trees if somebody had given me a big enough bottle of salad dressing.

Testosterone also makes you horny. I don't talk about it, because nothing I have to say about testosterone is the answer to a question about violence. It might be an answer to a question about love. The answer goes like this:

All of a sudden, it seems like everything in the world is in love with everything else. You can feel the breath of air across the hair of your forearms; everything is bidding for your attention, the soft caress of the table top across your wrists, the grass needling between your toes, the sun, the breath of a friend. You stagger around, drawn closer to everything at once. You want to touch, to be touched, with such a pure longing that it burns like sucking in breath before a glory hole. *Danger. Protective Gear Only: exposed flesh will burn in fifteen seconds.* There's no way to stop it. You can't stop breathing.

Don't mistake the feeling; it isn't sex, its that weird hopeless need that made you rock back and forth when you were a kid, made you jump out of trees just for the feel of the air and the ground on your skin, hold teddy bears tight against your chest, clutch wads of Kleenex when you were crying. So you reach out to someone, something, and all of a sudden you've got this *huge* hard-on you weren't expecting and it drags you along like a runaway train, sucking everything into some irreducible slush of confusion and desire. You find yourself doing what my old friend Joe used to call the please-baby please-baby please, and somewhere off in a corner you're sitting there thinking, *wait a minute, all I wanted was my teddy bear and now I'm that god-awful dog the neighbors had that wouldn't quit fucking the furniture.* The world loves you like the first sunny day all year, or the bottom drops out and you want to die, and the whole time you're just totally bewildered.

Nobody likes to look at the picture of their own face, desperate, begging. So mostly, we don't talk to women about it. So mostly, we don't say anything when we fuck each other.

One of the first things I noticed about testosterone was that women don't seem to need sex. Not that they don't like it, love it, do it all the time, get horny, fuck around, whatever. But women seem to need sex like you might need, say, chocolate. Men seem to need sex like you might need, say, food. I'm generalizing again; let's say we're not talking about sex. Let's say we're talking about the night my brother came home to an empty refrigerator and ate five pounds of chocolate because it was what was there. Let's say we're talking about whatever makes you think that, if you can't get laid, it might be almost as good if you could pay somebody to just rock you back and forth for a while. If you're a little more experienced, you might think, hey, if you can't find somebody who'll rock you back and forth for a while it might be almost as good if you could pay somebody to just get laid, and if you can't find either one you could just run into a wall a few times and at least that would be some contact. I used to have a feeling similar enough to recognize it later. Back then I called it loneliness.

Lonely people do stupid, crazy, painful things, and it's their own damn fault.

You're hard all the time, your face breaks out and you shave and you're covered in stubble and you don't shave and you've got that scraggly-ass nerd beard. You start snoring and your feet stink and you're hungry all the time and your clothes don't fit, you leave hair all over everything you get within a hundred yards of and you've got to have something from someone you care for and every time you reach out you just wind up, surprise, hard again. I used to watch my partner sleep at night, the curve of ribs rising and falling with each breath, and I'd think, "Must be a woman; doesn't need much of anything." A person like that seemed so self-contained, perfect as the plastic tubes of paint that spring back into shape regardless of how empty they are, or how full. I've got a whole drawer full of the old metal ones that came shiny and smooth and twice as beautiful. When you opened them they peeled and wrinkled and folded up small and hard and useless, tearing at the seams, squirting unwanted pigment everywhere. They don't make paint in metal tubes anymore; they're obsolete.

When I was a little kid my mother brought me a T-shirt that said, "A woman needs a man like a fish needs a bicycle." I wore it a lot. I liked the little picture of a fish on a bike; it seemed funny and absurd, like a Dr. Seuss book.

A friend unhappy with her husband tells me, "Men have testosterone poisoning." As gently as I can, I point out that I've been taking testosterone for years now and it hasn't poisoned me yet. She looks stunned. "You've been taking *testosterone* all this time? But you're not a total asshole!" she blurts out. I'm not sure where she thinks my beard comes from.

I don't get angry at her. Women say things like that all the time. Men do, too.

These days I run a theatre group for folks from the street. We go around the circle, each naming our drug of choice, playing it out as a character. One poised young woman says, "I don't do drugs."

I say, "Choose whatever works."

"Okay," she says, "I'll take Ego." She swings her hips, eyes flashing as she smiles, miming lipstick, kissing into an imagined mirror. A drug counselor and I "support and empower" her. She's a young woman with a tough life. She needs all the power she can get. He's a trained professional, my colleague from the hospital; his tall, spare body stretches undefended, his rugged handsome face open and supportive as the actors pound and laugh and writhe through Meth, Crack, Alcohol, Heroin. My turn comes. I'm still pretty naive about these things.

"My drug of choice," I say, hesitating only a little, "is testosterone."

The drug counselor leaps from the chair next to me and runs across the room.

"I'm moving over here 'till you're done," he calls over his shoulder. "Man, that scares me."

It's a joke, son. You're supposed to laugh.

I never get angry now. If I got angry, I would look just like my stereotype. But I remember the night I watched Ben Vereen on television, telling anecdotes about his early career. Sometimes, he said, he was forbidden to walk through the front door of the theatre where people paid to see him perform. As he spoke his face was a pleasant, chocolate-colored mask. His diction was absolutely perfect. You could cut yourself on the creases of his pearl-gray casual clothes. I see my face in his face and it frightens me; you can fight so hard for respect that you lose the ability to feel anything at all.

Men ask me if I have any regrets about the surgery. Sometimes their voices are high and strange, almost wistful. I have male friends and lovers with the tall, spare, strong-featured, tightly muscled, well-hung bodies associated with high testosterone levels. They have the kinds of bodies I always wanted. When talking about the behavior of men they don't like, they all use the phrase "testosterone poisoning." Each is ashamed of some feature of his body associated with high testosterone levels: a prominent Adam's apple, pattern baldness, a high sex drive, five o'clock shadow, sex organs that can penetrate another person's body, an intense need to move and touch.

Women ask me if I'm treated differently now. One day I saw an old acquaintance on the street, a woman I hadn't seen for a while. She'd been told about the testosterone, the surgery. She walked briskly over to talk to me.

"Hello," I said. She didn't say hello.

"So," she said suddenly, "people must treat you a lot better than they used to."

"Well," I said, "yes and no. I treat other people a lot better than I used to, and they treat me better in return. It's sort of a general rule that took me a long time to learn."

She continued speaking in my general direction. "So," she said, "you must automatically get a lot more respect now that you're a man."

"Respect?" I said. "No," I said, "not really."

"So," she said, "it must be great. You must be making a lot of money, too, getting rich, everybody listening to you, people doing whatever you want. Your life must have gotten real easy overnight, huh?"

"No," I said, "not really. Nice to see you again. Good-bye."

Sometimes I tell anecdotes about my new experiences. The times, filled with an astonished joy at my new fellowship with human beings, I smile radiantly at each passerby. The way I watch women reply by dropping their eyes and crossing the street to avoid the potential rapist. I used to think women smiled a lot. Sometimes they smile. Usually they avoid me. Occasionally I get the hate stare.

The women to whom I tell these stories rarely get angry. They do, however, really prefer to know about all the ways men treat me better than they used to.

When I started taking testosterone, my mother started to respond to questions from me by saying, "I don't know. Talk to your father. You're his now."

Roz Chast drew a cartoon once, a window with a lurid sign reading, "Adult Books." Underneath, the titles were: *What Is a Mortgage? Cutting Back on Cholesterol. Making a Will.* The basic theme of my lifelong conversation with my father has been the importance of a 401k plan. I love my father. I honestly don't believe I was adopted. Actually, he's the most forthcoming with his children of any man of his generation I know. Unlike the fathers of all my friends, he's actually willing to have a conversation with his son. For years I learned a lot about the importance of steady work and health insurance. To learn more than that, I had to learn to reveal more about myself, a lot more than I had thought was respectful for a man to share with his father. And my father had to start dying. It's taken us years to find a way to talk that has any personal context from his life at all. For most of my life, all I knew was that he tried hard. Once in a while the mask did slip. One day shortly after the Bowers and Hardwicke decision—in which the Supreme Court ruled that laws criminalizing private consensual sex between adult men were constitutional, based on the appropriate legal precedent of burning homosexuals at the stake—I was having dinner at my father's house. In the midst of desultory small talk, Dad suddenly slammed his hand on the table between the roast chicken and the herbed filet beans and burst out, "I can't believe that damned sodomy decision. What were those judges thinking?"

To this day I have no idea where *that* came from. Though thirty seconds later we were discussing chutney, ten years later his comment was my grounds for thinking perhaps my father would be up to really accepting a sex change. He was. As long as we didn't have to talk about it. Few men in my life have given me so much consideration.

When I smile at people on the street, most men walk by silently or bob their heads in a curt, businesslike acknowledgment of our shared humanity. I had a lover once I couldn't talk to. He couldn't talk to me, either. Every once in a while, when things got tough, we'd turn to each other and say,

"Looks like a hot day."

"Yep."

"Plenty more comin', they say."

"Yep. Corn's looking good, though."

"Yep."

"Yep."

Then we could laugh together, or make love, and things would be better for a while. I love men who smile. Young men smile back, sometimes, and young women, too.

Men do tell me something I never knew before I started taking testosterone. My best friend in LA is a blond-haired, blue-eyed, six-foot-one-inch, 250-pound ex-Marine. When I tried explaining to him why I was taking testosterone, my plans for surgery, he told me he admired my courage.

I said, "I just don't want people to think I'm some kind of damn role model for women. What I'm doing would be a horrible thing for a woman to do, thinking that's what it took to get a job or respect or some kind of power."

Joe pulled his eyes off the Hollywood Freeway long enough to give me an astonished look. "But you are a role model for women, going through all this shit to get what you want, I mean, a tremendous role model."

Okay, I thought, *that* wasn't what I meant. Finally, in desperation, I told him, "Look. Imagine one morning you got up, walked into the bathroom, and saw some pretty little woman in the mirror. How would you feel if tomorrow you turned into a woman—five foot three, a hundred pounds, nice big tits, the whole thing?"

Joe pulled into the parking lot of our favorite late-night diner. As he shut off the engine, I looked over to see how the thought of himself as a woman was affecting his emotional balance. He had the beatific smile of a man in a dream.

"Well?" I said.

"The first thing I'd do," said Joe slowly, "is buy the most beautiful dress in the world. One of those Chinese embroidered-silk jobs, with gold beads, dragons and phoenixes and everything. And I wouldn't have to care how much it costs, because I could get it on somebody else's credit card. They've been buying shit on mine for years, so I know just how to make that happen. I'd wear it whenever I felt like it, and I'd walk right up to any man I wanted."

"Oh, yeah, I'm sure sex would be a wonderful experience."

"Why not? I always wondered what it felt like. Besides, it would be great to just lay there and let somebody else do all the work."

"I'm not talking fuck-fantasy here, Joe. I'm talking real life."

"I know exactly what you're talking about. You think I don't know?"

"You mean you'd like being a woman? All the time? In real life?"

His voice was bitter, but his eyes were alight. "You're damn right I would. I'd love it. I'd live it to the hilt and savor every minute. I'd dress to the nines and walk off the street with my discharge papers into a yuppie office job instead of night security for a mini-mall in Compton because I'm just another big dumb fucking grunt ex-Marine. I could wear real clothes to work instead of a three-hundred-dollar monkey suit I can't pay for. And if I wanted something I couldn't get myself I'd just act helpless and somebody would help me, instead of being scared out of my god-damned mind and having to go out there and do it anyway, not just for me but for everybody else, too. I could do things that would make guys beat my head in, or get me fired, or put in jail now, and come out smelling like a rose. I've been watching women my whole life. And I'd go dancing—man, I'd dance. I'd put fresh flowers in my house every day. And when I went on a date, he'd be the one to bring *me* roses, open the door for *me*, bust his ass for *me*."

Joe pounded one ham hand on the steering wheel. "It would be great for once in my goddamn life to see somebody want *me*."

I sat there and stared at Joe.

Finally I said, "Okay, maybe that wasn't a good example."

"So what's a good one?"

I thought for a minute. "Imagine you get up and look in the mirror and you look just like Joe. You look down at yourself and there you are, Joe. Time to go to work, Joe. You get to work and you realize everybody else thinks you're a pretty little woman. Now imagine it's always been that way."

"Yeah, okay, that would suck. But being a woman, that would be great."

"Well, so why don't you go out and get a sex change?"

Joe laughed. "I said it would be great to be a woman. I didn't say I was one."

My friend Jonathan leans forward and confesses, "You know, when I first realized I was attracted to men, I thought I had to be a woman."

"Did you know there were men who loved men?"

"Oh, sure, my uncle was gay."

"Then why did you think you had to be a woman?"

"I guess I just imagined falling in love. I imagined my boyfriend giving me roses, kissing me in the park, holding hands, you don't see two men doing that in public. Feeling safe and accepted. Being protected. I liked thinking about a big strong man, his strong arms holding me."

"So did you ever think about a sex change?"

"No. I never really felt like a woman. It just seemed like the thing to be."

I shake last night's crop of lost hair off my pillowcase. There's a letter from my mother. I open it and read about the worst storm in a hundred years; as she writes, trees exploded by ice lie across her city's streets, the leaves still green and wasting in an indifferent light. The roads are closed. The only sound is falling branches, the creak of a neighbor's roof, its ribs caved in. They spent last night sleeping in the basement. She tells me last night was like war.

In the center of it all, she dreamed her daughter came back. Her daughter came to sit beside her, wearing clothes borrowed from Elizabeth Taylor. She was new from chest surgery, smelled like Chanel No. 5, wore silk and gloves lined with fur: rich, famous, she'd foiled the last barrier to power. Her beautiful lesbian daughter came and touched her face and sat beside her in the sound of trees dying like men's machine guns, and told her everything would be all right. My mother dreamed she could sleep then, in her daughter's arms.

She sends me the poem she wrote for her daughter. She says she knows I'll understand. I read the poem and know that in a world where women can't love men and men can't love each other, no one will ever love me that much.

Then I go back again to visit. I sell the jewelry I make when I'm short on rent money to professional women, my mother's colleagues. I use her beautiful house as a front, take advantage of the comfort and space and catered food that make the conversation and the money flow. The women return to their lives, secured with gifts and fresh ornament. I make rent. Everybody has a good time. Afterward my mother and I fight over whether women or men have an easier life. This is not the conversation I want to be having. Again.

Later I fly home on the ticket I didn't have the money to buy on my own. My mother buys me plane tickets, underwear, shoes. "You're my *child*," she tells me in Mother Voice, which is supposed to explain everything. A woman friend picks me up at the airport. I don't have a car. She doesn't have money for a car, either, but she's got a husband, and he's got rich parents. I'm grateful for the free ride.

At home I slip up the fire escape stairway, trying not to wake Tim on the first floor. After ten years of AIDS, his neuropathy doesn't let him sleep much. The lights are out in my apartment. For a couple of minutes I stand quietly outside Dawn's bedroom door, wondering whether to wake her and say hello. She doesn't much like nights. Besides, she was probably up late discussing the latest novels with a woman friend; they often do this, sharing a taste for favorite books from a genre by and for women. The protagonists of these books are always tall slender beautiful elflike hairless gay men with infinite emotional sensitivity and tireless giant penises erect only when desired by another. Acne and pattern baldness are unknown on their home planet. I try to shave quietly, trim my beard close so I won't look like a cut-rate extra from *Deliverance*. I remember to clean the loose hairs out of the sink trap again. Then I go to my own bedroom, sit down, unwrap a 21-gauge needle with a 1 cc syringe, and put this week's dose of testosterone into my leg.

I knock gently at Dawn's door a couple of times, but my partner is a heavy sleeper as long as I'm not there. The next thing is to push wide the partly open door, so the light from the hallway falls onto the bed. She lies quietly, her face perfectly open in sleep. I feel the shock that sometimes comes when seeing someone you love for the first time after an absence— Can eyelids be so miraculous? How could I have failed to notice? I take a long, slow breath, get ready, and step into her room.

She startles awake with the same scream as always, instantaneously strangled. Since I transitioned, she's done this every time I wake her, and whenever I come unexpectedly around a corner or out of the bathroom. If for some reason she thinks she's alone in the house, it happens when I speak. It never used to happen. At home these days, I'm always careful not to get too close, to signal my presence and location in advance with throat clearings, random handling of objects, snatches of song—a technique I learned from hiking in bear country. Screaming, she bolts half upright, then catches herself and blinks at me sleepily.

"Love you," she mumbles. She pats the bed for me to sit. I reach across to touch her shoulder. She flinches. I get up to go.

"Hi, honey," I say, "I'm home."

Men

There was a man with the band whose high cheekbones, shadowed with hair, dark as the guides in the centers of flowers for bees seeking honey hidden in the throat, led inevitably to his perfect lips. The color for this love is cocoa with ashes. Will it be the same forever? Was love always this way, when I wasn't looking? I told the man who was my lover, before we went to bed together, how the growth of hair across my shoulders stirs at the slightest breeze of his passing, of smiles from waiters, men in bar bands. Each hair erects at the faintest movement, high in the air, keyed to a tiny sensor in the base I never noticed, deep inside the skin it's sniffing like a dog for sense or at least sensation, this pelt we wear instead of armor. One inch from your skin, my skin. I love you. I love you like an instinct, the way retrievers go to water.

Something trembles, sometimes constantly, when you take your shirt off, wet or sweating, and it rises, itching to be touched and fluffed out, held a little. It makes my skin ache. You rubbed your beard close against mine, that night, over my lips, across my face, and you said softly, "I like this," with wonder. You'd never felt it before, either. Women seem indifferent. I love you the way I used to love my armor. I never needed any thing before.

"What?" the man says in the mirror. "What? You talking to me?" Old scars open, skin erupts. My fingernails weaken. The sculptor's clay rides under, thick with sulfur, builds areas of pressure underneath the skin that ache for release, need to be lanced. Women seem to have no problems. We adjust. Push softly now, and steadily. Do not claw for depth; behind the faces we are all imperfect.

Jack London wrote at length of how a hair sometimes does not grow out, but turns instead against itself, rankling in the skin until it is drawn or drives itself out. I read Jack London all the time when I was a kid; the part about the hair was the only thing he wrote that I didn't think I understood, then. He wrote adventure stories, boys' own. Sometimes these stories are even honest, but you won't know until much later, when you're grown up, and sometimes not even then. An old buddy and I sit up all night talking. He draws a pillow in against his belly. It's his habit sometimes, cradling something soft that you can't see through close over his crotch. It's not something I do. Maybe I should, depending on your perspective. I have to draw dark coils of stitches through my skin, leaking pus. "They're supposed to get infected," someone I love tells me, "a little. That's what drives them out." Scars swell up to follow. Someone says the tendency's genetic. Do not mind them. Set your own course. Sometimes a man's gotta do what a man's gotta do. Sometimes a man's got to write pleading letters to strangers in airports who wear one gold earring through their perfect skin, whose lips swell as if stung to a manicured edge, whose disappearing eyes will stand in judgment of the way you swing your heavy baggage through one smooth pull in your muscles, without feeling any of the old effort deep inside your joints at all. He keeps on looking till there's contact, and that's all. You know already he won't call you, because you're not supposed to tell another man your name. There are rules to this game. "Walk on," says the old man in my headphones. "I'll walk on." The women in the room will not have noticed. Thousands are walking past the gates whose lighted signs say New York Omaha St. Louis Madison Los Angeles San Diego.

On the computer, errors render women as men and men's as ms, prefixes, manuscripts. Stop swinging your fists when he doesn't fight back. Start hitting the walls if the man just won't fight. Stop hitting walls when you find one that's solid, live there the day you can finally hit something as hard as you wanted. Something breaks and bleeds under your fists, indeed, just the way it happens in boy's own adventure, only what breaks is your own hands. Nothing else changes. Sometimes new hairs get caught inside the skin but can't stop growing, turning inside, rankling like stitches. On a page my mother wrote, a woman says the difference between men and women is that women are afraid and men are not. I'm still in the airport. That man is long gone. I'm going to keep on walking till I find my way back home.

If you want to survive you must find a way to love what you are.

Service

After twenty-five years of gaining trust and providing help to people on the streets, the agency where I work has moved into a new building, a secure and brightly painted concrete institution. Suddenly no one who works there admits we are anything like the people we serve. We are certified professional service providers. We understand the problems of our clients only because we have had extensive academic training in the problems of marginalized people.

Perhaps if we had given trust and accepted help from people on the streets, things would have been different. But we have always been like the people we serve. We knew the same rules of survival: don't owe anything to anybody who looks like they can hurt you. Unless you make real sure they can't hurt you back.

For six months I pass the self-locking steel gates, the keyless-entry, ID-card activated front doors with the laser-etched brass plaque thanking the Bill Gates Foundation. I walk through the third set of locking entry doors and into the waiting arena whose miasma of distrust is now overseen by a woman who turns tight lips and crow eyes to me each morning from behind the "welcome desk," triggering sudden memories of elaborate lies, six-hour waits for medical care, and mandatory psychiatric evaluation. We are now required to wear ID badges at all times, so that staff instantly can be distinguished from clients. I often forget to do this. Occasionally I also forget which doors lock automatically from within, trapping me in the stairwell. Because I have staff keys I can escape this self-made predicament, but only by either leaving the building entirely or by going up into the muted administrative offices where people in muted office clothing debate in muted tones the merits of seeking money from faith-based initiatives and abstinence-education grants. (Times are tough.) Then I go back down through the extra set of security doors that separates this space from the waiting arena, through which I have to pass again to get to where I work.

One day I cannot do this any more. I move back into the most elabo-rate of the buildings where we used to work, an old wooden house in a semilavish state of disrepair. The staff in the concrete institution is not sad to see me leave the premises but does not hook up any communication between the old building and the new. Though I develop and coordinate programs, I am a man who does not speak or dress in muted office tones and my job title is not in a managerial category, which bars me from the regular meetings in which we communicate with each other about our work. I sit alone in the house for a long time. I understand that as long as I am there, they will be somewhat less likely to forget that before the secure and brightly painted concrete institution existed, we all worked in places like this. The empty room I choose to sit in, through whose leaky windows pour indifferently cold wind and magnificent light, is where the institution's director used to sit. While she sat there, I worked for her out of a ramshackle studio building down the street, with plastic bench chairs and a kitchen for pizza and rats in the basement and gouged wooden floors where my students and I could play hard and make a lot of noise. It was condemned as unfit for human habitation and demolished. The new concrete institution rises from the space of its foundation, which was the wrong size, too small. My students wanted to place gifts in the hole left behind when the builders demolished the old foundation, but the man-agement wouldn't let us. Apparently there was some concern that any-thing our theatre group put under the foundation might weaken the new concrete. My students joke that the new institution's foundations must at least have included a few vials of meth. I gird my loins and go there when I must or when I can.

Eventually the agency director decides to renovate the old house. The other programs, it is explained, are having a lot of trouble working with certain people. Programs for these most troubled individuals will move to the house. I will be returned to the institution to make room for those who have trouble functioning in the institution and need another place to go. These most troubled individuals flee the institution gratefully. I can escape only when I am with them, the "highest-risk, fringe-identified, disturbed, resistant clients"—too male for the secure and cheerful institu-tion, too physical, too sexual, or too queer. My space in the house will be rented to someone else, because there is a man who runs an organization that needs a lively, open-door, noninstitutional kind of headquarters. I am told this is because he is Latino and works with other people of color. I have learned that the institution's understanding attention to his needs is called cultural competence, which is important in dealing with people whose native language is not English or whose skin is brown. I remove to the institution. I scheme and beg for room someplace everyone can recognize as a space for performance.

One afternoon, after a couple of hours over at the house and the park with a group full of guys who are all gangsta'd out, I return to the institution to discover I do not have my institutional keys. I have already been reprimanded several times for accidentally leaving the door to the room with the pool table unlocked behind me. The pool table is very valuable and precious to clients, I am told, and if I leave the door unlocked even for a moment when no staff is present, clients may damage the pool table. I must never leave a door unlocked. I race into the arena to find an institutional staff member who can lock the door.

She is new. She does not know who I am. Her smile fixes in place as I tell her I work here, while her eyes evaluate me for danger, the chance of delusions. I know the look. To my relief, a staff member who knows I do work here takes over, and the first woman quickly makes her exit. I explain about the door again; I'm impatient, the guys are waiting, I was supposed to be somewhere else twenty minutes ago. But she steps back and her body grows rigid. Suddenly I realize I am still in the guys' friendly mode, talking fast and loud, making big gestures. But it is too late. She is already staging an intervention.

As she backs me away from her staff area into the arena, telling me my behavior is unacceptable and there will be consequences, signaling for backup, I do nothing. I am paralyzed by a combination of confusion—because she *knows* I work here—and terror. Perhaps she will call the police or the mental health emergency response team whose phone number is posted by every desk. I am a man standing in a space devoted to service. I am not wearing muted office clothing. I am not wearing a white doctor's coat. I am not wearing my special magnetic staff ID tag. I am wearing my mother's Hopi Wonder Woman bracelet, chef pants, one diamond earring, one red sneaker and one blue sneaker. The emergency responders will not know I am not one of those disturbed, resistant clients who can't function inside the institution, and they will do to me what they do to them—lock me up inside another institution, an asylum, a boot camp, a jail, beat me or drug me or kill me if I try to escape, if I can't fit in. All I can think is, *she knows who I am.*

Later she will report to my supervisor that she staged the intervention because my behavior was antiwoman. Shortly afterward I will return and back her up into her own staff area, using the politically correct professional social work language and the office hierarchy of middle-class white male gesture patterns and tone of voice I have learned to perform, because I realize she has seen she can reduce me to the status of a disturbed, resistant client, and this is what I must do if I don't want the people who work in the institution to keep doing it to me over and over again.

Then I quit my job and go to clown school.

Clown school is not as different from the institution as one might have hoped. I learn a lot from this discovery.

A year later I am back. The agency has added offices for the high-risk staff in the old house. I will once more be creating and supervising my own programs, but once more I will not be officially in charge of them. After a year of clown school, however, I understand that if you want the authority, you serve time in the institution.

My old supervisor promises things have changed. She's right, in a way. She has hired someone to serve the time in the institution that both she and I can no longer stand. Llewyn is willowy and straight, with quiet intelligent hands and a noble brow, clear eyes in a clear face framed and traced by cascades of ethnic jewelry and fine indigo tattoos. Her voice is soft, articulate in a medium register, and absolutely clear. She comes to us from the royal house of another world. I know instantly she knows the street and that she's from the world next door to my own, perhaps even a noble of the same house in which I am a fool. After a few days I am given to understand that Llewyn is using the male pronoun at work and some kind of gender-neutral pronoun elsewhere.

What the hell is a "gender-neutral pronoun?" It takes me weeks to adjust to the idea of not seeing hir as a woman. When I finally do, I say "sir" one day, as I am always careful to do for my crew of gangsta'd-out guys, and the pain I see in Llewyn's face makes me want to weep.

"I'm from Nebraska," I say. "There's something about respect in an honorific. I haven't been able to find one without gender."

"Sensei," Llewyn says.

"I thought 'sensei' meant 'master.' I wanted something people can call each other, that doesn't imply an unequal status."

"Sensei is like that. It means, roughly, 'learned person.'"

"Okay," I say. "Cool. Sensei."

I don't speak Japanese. I don't speak gender-neutral pronouns. I'm trying hard.

Llewyn wants to turn the house into a Trans Resource Center.

"What about the folks who come here who aren't trans?" I say.

Llewyn shows me the new description, which says the center is "for people marginalized because of their gender." "That includes men," ze explains, "especially the kinds of guys who come to your men's group."

I say that the guys who come to the group are comfortable with me, and with trans folks mostly these days, but probably really wouldn't personally identify with the language of gender marginalization. It isn't something people think applies to men.

After a while a different group of young men appear, trans guys, Llewyn's new volunteers. They bind their breasts, talk tough, their pale beardless round faces watching me suspiciously. On the way to the house one day, I say hello to a new one. His scowl fixes in place as his eyes evaluate me for danger, the chance of delusions. He backs up into his area, keeping the door to the Trans/Identity Resource Center covered. I unobtrusively dangle my staff keys where he can see them. He glances across the street at the institution, back at me, stares down at nothing, and spits at the concrete. He is wearing extra-baggy, extra-heavy, extra-long cut-off shorts and layers of wife-beaters under white T-shirts, the ex-dyke tranny boy uniform. I am wearing tight jeans, one T-shirt, one red sneaker and one blue sneaker. I make quick light conversation about the heat, modulating my voice, smiling and telling him what a relief it is for me to no longer have breasts to bind in this weather. It's a lie. I never bound, but he does. He looks at me and smiles. He gives me room at the front door.

Over the weeks the new crew of the gender marginalized mines the files. They find the tranny scrapbook I used to do with a couple of working girls, who'd help for free when they were sober, or angle for food coupons

I'd give them so they wouldn't have to trick so much that night for dope money. We used to dream we'd get enough done so we could stash the book under the counter somewhere other trannies could find it and the more problematic staff people would not. We used to dream about trannies creating some kind of help for each other. Inside Llewyn's newly remodeled Transgender/Identity Resource Center building, the crew throws out the clumsy, outdated scrapbook and starts on a resource handout. I offer to put it together. I edit down a single-page flyer, small enough to slip secretly into a pocket or read behind a magazine during a six-hour clinic wait, clear enough for somebody who isn't great at reading to read. I include the quick blood clot test I didn't know until too late—press a fingernail on the arm or leg that hurts, let go, see if the nail turns back from white to pink. If not, get to the ER. I include a short description of how people get access to hormones and surgery and legal ID, what these things do, emergency numbers, information websites, and, at the end, one sentence: "No matter what people say, you have the right to decide what happens to your own body."

It's the short list of what could have saved my life back then, in a form I could have found and hidden, tolerated and used. I show it to Llewyn, who smiles sweetly and inscrutably as always and does not say out loud that perhaps my idea of something small in simple language is founded in contempt.

Llewyn reassigns the job to hir crew members, who produce a thick oversized book with a bright red cover that says *Trans Resources*—over fifty pages of applicable transgender-related laws, medical guidelines, civic regulations, legal aid, trans-friendly medical providers and women's services and businesses, with reviews, all written in the most up-to-date conventions of language acknowledging the full range of gender-marginalized identities.

One day the crew cheers. The guy I met outside runs to Llewyn, yelling, "Hey, I found two great medical info flyers somebody did on this antique computer, one about estrogen and one about testosterone!" It will be nice to see them finally printed and available, I think. I go teach theatre at the dance studio. I go often to wrangle to retain our space, politely, in modulated tones, with the well-known modern dance company director who's unsure about our barbarian physical theatre thumpings. He's a very correct man with perfect posture and an Ingmar Bergman face and an obsession with the flawless perfection of his studio flooring. I go home with my new boyfriend, who's young and hung and white and energetic and can't figure out why I don't know that being older obviously gives me the authority in our relationship. Llewyn is a friend. I back away and let the gender marginalized do their work.

One afternoon Llewyn and I sit across the stairwell from each other, and Llewyn says, "The Trans Resource Center is about to open, and I need to set the hours. I want it to be open every day. We can do that if we move the men's group back to the main institution building."

"We've got two rooms right here," I say, startled. "We can run them both."

"Well, there are issues of access."

"We've got doors to shut between the rooms for privacy. It's only once a week. And hey, I think it's a real good thing for folks in these two groups to start respecting each other. I can get with the guys on it now. I know they can be noisy, but we'll work that out. These guys know how important it is, respect."

Llewyn doesn't say anything.

"Access?" I say finally.

"People from both groups would go in together through the front door and through the same hallway to get to the bathroom. If people aren't comfortable, it's an access problem. I'm not going to send trans people around back through the alley to use the bathroom."

"And I'm not telling black guys they have to go in the building through the back door. Come *on*, Llewyn."

"That's why we need to move the men's group into the main building."

"Back to the institution. Yeah, the guys do so fucking well there. Every black man on staff has quit this month, and a uniformed security guard starts patrolling the courtyard next week."

"My priority has to be the Trans Center. Other people have at least some alternative places they can go. There is no safe space for trans people, anywhere. This space has to be *safe*."

"For some folks, singing 'Come to Jesus' in the bosom of the church does not count as a safe alternative. The Promise Keepers do not count as a safe alternative!" I am furious. Why am I so angry?

Llewyn doesn't say anything.

I walk to the bathroom through the same hallway as these guys every day. I go through the same door. "Are you saying," I say slowly, "that you think the guys in my group aren't safe for trans people to be around? Is that what you're trying to tell me?"

"No. It isn't about the reality. You know I don't believe these guys are going to come in here and hurt somebody. It's about somebody who's so scared, so scared even to come here, so scared even to stand outside this door. It's got to be safe here, so safe . . . if a tranny who is just getting started and this is her very first step and she stands outside that door and listens and hears all these *guy* voices . . . it's not safe."

Something chokes me. I stand up. My head and shoulders make a kind of twitching movement, but nothing comes out. If I were Samson I would pull these walls down.

"I'm gone," I hear myself say. "You stay here and you think about it."

I walk blindly through familiar streets for an unknown length of time. I am thinking about what I would have given for one guy voice in the years I searched for someone, anyone, like me at all, searched for service and found pink fleece suits and Lee Press On Nails and listening to my counselors scream at me about their lesbian oppression and watching my partner cringe from me and idolize anime girls and hearing domestic violence professionals lecture on how men don't need help because 95 percent of violence is caused by men, over and over again, men's high-pitched laughs after they tell me they've been raped again, rooms full of women in wigs talking about electrolysis, and interventions, which means I have to leave now or someone will call the Nazis, because my voice is a guy voice and there are no guy voices, not in a safe space, no big voices, no rude shouting laughing deep and open from the belly voices, no men's voices in safe spaces at all. Go to the hospital, go directly to prison, hit the showers, do not pass Go, do not collect two hundred dollars. Go away. Disappear. Just go.

I go back. Llewyn is still sitting on the steps. "I can't explain," Llewyn says softly, "what it is like for me when people just disappear."

I sit on the steps. "I'm still here."

"So am I," Llewyn says.

"My voice is like theirs," I say.

"So is mine," Llewyn says.

We sit together for a while. We have been here too long to be weeping, quite.

"It's impossible," I say softly.

"I know," Llewyn says. "But we can try."

Note: In 2006 federal changes at the CDC made the successful Trans/Identity Resource Center ineligible for renewed funding. The institution responded by closing the center.

Flaunting

The thing that makes fags different from any other minority, people tell me, is that we can disappear when things get tight. Other people can't take a day off from the fight, 'cause people can't change their skin to match their background, so they tell me. This is the difference between gay people and "people of color," for instance, or between "postoperative" and "pre-op, non-op" transsexuals, or between transsexual men and transsexual women, or genetic women and transsexual women, or "pretty" women and "ugly" women, or "normal" people and "abnormal" people, or just passing, which is a word black people made up to talk about black people before gays borrowed it to talk about gays, and transsexuals use it sometimes to mean either pretending to be something that you aren't or pretending to be something that you are. I couldn't go to a queer Halloween party once because the only rule was that you couldn't come in costume and darling, I had nothing to wear.

I can't stop looking in mirrors. I can't stop looking in mirrors because I like the way I look. I can't stop looking in mirrors because I like the way I look and it surprises me that much. A bunch of Marines starred in gay porn movies a few years back, and when the whole story came out there was scandal. A writer asked some Marine why he and his buddies wanted to be in *gay* porn movies and he laughed and said, "Marines like to be looked at."

When you don't flaunt, it doesn't show, which means you've got privilege (official het-er-o-sex-u-al privilege, official white/male/Anglo-Saxon/Protestant/rich/patriot privilege, fill-in-the-blank-with-serious-news-story privilege). If you do show it, then you're flaunting, so people won't take you seriously (but they'll look at you and take you anywhere). When you flaunt it, you've got privilege (victim privilege, queer/black/women's/ex-o-tic/pagan/poverty privilege, fill-in-the-blank-with-sexy-feature-story privilege). If you don't show it, people will take you seriously (but they won't take you anywhere).

Vito Russo, in his last year, flaunts his footage from *The Celluloid Closet*, tells me when a man is dressed up as a woman, people love to watch him flaunt, but they don't want anything real to show. Men aren't supposed to find real power in women's things. Vito thinks that's bullshit. So do I. We both love monsters.

I go to the pride parade.

In Wisconsin the pride parade is strewn with tiny clots of protest. One man holds up a sign that says "Rights, Yes; Pride, No."

I go to the pride parade. People watch the beautiful boys flaunt feather boas.

In Southern California the pride parade is laced with men and women holding rolls of stickers that say "Speak to Your Brothers." As they walk past, laughing, they touch the stickers to the bodies of only the most beautiful men in the crowd. None of them looks at me. None of them wants me to speak to my brothers.

Everyone thinks I'm a woman who finds power in men's things. I stop going to the pride parade.

I go back to the pride parade. I go back because I've stopped wanting to be looked at. So I watch the people flaunt, motorcycles, leather, feather boas, dancers, lovers. Steel and sequins in the park, and a woman in a tasteful dress stands beside a chino man in penny loafers. They look so very, very normal, as if they've been flown in fresh from Orange County. Behind them a big banner flaunts: "Transsexual." Information. Sideshow. If it weren't for the banner, I wouldn't know.

I wear hot pink Spandex to flaunt the muscles in my shoulders, like the beautiful boys do down in West Hollywood. One of the women doesn't like me. She wears her Spandex to flaunt her breasts, which took her a hell of a lot of work to get. She was the woman in the tasteful dress. She tells me I shouldn't dress like that; if I want people to take me seriously I cannot let my body show. I have to button down. She says I have an image problem.

I had surgery because I had an image problem.

My friends have to tell me after surgery that I probably shouldn't wear my body suits anymore. Men don't wear women's things. I look like a drag show. On a trip to LA I find the hot new queer men's fashion: body suits. And I've cut up all my feather boas to cover masks with.

I go to a meeting of Speak to Your Brothers. I decide not to flaunt. I want to be taken seriously. We talk for two hours about coming out. Everybody recommends it, everywhere, without exception. One of them mentions a crazy guy who told his HIV status to everyone he met. Everyone suddenly agrees that there's a time and place for everything. Some things aren't appropriate for right away, they say, some things you don't flaunt, 'cause people just don't want to know. Once I mention being in the hospital, and someone asks "For what?" I tell the room I had a blood clot, and the room says "Oh." It doesn't occur to me until after my own sweat dries just why they would be so tense about asking. Everyone takes me seriously. Everyone listens (but there's not much to say).

Linh talks at the meeting; Linh's a drag queen. When they asked him about coming out he laughed from his belly. "I was so tense before," he said. "Now I just have fun. Celebration, everything. So much artistic, so much culture, so much life." They ask me about coming out. I don't tell them much 'cause certain things like sickness (and how I loved a picture of a naked woman with a tattoo flaunting bright across her breast cancer scar) you just don't flaunt (so that I found the woman's photo while I looked in vain for pictures of somebody, any man like me. My mom the breast cancer survivor was the one who ended up telling me about what to expect from chest surgery). I don't tell them somebody has to flaunt it (so there can be pictures, stories, so people don't have to believe that they're the only one, remember?). I don't tell them (now that there are pictures and stories, maybe people know just what my scars are. So now before the meeting if I flaunt that tight white fag T-shirt I wonder if anybody will look at me, talk to me. I am wondering if I show).

Linh is nice to me. He gives me a ride home. He asks me questions, encourages a flaunt. I tell him in the car. He asks how big my cock is, if I come good. I tell him. It's nothing personal. Often total strangers want to look at my cock, especially if they're doctors. Linh and I exchange phone numbers. He says he'd like to have a cup of coffee sometime, he could dress and we'd go to the drag show.

In Vito Russo's flaunted footage there was a scene from *Outrageous*, a film about a crazy person and a drag queen. One says to the other, "Do you know what it's like to see a really good-looking guy and know that all he sees is a *drag queen*?"

I go to the pride parade. I strip down and paint my body black. I paint my scars in red, because I'm not sure how much they show from a distance now. It's like Linh said at the meeting.

If you got it, flaunt it.

My partner, who has never been a woman, tells me she is changing his name to Daire. Though most strangers, as well as friends who know him from the Internet, describe him as male, old friends still use female pronouns to describe him in person. In person, as the years go by, he looks increasingly like John Wayne thinly coated with Leonardo DiCaprio. I ask if he is changing pronouns from "she" to "he" and Daire says no, but the breasts are getting to be a problem. If you think I understand all this, you will be profoundly mistaken. I am, however, deeply relieved that he has finally stopped trying to be an anime girl.

I remember the moment I became a man. It took a lot of reading to get ready for. I was sitting on my front porch, arguing with myself, and a book by Kate Bornstein, and with anything and everything I could get my hands on. I'd been arguing because, basically, the sum of my life experience up to that moment was: If I wore a slinky dress, I was displaying female power. On the other hand, if I wore a three-piece suit, a jockstrap, and the clean manly scent of Old Spice, I was displaying female power. Every story, every ornament, every possible mode of communication between the self and another, every encounter with culture, in the body of a woman, became a statement about womanhood. What is more, the stronger the *masculine* associations—a piece of clothing, a gesture, an identifying word like "gay" or "cowboy"—the more powerful the statement is supposed to be about the nature of *women's* experience. *Femme* is a word for female. *Butch* is a word for female. And in this culture—white, middle-class, TV-anchor-accent culture, academic culture, Hollywood culture, my culture—a butch in a tuxedo is supposed to be a stronger image of *female* power than a femme in a slinky dress.

As a result, in my life, every direct means of communication between the self and the world was corrupted. In this culture, there is nothing that does not become female in association with a woman.

For a man like myself, the signifiers of power are reversed as well. The ornaments of masculinity become ordinary objects, holding little power except as negative symbols of habit and expected role. (Interestingly enough, people seem to have an easy time understanding why a woman might find no power in pink dresses. But people are often mystified to discover that I find no power in ties and aftershave.) In the same way, the ornaments of power in feminine form—jewels and feathers, makeup, artifice, subversion as bravery, subversion of authority by means of guile, wit, costume, sex—are unspeakably attractive; they are signifiers of vast and transgressive power. That they can be symbols of a vast and transgressive *male* power seems obvious to me. Any man can walk down an American street in a leather jacket, but it takes a fucking powerful man to walk down an American street in a dress. Or, for that matter, in a leather jacket ornamented with feathers and jewels.

My resistance to transition came from the script of female power; if everything became a female symbol in my hands, what use was there in trying to be a man? What communication is possible if the most powerful and terrifying, monumentally difficult act of reclamation—to put on a dress—seems to others to be entirely ordinary, even conservative? These were questions that ruled my life; others I have heard asking parallel questions have been femme women, drag queens, and queer leathermen. Later I learned how to work with men who were trying to be gangstas and men who were trying not to be gangstas, because I recognized in them the same questions, under the ornaments of race. Mine were shaped by the ornaments of gender. Sitting on my front porch, I became a man in the moment of understanding that if I changed my body, I could wear a feather boa.

I wish the story had turned out so simply. What I have discovered in the years since I changed my body is that my culture's script for men is much more narrow. What a man touches doesn't become male by association. Feminists talk about the prejudice of female contamination, but every weakness is a strength, from a different perspective. The privilege of female contamination is that, in my culture, whatever women touch belongs to them. Men are allowed only those aspects of culture that women can't touch. And these days women can touch almost everything. This is the only way I know to explain why men are expected to feel so strongly about football, baseball, basketball, beard-shaving products, infantry combat, male homosexuality, and erectile dysfunction.

As hard as I tried before my transition to make the suit coat, the leather jacket, the jockey shorts say *male*, they remained stubbornly female ornaments in female hands. And now, as hard as I try to put on that feather boa, it remains equally stubbornly a female ornament, though my hands are now quite visibly male. (If my hands holding a feather ornament were both male and brown, of course, my story would be somewhat different. But that is someone else's story, and they will have to tell it.)

What I wanted so desperately before my transition was to become male by association. The idea that manhood could be durable, even contagious, seems so foreign to people that even now when I am bald and bearded, when women cross the street to avoid me, when I can put my erect penis into another person's body, when I struggle against back hair and middle-age spread, there are many, many people who are convinced I am a woman. The fragile male ego is a social construct, not a personal one. Penises and pattern baldness prove astonishingly durable. It is group acceptance as a "real" man that is delicate, and easily removed.

If I had been a woman, I would have lived—probably unknowing—in the boundless lap of a luxury for which I know no name. My nightmare would have become—if I had been a woman—only the right to remain a woman, no matter what I did. And the more I used what were historically men's stories, men's ornaments, men's symbols and styles to express my self and power, the more clearly and truly others would have seen me as a woman. But I am not a woman. I want the same right to a nonnegotiable identity—as a man.

That I do not have it quickly became obvious to me. What took me a little longer to realize is that, in my culture, no masculine man does. If we do not toe the line, suck it up, suck it in, and follow orders, soldier, we cease to be "real." We don't become women by not acting like "real" men. Socially speaking, we simply cease to exist. Because my body looked acceptably feminine in the past, a black leather jacket rendered me as a powerful woman. Because my body looks acceptably masculine in the present, a feather boa renders me neither as a woman nor as a powerful man, but merely as grotesque. Like my partner's breasts, the combination does not communicate anything to others except that something in the communication loop is wrong.

I am not a feminine man. A childhood in Nebraska and thirty years of carefully cultivated adult manliness will not make you any taller, but it will make you what gay men used to call "butch" and now call (God knows why) "straight acting and appearing." Rather unfortunately in my more androgynous partner's case, so will being five foot ten and built like an Irish footballer. Feminine men can follow the women's script, in which the ornaments of women's power are expansive and contagious with femininity. But if I were a feminine man, a feather boa would still not render me a powerful man. It would render me female by association. A female ornament in feminine hands communicates female power. A female ornament in masculine hands communicates only that the item properly belongs to someone else. Unless, of course, you are a woman.

There are many people happy to share with me their deep certainty that I am attracted to feather boas because I am a male homosexual, and male homosexuality is a kind of femaleness, a spiritual (or genetic, or hormonal) transsexuality. Many of them, God help me, are gay men. They're feminine gay men, offering me the escape route into female power that allows them to exist. Since I am already an actual transsexual, however, it's difficult for me to keep a straight face when hearing the same arguments invoked to explain me as essentially feminine and therefore gay that were previously deployed to explain me as essentially masculine and therefore lesbian. But feminine gay men are often kind to me. Masculine gay men like myself are more likely to be uncomfortable with the sense of female encroachment that they feel I represent.

I sympathize, in a way. As a masculine man who loves men in this culture, I would probably be uncomfortable with the idea of female-to-male transsexuality if I were not also a female-to-male transsexual. For instance, while preparing this book for print, I have read two separate reviews in which famous women writers describe the way a male author uses traditionally masculine themes as evidence that the author must be a woman-hating closet case. A male critic has written a review in which the film *Brokeback Mountain* is described as "a women's picture." And my partner has been taken to task several times as an inappropriate male presence in a subculture increasingly defined as "women's space." I visited one of these

Internet spaces recently, to be welcomed with the promise of creative challenge and conversation about rebuilding images of masculinity in popular culture, and lots of hot gay male sex. This on a background wallpapered with the symbol of Venus as a firm reminder that the discourse is for women only. That people can feel entitled to use women's power to deny men ownership of our own lives makes me distinctly queasy.

I walk into the bookstore for the first time. There's a pink triangle sticker in the window. I've just come from the gym; I'm wearing a black leather jacket, jeans, and cowboy boots. The woman at the counter spots me at the door and smiles reassuringly. She looks like Peter Pan. She shouts across the store, "Women's books are this way. I can help you find what you're interested in."

She walks over, moves in to touch my elbow. This total stranger keeps wanting to pat me and chat like we've known each other for years. I came in here to buy a Raymond Chandler novel. Who the hell is this woman? What does she want from me?

I walk into the coffeehouse for the first time. There's a pink triangle sticker in the window. I've just come from the gym; I'm wearing the same black leather jacket, lifting gloves, sweats, and sneakers. The woman at the counter spots me at the door and gives me the hate stare. She looks like Peter Pan. Awkwardly, I order a fancy coffee drink. She slams a cup of black coffee on the counter. Her eyes never leave me.

"That's what you ordered, right? That's what you ordered. What's the matter with you? Pay up."

Who the hell is this woman? What does she want from me? I've looked like a man to other people for several years now, and I know. She wants me to leave. I do.

For years after my transition, my partner, who had been given a female name and taught the story that he was a defective woman, could not treat me with respect. It took me about six days to figure out I was expected as a man to solve this problem with my fists. Which, of course, was why my partner was working so damn hard to convince me I was powerless. I knew using my fists on my loved ones wouldn't solve the problem, but (listen up, guys) I quickly learned that refusing to use my fists on my loved ones didn't solve the problem, either. It took me about six years to learn what kind of power I did have. I learned about it in clown school.

All classic clown scripts include space for three roles. Clowns being desperately serious people, we call these roles One, Two, and Three. Since I'm not such a serious clown, I like to call the roles Top Banana, Second Banana, and Banana Peel. Top Banana is supposed to be in charge. The other side to this story is that being in charge is a terrible position, because other people always want to be in charge, and there's nowhere to go but down. Second Banana is the servant role, the second-class citizen. The other side to this story is that if you don't go up from here, you're in imminent danger of going down. And, less obvious but equally important, if you don't go down from here, you're in imminent danger of going up. Choose your enemies carefully, you will become them. The Banana Peel is, well, that thing the other two slip on, the odd one out. The Banana Peel story is: as long as you've got nothing, you can't lose. If you win, you go up, and one step up is the role of Second Banana. Which is why so many Third clowns are tramps.

When these roles change, what happens is either a tragedy or a clown routine.

As a female-to-male transsexual, staying exactly the same person moved me from being a first-class woman to being a second-class man. Now that's funny.

After forty years of scientific investigation, I have become a drag performer.

The Amazing Jeremy Isinglass dispenses with a wig, of course, and wears Joel Grey whiteface, white shoulders, and a lovely white throat down to a medical corset trimmed with ermine, and scarlet satin opera gloves, a matching red satin jockstrap with a single pink marabou accent, dancer's tights, and black and white Italian go-go boots with Cuban heels. As some readers may know, satin opera gloves are extremely slippery, and really first-class Italian leather-soled boots have heels as slick as ice. Since Jeremy dispenses, of course, with my glasses as well, I quickly discovered that this role involves largely dispensing with my ability to pick up objects, move, or see. This is how I discovered what it is to have high status. What my friend Joe the ex-Marine knew so many years ago from watching women,

I learned from Jeremy; that if you need something you cannot provide for yourself, you must stand still, glance meaningfully between the object of your desire and an appropriate servant, and wait.

The rub, of course, involves choosing servants who will serve. The most difficult thing about Jeremy is that his success depends totally on the goodwill of those who play the role of his Second Banana. If you are the Amazing Jeremy Isinglass, I do not recommend seeking service in a gay bar whose usual entertainers are go-go boys who look like Arnold Schwarzenegger.

Some Top Banana characters lose status in these situations, becoming Second Bananas to their would-be servants. When I do drag king shows, in which the performers and audiences are usually lesbian, my character is Morris Schmorris—a little bald guy in glasses and tiny shoes who runs around busily but ineffectively, wearing a suit and a cigar far too big for him. This is the classic Jew clown, a Second Banana.

Some top characters can't trade away their high status, and if not respected will become outcast by merely standing still. This can still be a comedy routine—the Top Banana becomes a tramp—but it's often very dark comedy. As Llewyn likes to remind me, the other classic Jew clown is Jesus. This is a story Llewyn performs in the guise of a femme transsexual in whom most people fail to recognize a classic, androgynously beautiful woman. Since I am a man, and involved with race, I would be more likely to create such a story around the voluptuous horror of Michael Jackson. But I am not eager for martyrdom. I take Morris rather than Jeremy to drag king shows, where women delight in having status above him.

The most difficult thing about Morris is that he's easy to abuse. He struggles constantly to be Top Banana. He also knows it's a terrible role. Whenever he has a chance to actually win the top spot, he hesitates, is lost, and knows enough to blame others for his failures. Like Shylock, he easily veers into stereotype.

The most important thing I learned in clown school was the difference between roles and actors. All clown routines are based in conflict. The roles wrestle desperately with each other for authority and power. The character's role is often to make the other characters look bad. What makes a routine into clown instead of tragedy is when the *actors* understand the basic rule of play; no matter what the role involves, your work as an actor is to make your partners look good. They'll be doing the same for you. In any of my clown suits, I can remind the other actors that how much they need me in my role is exactly how much my role depends on them.

The Myth of Fingerprints

The room is full of teachers and students, sitting in a hotel basement, talking about discrimination. Someone's holding up a piece of writing.

She says, "This is the document we came up with. We tried to make it the last word on the subject of equal treatment. It's pages and pages and pages long—everybody you could possibly imagine is included."

I wonder if I'm on the list of everybody you could possibly imagine.

So when my turn comes to speak, I tell the people in the room the Word. Transsexual. I'm calling it the T-word to my friends these days. I've been playing a lot of word games. After I identify myself with the T-word, I look around the room. Am I still in the human being club? I'm not sure. Press on regardless.

They can add the T-word to the list now. But adding another word to an endless list seems pointless, almost childish: I get in the special people club? Who doesn't? Will you love me now? Do I get a secret decoder ring?

What I'm looking for I can't find on a list of categories. So I tell them to forget about protecting our own categories. Who the hell *we* think we are doesn't get us hurt. People hurt us because of who the hell *they* think we are. I almost drowned in the ocean between my sense of myself and other people's imagination of me, and right now I want to share my rescue. Right now, my sense of myself is as a man who thinks he can stand in front of fifty strangers and fill the ocean up with words. More fool I.

Later a few women stop me to talk. As usual in these situations, other men don't talk to me. The moment I identify myself as transsexual, their eyes rise slightly to stare past the top of my head, into vacancy. *Women's things.*

A young queer punk with starched white hair and multiple nose rings says she thinks I had a great idea, but she's not sure it's practical. She wants people to accept her personal identity category, and she doesn't think they would accept her if they also had to accept something really weird, like me.

Someone else says pleasantly that a lawyer friend explained all the answers to her; she has rights because she was born in her category. The correct word for her category is Lesbian. She doesn't tell me her name.

"It's not a choice," she says, over and over again. "I didn't choose to be a lesbian. I was born this way. You chose to have surgery. You chose."

"No," I say. I wish I were on an island somewhere far away. Maybe I am. Maybe that's the problem.

"You don't understand," she says brightly. "It isn't personal; this is a legal question. You chose. So your condition is voluntary. I deserve protection, I didn't choose to be this way. People like you don't deserve protection."

She smiles at me. From where I'm standing, I can feel the waves of hate.

Deep down underwater, I imagine her in the moment before her first woman lover. The hand that softly touched her hand, her cheek, the moment when she could have said No, gone home, closed her eyes and thought of England, oh, for the rest of the rest of her life. I could have done that, too, with testosterone and surgery, or men. Neither of us did. That's why we're both here now, playing enemies. For the first time, I feel the deep, distant pull of the current, like breathing in sympathy. We make a lot of choices; I don't want to forget making mine. As they used to say in *Star Trek*, there are always alternatives. Today I choose to follow her lead and not be personal, so I tell her a lot of words instead.

"I wanted to choose to have surgery. I wasn't allowed to choose. A psychiatrist and a psychiatric social worker both had to certify I had the appropriate mental illness before I was eligible for treatment with hormones and surgery. Legally you're not entitled to protection because of your inborn qualities, but I should be. I am not federally protected from discrimination only because Jesse Helms added a specific provision to the Americans with Disabilities Act to disqualify transsexuals, who would otherwise have been covered along with all other people diagnosed with an illness on the DSMV list of recognized mental disorders. Homosexuality hasn't been listed in the DSMV since 1973. Legally it is neither a mental illness nor a physical disability, and is therefore not a medically protected category. Where homosexuality is a legally protected category, it is considered similar to religion, a personal matter. Legally speaking, you chose and I didn't. This argument is yours, not mine. Nothing personal."

Between us rustles an ocean of scientific papers: words like *inborn, genetic, hormonal,* identification by the shape of ears, brains, skulls, lines on our palms, our fingerprints, the pages rotten with hope. (We'll be cleared of responsibility for our dangerous deeds, proved innocents.) The only language to describe our differences is a lexicon of prejudice and disease. The only words that count to describe us are the ones we don't choose. She's a "lesbian" because she's "like a man." I'm a "transsexual" because I'm "like a man." She hates me because I'm "like a man." I'm a "faggot" because I'm "like a woman." The beautiful fag cruising me before I said I'm "transsexual" won't look at me now, because I'm "like a woman." A "straight" might beat up the beautiful fag tomorrow because he's "like a woman." I don't say any of these words, we're not being personal. Just the facts, ma'am.

A friend of mine breaks in, outraged. "Would you call yourself insane? Abnormal?"

Deep down underwater, I remember trying for hours to decide to lie in the psychiatric evaluation. I could have played straight, just a regular guy. Psychiatrists can refuse consent for surgery if you're not their idea of a real man. Faggots, for instance, aren't a popular ideal for real men. We're supposed to *want* to be women. Besides, according to the official psychiatric explanation, I'm supposed to want to have sex only with women, because I'm supposed to be a normal guy, because I'm supposed to be an abnormal woman, because I'm supposed to be a self-hating lesbian. When I started my transition, I'd promised myself I'd never lie again.

Deep down underwater, I wouldn't call myself anything anyone here has said. I don't believe in this entire conversation; everything we've been saying is a lie.

For years I was cast away from everyone because I was always lying. It didn't matter what I said or did, where I went, or what I wore. Everything lied to the world about who I was, when worn on my skin. In ways more subtle and corrosive, my own knowledge of myself was a lie, proved false by the failure of that self to reach anyone though the impenetrable barrier of my own skin. The horrible thing about living underneath a constant lie is that, eventually, you wind up with nothing but contempt for a world so easily fooled.

When my desperation rescued me, I took hormones and had surgery until I and other people could see me in ways equally close to how I knew myself. I'm a man. Now all I have to do to make the images line up is be all-powerful, never get hurt, be capable of anything, and never, ever be afraid. No problem. Jesus was God, right? Wrong religion; my mother's people are my people, and we're still waiting for the Messiah.

And when my desperation rescued me, I gave up lies with the fervor of a reformed junkie. Now all I have to do is always tell the truth. No problem.

The water is getting deeper. People wash past me in the current, freaks like and unlike me, people who wound their skin in desperation, are denied jobs, have to hustle on street corners, get killed and lie in unmarked graves because nobody has to care. People drown here. People are drowning everywhere. Maybe the right words would save them, gain them authority, respect, provide practical help. If words are useful enough, do they become right? If they're right, do they become true? If I accept words for myself I didn't choose and don't believe, the world will help, understand, and accept me as they say I am. But if I can't choose my own words, I will always be lying. I promised I'd never lie about myself again. By now I'm so far under I can look up through uncounted layers, mixing like paint. In geology we used to call this sort of territory "suspect terrain."

When I was a kid I used to escape by falling through time. The ground under my feet disappeared, becoming the surface of an enormous shallow sea. Around me shoals of antique fish swam. Crinoids waved, easy in the diffuse sunshine. Human beings were still unspoken, more bodiless than jellyfish. Trapped between layers of ocean become solid rock at Weeping Water, Nebraska, I used to wonder if fossils felt the weight.

I want to find the words that never lie. I can't find the words.

Afterward my friends congratulated me for winning the argument. All I could think to do was tell my mother I was sorry.

The words I'd failed to find again were what I'd wanted to give her from the beginning. For years each time we'd tried to talk about what was happening to me, to her, to us, I would construct elaborate arguments. When

I was satisfied these were, at last, the perfect words, I'd throw them out to her, sure that the ocean between us would at last be bridged, filled by me. She'd read experts on "the subject," whatever subject seemed to separate us; the words for our differences are endless, and they don't matter. Each time she found a theory attractive, she'd toss it in my general direction to see if it hit the mark. For a while I'd wonder who the hell this stranger was; the message certainly didn't sound like anyone I knew. Only she knows what she thought of my efforts.

In time we became castaways on separate islands, each throwing the other the life preservers that had saved us, and left us marooned.

I've spent my life fighting against the words other people offered to describe me. If I didn't like their words, the answer must be words of my own. People said "she"; I fought for "he." I got the word "he," complete with expectations of violence and invulnerability and testosterone jokes and shaving products advertised as the high point of my existence. So I fought for the word "I."

But the first person is a desert island, the world's smallest ghetto. People on the edges of the known world fight to articulate and define what we know has never been spoken. We live in the thin ends of the bell curve, where the line of our lives comes close to the baseline. But somehow we end up not speaking from that basic common ground of human life, instead locked into that tiniest of spaces between our experience and the bottom line, confined to case studies, speaking as curiosities. It's talk-show chic; the most popular exhibit in the circus used to be the sideshow, where they dressed up the freaks as members of "primitive tribes." Being the first to see tribes no civilization has ever reached is a wet dream invented by people who want a peek in the sideshow. But sometimes people look into the sideshow in order to find themselves there. Drawing the line of your life in the sand and standing behind it to say, "This is my unique experience, you wouldn't understand" just translates to "Put a picture of me in the *National Geographic.*"

Every word I've used to name myself has sometimes been a lie. Every experience I thought was unique, I've heard from someone else's mouth. I don't know. I'm no longer sure of anything. I call my mother for advice and she says, "I don't know. I'm no longer sure of anything."

Maybe we weren't stuck on separate islands. Maybe we've spent years in a Three Stooges routine, up to our eyeballs in the same ocean and hitting the person next to us over the head.

So now I fight for the word "we." The right to say "we" means the right to talk about "us" and mean "human beings" instead of "members of my tribe, people with my rare disorder," just like the "normal" people do. It means the right to go beyond intimate confessionals, outraged broadsheets, and heartwarming stories: to take a look at the life I've lived and see something of what life is like.

But "we" is just another word.

Saying we're really all alike after all is sometimes just another lie. My peculiar gift, as silly and symbolic and inescapable as a clown suit, is that this lie only shows up when I take my clothes off.

This room is so full of men that by halfway through the meeting we're piled up like baby rabbits, clothes shedding in the heat. It takes hours to get through our various concerns. Finally I give up all sense of propriety and recline into the man beside me. His quick, slender face smiles. Later, half asleep, I reach out and place my palm against his stomach, overwhelmed by the sudden closeness of another heartbeat, by the miracle of breath. After the meeting's over, we remain lying comfortably side by side. I feel absurdly as if we're floating in an ocean somewhere, watching stars.

At his house he offers food, lights candles, shows me the way into his room. It's light, pleasant work. He kisses me. I ask him how he came to be here. He tells me he's a psychologist. I want to laugh. We kiss some more. Does he like his work? He loves his work. He strokes my chest. We talk some more. We kiss some more. Everyone else I've known disappears under the surface of sex or sentiment by now. His flexible, honest face remains the same, happy with small talk, or conversation, or kissing with an unhurried insistence. He wants to make love. He doesn't mind feeling how much he wants me, or that we both know his plans ahead of time. I limber up explanations, but I'm desperately tired of words. For a moment everything is perfectly simple and right and true; this is how life happens. We drift in the current, touch, float together for a while. We don't have to say anything at all.

Then, of course, I recollect myself.

Slowly, carefully, I describe what I think of as my unique conundrum;

love comes suddenly out of nowhere, filling up all the empty space be-tween myself and other people, as irresistible as ocean. So where does it go when I take my clothes off? If love isn't a mirage, how could anything make it disappear so instantly? The idea fills me equally with rage and de-spair. He winces and says, "It's such a common problem to run into. There are so many people who can't tell the difference between having sex and making love." I know the difference. Having sex is what he won't want to be doing with me in five minutes.

Casually, I ask him which one he prefers. He rolls over to stroke my beard gently. "Making love," he says, "always." Deep down underwater, I note that I don't think he's lying. It frightens me; I'm used to lies. So I start unreeling words. I tell him *handicapped*. He looks blankly down, feels for a nipple. I look lovely in his eyes. I say *my appearance*. "I know how you feel," he says. "I'm a gay man, and I'm not a youth any more." We talk a little. I'm desperate not to say the T-word, not to do anything that would maroon me alone again on my little island. A vague sense that I might not have to go back there tonight is making me crazy; now every-thing depends on my finding exactly the right words. I say *surgery, scars*. He says, "It's okay. We're none of us exactly what we want to be." He kisses me. "We're *making love*." And for an instant, I can believe.

Almost the strangest part of wanting is knowing that the more you let yourself want something, the worse the idea of not having it becomes. The strangest part is the way that, the closer you get to having what you want, the more afraid you get. One clear instant of belonging, a *we* with me in it, was enough to uncoil a watch spring in my stomach and send me across the room shucking my shirt and sweatshirt. Here. Just get it over with. I let him see my scars.

He leans over and strokes them easily. "What are they from?"

I say, *Where they took the breasts off*. Just get it over with.

"Oh, you had that condition, what do you call it, where men get breasts . . ."

Gynecomastia. Yeah. Sort of.

His fingers stroke wide, slow circles. His eyes linger. "I think you have a beautiful body," he says. He means it. More digital friendly persuasion. "Is that all you're worried about?"

There are more scars, they don't show . . .

My mind freezes up completely. He's not acting right. He obviously hasn't understood any of the words. All I can do now is say the Word or take the rest of my clothes off . . .

The worst imaginable ending is the one where you almost get what you're looking for, then the door that slams in your face at the last possible moment, the last image of hate and disgust in the face of someone you thought was a friend.

I had a sex change, I said.

Kneeling at my feet, hands lapping at my chest, he freezes exactly the way most men, caught making love to another man, would freeze when a woman walks into the room.

"I guess," he says slowly, after breathing a little, "my only question would be, do you have any regrets?"

And words, words, words. He laughed sheepishly, went to sit on the couch, made little noises about the unpredictability of desire. His own prejudice surprised him, he said, the way they say we all hide our racism. When I got up to put my shirt back on, he averted his gaze from my naked chest while he thanked me for raising his consciousness. I looked at him and thought, I can't afford to want anything, but I want to kill you, white man.

Finally I managed to ask him about the woman in the room. There wasn't a woman in the room, but I couldn't find the words that didn't give people the impression that there was. I asked him for the right words. He stared at me and said, "Well, why did you use *sex change*, then? It certainly implies your sex has changed."

"I said a lot of other words. You didn't get any of them." How did I know? I knew he didn't get the truth because he didn't start thinking, "He was a woman!" People do that when I say *transsexual, sex change*.

He's right. I've been telling lies again.

So what if I said *birth defect*? That's what the problem is like for me; I could say . . .

My mother's voice: "You mean female bodies are birth defects?" Another lie.

"If I said I'd had *plastic surgery* and you found out what kind of surgery later . . ."

"I'd probably feel like you'd lied," he said.

"So what am I supposed to say? What am I supposed to do, just whip off my Calvins and . . ."

And what? The fear of violence is an easy blind alley to get caught in, in front of a man whose soft hands have never made a fist or held a gun, an unarmed man you could break in half. And what? And watch love evaporate into pity, hatred, disgust. I stood there and watched his face twist up, and suddenly I realized we were together again. He was as afraid of his own reaction as I was, as afraid of my own as I was. We were both frozen in the fear of who we might have been.

The worst imaginable ending is the one where you almost get what you're looking for, then the door that slams in your face at the last possible moment, the last image of hate and disgust in your own face, the face of someone you thought was a friend.

Seeing something horrible is bad, but seeing yourself as something horrible is worse. The worst thing of all is not knowing what you look like.

And there's no word I can say that will release me from the fear of the worst imaginable ending. There's no word he can say that will release him, or me, or us. All we can do is to reveal ourselves and see what happens, or choose to try not to and see what happens. My new name, like my old name, like every other word we're called or call ourselves, hasn't saved me from responsibility for my own skin and my own life. No word for us is us. Words won't save us. Words weren't what saved my mother and me from our exiles on separate islands. What saved us was we talked until we realized we weren't looking for the right words to unite us but for the sound of love in each other's voices.

So what happened then? Imagine the best imaginable ending; what it is, I can't say. This isn't the end of the story, but this is where I run out of words.

Token

In the mail this morning is a formal invitation, printed on expensive cream-colored paper. It officially invites me to another formal luncheon honoring Professor Hilda Raz. This week it's for her contributions to medicine and the humanities. The contribution she made to medicine and the humanities was in gender studies, including a book of poems documenting her responses to the sex change of her son. Last week another award from women's studies. She goes to the award ceremony. She goes to be interviewed for the radio. She goes to be a consultant on a national television program about transsexuals. Meanwhile, her son does odd jobs to pay for a class to work some more on rehabilitating the sensory function in his chest. After the ceremony she calls him to thank him for his great contribution. She says, "The award is really yours, you know." He chats and smiles and tells her she deserves the honor.

He knows that when black people were shot and lynched for the crime of helping black Americans register to vote, nothing changed. Nothing changed until someone stood in the line of fire who was white. He knows a little of what a lot of black people must have felt when America was suddenly outraged at the murder of these brave white people. And he goes to his own home every night, leaving behind children and colleagues who will sleep on the street. People who've never had to worry about being killed or arrested every time they go to sleep tell him how brave he is to work with "the homeless." So he also knows a little about what a lot of white people must have felt. The bravery of people the system cares about, who go on knowing, perhaps, that their lives matter—as their coworkers', friends', and families' lives do not—to a larger world. And that this won't necessarily save them. What he doesn't know is a way for any of us to escape collusion.

Being me, and therefore eager to spare himself pity and other people pain, he doesn't tell Hilda any of this. He imagines, I have no idea why, that she doesn't already know.

On the television the same evening is an award ceremony honoring a woman who has made a film about Robert Eads. Robert Eads is a man dying of ovarian cancer after every doctor he could find refused to treat him. He's transsexual. Here's the woman, who is not transsexual, winning the award for Best Documentary at the Sundance Film Festival. Robert Eads is not there. Robert Eads is dead.

On the television they show pictures of the filmmaker with Robert and his transsexual partner, Lola. The filmmaker's voice is heard telling us she'd thought of the film at first as a story about prejudice, but eventually decided it was really a story about love. Her voice is brave and honest and true. She says that some of her best friends are transsexuals.

Here's me, reminding myself that Robert and Lola couldn't get people to listen to their own stories. Just like the homeless people to whom I teach theatre and whose best stories I file in my mind as future material.

On the television now is a story about *The Laramie Project*. A group of gay men, well-established big-city theatre artists, talk about their work in response to the life and death of Matthew Shepherd. How painful it was. How afraid they were to go to Laramie. How open and welcoming everyone was to them. Here's the Robert Eads filmmaker again, describing how Robert told her his greatest ambition at the end of this life. He said his pain would all have been worth it if just one straight person would see trans people as human beings. On the television now is footage of gay men whose pain was worth it, big names in the theatre as a result of *The Laramie Project*, with a lucrative contract from HBO. Matthew Shepherd's not there, either.

On the television the well-established New York actor Harvey Fierstein lambasts his gay audience because someone he met didn't believe he was a gay man. She'd told him, "If you really were gay, you'd be ashamed to say it out loud." He's outraged at the denial of his identity. He's not used to it. It happened because, he says, of prejudice: gay men like us use phrases like "straight acting and appearing," and only a few characters on prime-time network TV are gay.

As I watch Harvey, I am thinking of my father's strong hands gripping the steering wheel as he tells me not to tell anyone I'm having a sex change, to think terribly hard before I do anything irrevocable that might change my way of relating to people, that might break the social contract. There I am, lecturing him on queer politics until I finally realize he believes that if I live openly as a man I will be raped and murdered. As he talks, Brandon Teena's rapists and murderers are standing trial a few blocks away. Lincoln, Nebraska is my hometown. These are the voices of my community. Dad, you were never a fool. You were right. You were right about Brandon Teena. Trying it is the only way to find out if you were right about me.

Here I am.

Here I am with my little black book of theatre projects, years' worth of my own stories that I have not been able to tell. Here I am with stories from the people I work with, the stories I don't feel I have the right to tell alone and they can't tell anyone but each other, and me. Here I am, whose only community is in the lack of power. Here I am, standing still.

In the mail this evening is a picture of my father. Here he is standing still, a man who certainly must not look as if he has Parkinson's disease. It's a disorder he tells me he believes he must hide to keep his authority, his work, the respect of others. The only way to find out if he's right is for him to try it. There's a kind of sadness in his eyes, a new expression that could of course be a consequence of the disorder, or perhaps of something else. He imagines, I have no idea why, that no one else already knows.

In the Feldenkrais class, his son works some more on expanding his flexibility, the back of his heart. His teacher tells him he doesn't have to try so hard. But not how.

I'm a gay man. But I'm not a real gay man in the eyes of many other gay men I meet, who find in me no stories about love. I'm a real gay man for gangstas growing into men, who struggle with me to meet each other's eyes and find a love there they can live with. They tell me about the one game guys everywhere know. When I was a kid we called it "Pile on the Guy with the Ball." They call it "Smear the Queer." The guy whose name is Knowledge tells me sex is all in the genes. To them, I come out. "It's a funny name for that game," I tell them. "I'm a queer." "If everything about men and women were in their genes," I ask Knowledge, "how could I be a man? I was born looking like a girl." The guy whose name is Niño meets my eyes as if I were Superman. "You just say it out loud," he says. "You're very open." Later he'll ask me what I'm afraid of. He cannot imagine any-thing I am afraid of. Later still he'll walk down the street in his baggy pants and brown skin through my world of people who cannot imagine anything he is afraid of. I tell him I'm afraid of cockroaches. He tells me he's afraid of mosquitoes. Tomorrow I will go tell my boss I'm not sure I can run a support group for lesbians and gay men, because I don't under-stand the lives of lesbians and gay men.

I once asked Quentin Crisp how he dealt with being afraid. He told me, "It's like the Blitz. You never really get used to it. You just go on."

I told my mother I'm happy for her. I told the truth. Of all the non-transsexual teachers, artists, and writers finding fame and fortune in recent years with transsexual subjects, there's no one I'd rather see successful.
I never asked Quentin Crisp about being angry. He seemed so open. So polite. I told Niño I'm afraid of roaches, so I worked with them anyway and learned to love them. To love and to respect all creatures. I always try to tell the truth about important things. And now I'm saying I don't know if there will ever be space enough to get rid of all this shit, or time enough for it to fertilize some sweet new growth in the world.

My Mother's Ring

In my mother's house a window overlooks the garden. This window is above the kitchen sink, a feature my mother once told me is her favorite thing about the house. It allows her to look out on the world as she's washing the dishes. My favorite thing about the house, other than the secret compartment behind the hall closet and my ferociously ugly bedroom curtains (ornamented with diagrams of knots I can't tie, but I never tire of their elaborate names), is the other bank of windows in the kitchen. These are larger and let in much more light. They look out on a tiny garden walled with juniper bushes, and these windows are in front of the kitchen table, from which you can keep one eye on the path to the door and the other on the suspended crystal egg lancing rainbows across the wall while you wait for your mother to do the dishes or make you breakfast. I'm a kid, of course.

Sometimes she asks me to help and I dry the dishes. At the time I do not see much point to this task, since if you would merely put the dishes in the draining rack they would be dry in a few minutes and later on someone, probably my brother, would wander by and put them away. I have pointed this fact out several times over the years, but parents are notoriously slow. As my own brain has softened with age I have found vivid memories of my mother and me standing by the sink, looking out the window, talking.

I am three years old. I keep having the dreams where everyone turns into skeletons. Going down endless stairs in an unknown museum to see the skeleton, skeletons who talk to me, and one horrible time my mother comes to kiss me goodnight and she—like everyone else in the family except me—has turned into a skeleton. She leans over my bed to kiss me with her grinning skull and she tells me that she loves me.

Later Mom and I are standing at the sink, doing the dishes. It is still light out. When I'm older, old enough to wear glasses and see over the sink, I would be playing with the treasures she keeps on the windowsill—a slice of transparent agate with a broken string, the miniature dish shaped from what was left of the failed pot I'd made at school, a tiny carved tiger's head with porcupine teeth, Apache tears. They change over the years. She always puts her watch on the windowsill before washing the dishes, the one with the woven gold band I like to play with. She says she takes it off to protect it from the hot water, because it's the most valuable thing she owns. But she never takes off her ring. I remember her hands down at three-year-old level, red and wrinkled as she lifts them from the sink and reaches down to me, drops of water running over the gold band honeycombed like the insides of bone, the single diamond.

"Mom," I say, age three, "what happens to people after they die?"

"Well," she says, hesitating only a little, "some people believe that they go to heaven, or to another place like this one, or different, and some people believe that when people die they get born again as babies, and some people believe that when a person dies they are buried, and that's all, that's the end."

She's hedging. I can tell. "What do you believe?"

"Well, honey, nobody can really know what happens, because we haven't been there yet, and people who die can't come back and tell us."

"But what do *you* believe?"

She hesitates again. "I believe that we each have a life that can be full of good things, and it lasts as long as it's supposed to. Then it's done."

"And we go in the ground, and that's all?"

She kneels down. "That's only what I believe. I don't know. Nobody does. People believe different things."

"And that's ALL?"

She stops hedging. "I believe people who die live on in our memories for as long as the people they loved remember them. When my papa Aaron died, my daddy lit a candle every day for a year to help remember him."

"Did you ever light a candle for anybody?"

"No, honey, that's something only the oldest son can do. But we do lots of other things, too, like tell stories. You remember I told you about how my mom, your nonna, fell into the well when she was a little girl, and how *my* nonna, your great-grandmother, jumped in and made her dress into a big balloon to hold them up, and rescued her? That's how my mom lived to have a daughter, and that's me, and I have a daughter, and that's you. And you look like my nonna, and you're like her in other ways, too, even though she died before you were born. So she lives on in you. People live on in what they leave behind."

I don't remember if this was the first time she told me her ring would be mine.

There was only ever one ring, my mother's. She told me once she'd thrown the wedding ring from my father out the window of a moving car, or maybe I read that in a poem. At any rate, I don't remember one. If my stepfather gave her a ring, I don't remember that, either. Maybe it's in a safety deposit box somewhere, or maybe she sold it when we needed money, or maybe she threw it away. My father's mother came to help take care of my older brother when he was born, and on the way home she was killed by a car. Her name was Sarah. I don't know what happened to her ring, or her mother's. My father told no family stories. Not until I had written this book.

My mother's grandmother didn't leave a wedding ring. She kicked her husband out one day, locked the doors, and flushed her wedding ring down the toilet.

Victoria wasn't a woman who liked fripperies. Afterward she sold their house and used the money to buy herself something useful, a grocery store. Her son dropped out of school and delivered the groceries in his little red wagon. As he got bigger, he bought bigger wagons and ended up making the family fortune from his trucking company. Why a grocery store? Did she like gardening? I asked my mother. Was she a cook? A farmer? No, my mother said. She didn't like much, except my father.

The fortune is lost, except for the fragment that was left to the women. My mother's ring survives, and a little money, passed on intact from her mother to my mother, and from my mother to me.

"It was the only thing my mother ever insisted on," my mother said. "She never even learned to drive until after my father was dead. But money was supposed to go only to male children, and she made sure you got an equal share." I don't imagine she thought I would use it to have a sexchange operation.

The rest of the legacy was entrusted to the men—a family home, respect, a fleet of green trucks with my mother's name in red and gold and the motto "We Move Everything but the World." One brother an embezzler, the other useless for anything but to stay home and do housework, I was told. Perhaps my mother's ring was bought by his wife the accountant. Perhaps it came from the grocery money. Victoria told my mother she bought a grocery because "No matter what happens, people still have to eat."

"Why did she kick out her husband?" I asked.

My mother said, "Nobody knows. His name was Samuel, that much I can tell you. But when I asked about him I was shushed. Years later, driving down the street with my mother and father, small in the back seat, my father barked out my name. He sounded fierce. He said, 'Look out the window' and I did, although *he* was looking straight ahead, not out the window at the broken old man walking by on the sidewalk. He said, 'That's your grandfather. His name is Samuel.' He said, 'Samuel is your grandfather.' He didn't say, 'Samuel is my father,' although he was. Nobody ever answered my questions about him. Finally my mother told me he'd done a bad thing, and I remember my father driving away."

Everyone in the car that day is dead, except my mother. Nobody remembers Samuel, my great-grandfather, or the bad thing he did. I used to like to imagine maybe he loved a man.

My mother's father was a prince of the Masons. He died of cancer when she was seventeen. He left behind a gold ring with a sculpted eagle I used to run my fingers over and the number "32" in tiny triangles of enamel—the highest grade there was, my mother said. She told us if we were ever in trouble, anywhere, we could go to the nearest lodge of the Masons and show them her father's ring. They would have to help us, take us in. When she got rid of her second wedding ring, my mother decided to wear her father's ring. It was far too large for her hand. The jeweler said he'd have to break the ring to make it fit her, and she told him to go ahead. He cracked the enamel shoulders and cut a chunk out of the side instead of the shank, where there was more gold. Maybe my mother asked me to size it first, and I said no because I was young and inexperienced with gold, because the professionals said changing a ring that much would be a hard job, because I was afraid. I don't remember. Now it looks like something you'd pick up cheap in a pawnshop, something broken. When my brother grew up and left home, he asked for his grandfather's ring, and that was what my mother had left of it to send him. I used to dream about restoring it, but my hands are my mother's size, and it's not my ring. My brother wears nothing but his wedding ring.

When I grew up my mother started hinting about diamonds. She wasn't talking about marriage. She was talking about portable property. You don't have to have a man if you've already got a diamond ring. At sixteen I was as dense as my brother the romantic but about different things.

"I don't like diamonds," I said. "They're fluffy."

"There are lots of different settings."

"I don't need a diamond ring. Someday I'm going to inherit yours. That's enough for me."

She laughed. "I'm not planning on going anywhere for a long time yet, and you're on your way in the world. Besides, not that I could do anything about it from beyond the grave, but you must never sell my mother's diamond."

"Who said anything about selling it? I wouldn't sell it, no matter what."

"Well, I mean if you were starving in the street I'd want you to sell it. I mean, sentimental value aside, it's a rock. You're a lot more important. But that's the point."

"What's the point?"

"Someday you'll want to pass my diamond on to your children. So you should have a diamond of your own. It'll be your graduation present."

"Mom! You're talking about something really expensive I don't need. I told you, I never wear jewelry. And I don't like gold. And a diamond ring is so, so, you know, *fussy*. I'm not that kind of person. If you want to get me something, buy me books for school or give me, like, money for food or rent."

"But someday you're going to have my diamond. Do you not want it? Are you not going to wear it?"

"Of course I will."

"I suppose it doesn't matter. You could be totally indifferent, as long as you *have* it. You pass it on to your daughter, she'll love it. Sometimes these things skip a generation."

"Mom, I want your ring. It's different. It's completely different. It's not like some kind of, you know . . . it's *yours*."

And it was.

Somewhere in the course of my senior year in high school my friend Rob, whose parents were Mormon, got his ear pierced and his parents kicked him out of the house and changed the locks. My friend Ivan decided a considerably more tasteful single earring than Rob's might be just the thing with Armani, and as usual I followed suit. Rob had been extremely concerned to explain that which ear you got pierced made a great deal of difference, as shown by the fact that he had gotten the correct ear pierced for being merely cool. Ivan laughed.

"Left, right, right, left. Who cares, anyway?" he said. He carefully arranged to have the opposite ear pierced than Rob's, and I had the same ear pierced as Ivan's, of course.

The week before I went away to college Mom asked me to come to Zales with her to get her diamond appraised. Sitting in the dental atmosphere of a commercial jeweler, Mom explained to me it wasn't that her stone was so valuable; it looked large, but because of the way it shattered when my grandmother hit the pavement they had to recut it, and it was too shallow for ideal refraction. The color was very, very good, but deep inside it had one single dark spot, a hidden flaw. Though I looked and looked I couldn't see it, but my mother knew.

In the parking lot she handed me a small box. Inside was one small, absolutely plain diamond stud earring, not from Zales. I stared at it.

"It's not great, but its good," she said. "I mailed a little something each week to the jeweler who made the earring. It was fun."

"Mom . . ."

"Try it on."

I tried it on.

"Now, wear it all the time. It's got a screw post so it can't fall out. Anything happens, you get into trouble, go to the nearest pawnshop and hock it. Don't be sentimental. That's what it's for. Anywhere in the country, it'll bring you enough for a bus ticket home."

Once upon a time, my mother told me, a woman got married. Something bad happened, she couldn't say what, but that night the woman drove home to her mother's house and walked up the driveway, her new baby in her arms. Her mother stood in the open door. As her daughter approached she said, "Go home to your husband. Go home." And she locked the door. The daughter was my mother, my mother said.

My mother told me a lot of family stories as I was growing up. We stood at the sink and she washed and handed me the dishes, her hands red and knobbly and the diamond gleaming among the knobbly dark gold pools across the band. As I got older I'd help with the washing, but the water she used was always hotter than I could stand. We'd make bread together, and as I got bigger I could keep up with her strength more and more, kneading, and I understood I was growing up. But I still couldn't take the hot water straight from the tap.

"It takes time for your skin to toughen up," she said.

"But it's not any easier, and I've been trying for *years* . . ."

She laughed. "I've had my hands in hot water for a lot more years than you have. You'll have time. Besides, I don't know if it's such a good thing to get used to anyway."

My mother's ring came from her mother's hand. I've never seen her take it off. I remember taking her hand as a kid and looking at the gold honeycomb setting, which I found ugly but fascinating. The diamond was the only thing I'd ever seen that was beautiful in the same way as the window crystal. In the grim awful days of winter, the kitchen's pastel pink steel cabinets turned the color of a corpse for weeks at a time and my mother would sit on the floor. Then the room would abruptly grow light. My mother's head would come up and suddenly, out of nowhere, the corpse-colored room would be lifted, wheeling and turning into shards of light, all the colors of visible fire. It happened more and more often, and then it was spring. By summer patches of rainbow lived on the kitchen walls, and I learned how to spin the suspending thread of the crystal and send them running across the ceiling like orchids, *Morpho* butterflies, tropical lizards. I learned the name for this: refraction. Reflection happens when light bounces off a surface unchanged. Refraction happens when light penetrates the surface, strikes something inside, and is changed. Diamond, I learned, is the most refractive substance in the world. This was why there was so much fire inside my mother's ring. Diamond is also the hardest substance. Nothing can destroy it.

Once upon a time, my mother told me, a woman married a man. She liked him very much, and they had gotten along very well until they were married and living together. He started to argue with her a lot, and one night he came home drunk and beat her. Since men are usually stronger than women, even though she was very strong she was not able to stop him. Afterward he fell asleep, and she realized he would beat her up any time he felt like it for the rest of her life, unless she did something. The next night the man woke up in the middle of the night not knowing what woke him. He opened his eyes and saw he was lying on his back and the woman was holding a pan of boiling water above his head. She said, "Next time I don't wake you. Don't ever hit me again."

And he never did. That was my mother's mother, your great-grandmother. They had a very happy marriage, my mother said.

When my grandmother hit the ground the diamond broke. My mother told me in the kitchen one night. She was doing the dishes. "I was doing the dishes," she said. "The first time after she died, I was wearing her ring. I can still see it. The stone just fell apart on my hand."

My grandmother had Parkinsonism, a progressive disorder that robs the brain of dopamine, a neurological messenger chemical that carries impulses to communicate rest, desire, spontaneous action. Dopamine is also depleted during depression, a neurological fact that explains a lot about why I never mastered a flying cartwheel and spent much of my year at clown school standing like a stunned ox while my teachers screamed, "Stop thinking!" and "Be funny!" My father has Parkinson's disease. After he was diagnosed, he sold off all the tools I remembered from my childhood at a garage sale, since he could no longer use them. I came home and found them gone. My Uncle Hugh's tools went in another sale, years ago. A fungus infection had destroyed most of his brain, and he kept on trying to go down to the workshop and fix something. I came home and found everything gone except the little Buck knife he gave me that last time, when we rummaged through drawers and turned the table saw on and listened to it hum like when I was a kid, and upstairs they decided the shop had to go. I shouldn't have let him turn the table saw on. I can't buy a house with a rec room and a basement, anyway. I live in a small apartment, far too small for anything but a jeweler's bench.

People with Parkinson's disease write very, very small. When I turn on my computer to write, I set the automatic font control to 14, two points larger than average. I think this is funny. I have to.

Unlike my father's, my grandmother's Parkinsonism was untreatable, a late visitation from a childhood bout of the 1918 flu. One year. An epidemic that killed twenty million people. Nobody remembers. Only the brains of old people who survived the flu in childhood sometimes remember, falling slowly into a helpless inertia that mimics the most severe forms of Parkinson's. My grandmother's name was Dolly. One day, after many years of it, she spent the afternoon dragging her armchair like a concealing bush in a Bugs Bunny cartoon across the floor of her room at the long-term care residence tower. When she finally got to the window, she climbed up and jumped out. It wasn't a flying cartwheel, but I still think it was pretty impressive. She was seventy years old.

The men in my mother's family die young, and in my father's family they disappear. But my grandmother's death cracked the ring. I remember my mother lifting her hands from the dishpan, cupping them as she describes the stone falling apart, water dripping from between her fingers. I remember my terror that the steaming water would destroy the diamond that was left, and everything would be gone. I remember her reassuring me—her mother fell from a great height. Hot water, even boiling water, couldn't hurt a diamond. My mother was not going to do the kinds of things that would destroy her diamond. She would be here, and the ring would be here, and the ring would still be here with me *someday*.

On my own, I looked up the difference between hardness and toughness. Nothing could scratch a diamond, not dish soap, or pennies, or the window crystal, not sapphires or rubies. But toughness was different, not whether you could be hurt on the surface, but your resistance to a sudden shock. Diamonds are the hardest substance on earth. But they're not so tough.

My mother described the way she had the stone recut, all the cracked and shattered places fallen away to leave a sound stone, just of an inconvenient shape. How she had the choice to make it small and deep or broad and shallow, and how she wanted to be able to see its play of light, even if it was imperfect. I agreed. She'd done just right.

She'd had to choose a new setting, since the stone no longer fit in the

213

old one. Her new setting was bold and irregular, unisex and unusual, but very fifties modern. It wasn't my taste, but it suits my mother. Her mother's setting must have been tiny and delicate as she was, Victorian. "What did you do with the old setting?" I asked.

"It's in the safety deposit box. It was too small. No use to me."

I looked at my mother's setting, which is so much my mother's ring that I loved and so much not what I wanted for myself. As a child I realized that someday my mother would die. Then I would do as she had done—put my mother's diamond into a new setting. But I realized then I could do even better; even if I chose to change the ring, I didn't have to put my mother's setting away. I could learn how to fix things, how to melt it down and make myself a new one from the same gold. My mother dying was an unbearable thought. But her mother's ring was hers, and her ring would be mine because no matter what happened, I was her inheritor. And what that meant was I would carry her with me, changing the shape of things, telling the stories, moving on as she had done. I would wear her ring everywhere I went and I would never, ever take it off.

In the year of my mother's sixtieth birthday, we went to the safety deposit box to admire the jewelry we visit every few years, including the stuff my stepfather gave her, which she never wears. "It will all be yours," she said. "You take after my papa Aaron, the gold dealer. He was a gentle man, a good man, and I loved him. I'm so glad you took his name. You're the only one who knows anything about jewelry, so you handle this stuff. Sell what you want, you'll know what price to get. Keep what you like, and wear it. It's tainted for me, but for you it will be fresh."

She took out a sheaf of papers. "I had my will done. There's nothing wrong with me, and I expect to live a long time yet. But it was time to have things updated; I hadn't looked at it for so long that your stepfather's name was still on some of the paperwork."

At home she shows me where she files the papers. We sit in the kitchen as always, the two of us at the table before the big windows, drinking coffee together, the window crystal spinning rainbows. She goes over the provisions; my brother will handle the paperwork, he's better at that; I'll deal with medical issues and portable property. "All the jewelry will be yours to deal with, though I hope you'll give individual pieces to whomever wants them. Except for my ring, of course, which will go to the girls."

I look at her. She shrugs.

"Tradition. It always goes to the daughter."

"I know."

I don't know why this is happening, but apparently my mother does.

"The girls'll grow up and have daughters of their own to pass it on to."

My brother has two small children, my mother's granddaughters. Their mother had been cool with the rest of the family, and my mother slowly learned over the years to bank her fires when in their company, but visits are still rare. They have their own stories. I don't see how they fit with ours. I see them in photographs, two laughing blond girls with intelligent eyes, posing for the camera in their Manhattan town house, at my brother's university, at their Montessori school. A few times a year they talk excitedly at me on the phone, tiny unfamiliar inflections. In the photograph their father sends they are wearing their favorite new costumes, plastic tiaras and pink princess dresses. They look beautiful. They are the future.

It's the first day of spring. Where I live we don't measure time by the calendar. Spring, in coastal Oregon, comes the first day it is not raining. It has been raining for several months.

My partner and I pile into Isis, my twenty-year-old car. This year Isis is half my age, and, I believe, can now be certified as antique. This is something I try not to think about. We intend to go to Sauvie Island, where a steel sign marked "WARNING: CLOTHING OPTIONAL! divides the sand between straights and queers. Behind the firmly clothed bathers are the associated U-pick berry farms, flower fields, and pumpkin patches; behind the queer beach are sterile hills thicketed with screens of wild blackberry and second-growth aspen dense enough to fuck behind, and beyond them, a bird sanctuary. It is to the bird sanctuary that we intend to go. Perhaps later, if we're both feeling up for it, we'll take a walk on the beach.

For some reason, though, I take a wrong turn before we reach the island and cross the Saint Johns Bridge. There's no turning back on the narrow hill, and the bridge itself has become a vast construction site; we stagger irrevocably across the river on a road that releases us fifty years into the past.

Saint Johns was the blue-collar town north of the black town that was exiled from Portland proper in those days, and for Saint Johns those days never ended. On the main street you can buy a tuna fish sandwich at the lunch counter, a pack of five dozen tortillas and a piñata at the *groceria*, steel-toes, flannel shirts, live bait, jackets with corduroy collars. The baseball caps that say "God Bless America" are not newly made. As slick young families explode money into town houses and condos downtown, Saint Johns will change as the black town already has. The shockwave drives hipsters and queers north toward the edge of the state, they drive the blacks and the freaks further still, until bohemian meets bohunk on the edge of town. On the main street of Saint Johns, the track-light taqueria and the flickering fluorescent now sit side by side. If I live long enough, I'll see the grandchildren of the folks I used to know, back to living downtown. My students who aren't sleeping under bridges and dodging paid cops from the downtown business association went to trailer parks beyond the suburbs. They grew up to be not cute enough to care about, and their downtown residence hotels mysteriously burned down. The condo towers that immediately replaced them will be residence hotels again, where the children of the babies in my old photo album will hustle when the slick young families move back to the suburbs again. Money changes everything, and nothing. Until then, Saint Johns is liquor and lunch and church and longshoremen, Mexican Spanish and Semper Fi and bohunks from the old school, and I know the place because I worked pickup jobs here in the old days, theatre jobs in cheap warehouse spaces here now, and Daire doesn't know the place but falls instantly in love. There are enough new coffeehouses and I'm enough years away from Nebraska and Labor World that I can appreciate what it doesn't have in common with universities and social workers.

We browse the flannel. We drink coffee, buy Jarritos soda and *pepitas*, wander down to the river. Under the cathedral pillars of the Saint Johns Bridge, wild chamomile blooms in the grass.

Daire, whose name used to be Dawn, says, "One thing I like about us is that we can enjoy things even if they don't turn out the way we planned. A lot of people can't seem to do that."

The brown Willamette River is innocent of life. A family picnics on the concrete boulders of the riverbank, laughing. A girl in an immaculate magenta dress and Mary Janes picks her way along the shore; her mother calls to her in Spanish.

"I love you," I tell him.

She puts her arm around me. "I love you, too," he says.

We stand on a boat dock and watch the water. Above us half-seen construction workers spray reflective beads onto new asphalt; the spray catches the air and floats down in brilliant particles of refracted light. A barge and a yellow and black boat like a huge bee make their way along the river. On the boat dock a drunk man with a beaten face hails us. I call back hello.

"See that?" he says. "That's a riven bilot."

"I'm sorry," I tell him. "I don't understand what you said." He tries twice more, and the second time I understand.

"What's a river pilot?" I ask.

"It's a rule from back in the last century," he says. "Any boat can go down the Willamette to the sea, but for every boat coming up against the current, you have to be guided by a river pilot. It's because of the shoals. All those guys from the ocean, they were coming up not knowing the river, they'd hit things they couldn't see and sink. It's too dangerous—where the snags are, the sandbars, every time there's a storm, it changes. But the river pilot knows." He tells us more, technical details.

"Were you ever a river pilot?"

"I like to sing," he says. He sings. "Hey, sing along."

I sing. When we get tired of it, we make our way back up the hill, detouring toward a building that Daire maintains is interesting. It looks like an ordinary brick industrial building, but I don't argue with architectural instinct.

Swallows are flying around the windows. "I want to go around back," Daire says.

I find a tiny marsh, a wildlife refuge. I spot a heron, an interpretive sign. The sign, in flowing script surrounded by portraits of native birds, says, "County Experimental Sewage Treatment Facility."

Daire calls. I follow her voice along a curving trail to where he stands on the periphery of a great circle of rusted steel pylons, cut off at waist height. In the center is an enormous tear of mirrored steel, falling into a pool of water.

"Thought so," Daire says. "I remember this from architecture school."

I remember one of my students, who used to leap up and balance on the bars of bike racks, the tops of fireplugs. I used to think it was impossible before I went to clown school. I vault up on a pylon. Daire doesn't follow. So I describe what I see:

From this vantage point, the teardrop reflects like a funhouse, a camera lucida, a circular mirror—reflects the whole scene, the refuge, the water, the sky. And the water reflects, too. It reflects the steel tear, but also the reflection of everything that's reflected in it, and the really amazing thing is that the water reflects not only the tear and its reflections, but also the water's own reflections of the same scene—the rushes at the edge of the marsh, a bird flying over, the sky—so you're really seeing everything at once from two different perspectives, at the same time. And the most amazing thing of all is that wherever there's a shadow you can see in the water what's inside, so you're seeing both the surface, more than one surface, and what's underneath, because water both reflects and refracts the light.

She watches the same thing from his own perspective.

"Daire?"

"Yeah?"

I tell Daire about my mother's ring.

"Just let it go," says Daire. "You can't do anything."

We look at each other. He doesn't say what she would have said a year ago—*you wanted this, you didn't have to do it if you didn't like the price.* He doesn't say, *Suck it up. Be a man.*

After a while she says, "I think talking about it would just make trouble."

"I don't want to just let it go."

"What's the point?"

"The point," I say, "is not about control and not about greed, and every way I can think of to talk about the ring either sounds like I think it's my business to say what choice she should make, or it sounds like I'm just trying to get more goodies than the girls."

"So what's the point?"

I remember watching my mother and her ring, every day, growing up. I remember listening to the stories she passed through it to me, teaching

218

me what we were, where we stood, how we survived, who I would be. My mother stands with her weight on the fronts of her feet, locking her knees, leaning forward like a racer reaching for the starting gun, braking herself with a constant, frantic pull upward all the way from her toes. She falls forward through everything, throwing herself ahead, braking all the while with terror, keeping up against the hunger of gravity by the force of will and sheer speed. I know it like I know my own body. I have her scars on my knees.

It has been ten years since my surgery. I imagine myself as ten years old, running home as I often did to report to my mother on the state of the wide world.

"Hey, Mom! Good news! You know those stories you used to tell me? They're about *us*! They're about *me*!"

"Of course, honey," my mother says in my imagination. "They're about women."

Of course, she wouldn't say that, because my post-transition ten-year-old is visibly a man.

She says, "No, no, these stories aren't about you. They're about women. I told you those stories because I thought you were a girl. I told you the wrong stories. I'm so sorry. It was my mistake."

"No, Mom, wait! That's what I'm trying to tell you. The stories you gave me, they're true. They're about me, and I'm not a girl. I'm a man, and they're *mine*."

What do you mean, it's not good news?

Growing up, I realized my mother's stories were about strong women, just as I realized that the story of Gilgamesh and Enkidu was about strong men. I had lots of role models, of a variety of genders. My mother's stories about her ring were her gift to keep me safe, a special set of stories about people just like me. I never imagined her stories as guides for being a woman. I was never told that these stories were only supposed to be for women. I wasn't a woman, and they obviously applied to me.

As a result, I have carried through my whole life a tool kit of stories about how underdogs and in-between people survive against the odds, fight and flee, destroy or support each other, escape poverty, and prosper in the face of silence, shame, and superior force. Stories, above all, about how to live your own life when, as Public Enemy says, it takes a nation of millions to hold us back. Stories about women? Yes. And they work. Each feminist tale of oppression and triumph in my life has also been lived by a man. The stories of these women never failed to give me hope while they kept me alive. For the past ten years they have helped me to survive, a man living a man's life in the world. Now they also make me ask questions about a greater victory, one that might come when we can look beyond our own survival. These cannot be only women's stories. I have lived them. I cannot be the only man who has. I do not understand how this could be bad news.

My brothers' girls might not have children. They might be lesbians. They might not have daughters. Their daughters might not wear tiaras and think they want diamonds. They could even be sterile, like me. I can neither bear nor father children. I have no legally valid right to marry anyone. I am not allowed to adopt children. And as a man of my race I cannot pass on my family line. My brother will have no sons, unless within the pictures of his girls they are better hidden than I ever was. My cousin Micah, whom I love as I might a son, has a mother who will give him stories of her own. When my generation is gone, everything I have will belong to the next generation, regardless of anything, it will go to my children and my children's children, the children of my brothers and sisters everywhere in the world. Everything I have will go to them, or it will be lost. We will keep only what we can share. My brother sends me photographs from the other coast in elaborate computer code, pictures of girls who know the world was made for them to smile in, in a format I can't read. What do I have they will want?

I looked at my partner and said, "All my life, my mother made a promise, and she made it to me. If being a girl is what matters, I want to know why."

Hilda Raz

The Book and Its Cover

Pale as she was, Ninsun turned more pale. But since she could not dissuade her son, she merely kissed him, giving him her blessing. | GILGAMESH

Aaron is my son. Sarah was my daughter. They are one and the same person, unlikely as it seems. I miss my Sarah, forever gone; but at the site of her disappearance, here's Aaron. Sarah was my companion, my connection to my English mother and to her mother, after whom I am named. Sarah was an unusual child, quick to talk and play, curious about the natural world, and beautiful, and I came to love her as myself. Myself in the next generation. Walt Whitman's vision, "the mothers of mothers." From her birth I wore her at my breast, as all mothers do, like jewelry, as I wore the cherished cameo my mother gave me, from her mother. As I wear my mother's diamond in a ring.

Aaron's favorite story was about the great king Gilgamesh, first written down in Sumerian cuneiform on clay tablets five thousand years ago. When Sarah and her brother John were children, we read it again and again in the Bernarda Bryson Shawn version, a careful, brilliantly illustrated, and widely praised book. I raced to the bookstore, brought it home. An account of the wild monster, Enkidu, and Gilgamesh, the king, who came to be companions past death. And pale Ninsun, his mother.

After Enkidu is killed, Gilgamesh is disconsolate. He comes to Ninsun and begs, "Tell me what way to take, Mother. How shall I direct my steps to find my friend?"

And his mother, Ninsun, says, "O Gilgamesh, cease your running hither and thither! Stay in Uruk, my son; take a wife. Have a child that you can lead by the hand. Such is the conformity of life!"

So my mom said to me, but not in so many words. "Oh daughter, stop running around. Be a wife. Have a child you can lead by the hand." I am Aaron's mother, but first and foremost I was my mother's daughter. My

223

mother was thirty-eight when I was born, a miracle child after her twelve barren years. Mom liked having a daughter, although maybe she didn't like so much having this one. I didn't seem to be anything like her in the next generation. We differed wildly. But in some ways we were alike. We loved to shop together, mostly for clothes. We found clothes for each other the way warriors find armor, for definition and protection. We looked for clothes to shape the girl, then the bride, the pregnant daughter, and finally the mourner. When a twin set and skirt, a dress, a suit went out of fashion, we discarded them. We shopped joyfully, obsessively. Mom's first gift to me after my marriage was a credit card. I learned the language of my body from my mum. I'm "dark, high waisted, small breasted, long legged, boyish, tailored." She was "petite, big busted, short, fair, rounded, womanly."

What my mother knew she told me, although certainly she kept some secrets. And some things she didn't know. How could she? Knowledge assumes different forms from generation to generation. Many daughters of my era read the anthropologists Ruth Benedict and Margaret Mead for the good parts, the parts about us. Then, tactfully, we told our moms, who seemed to be interested. They were learning from us as we were learning our several and sometimes conflicting identity politics and economics from global societies of women, women scholars, and women writers. However incredulous Mom's response may have been, we knew we were in this life together as women. Born in 1898, she had made the immigrant's journey from Europe when she was twelve. Her own mother, after whom I am named, had come from a Russian village to England, running from the Cossacks.

My generation read *The Diary of Anne Frank* and then we read novels like Marilyn French's *The Women's Room*, Rita Mae Brown's *Rubyfruit Jungle*, and analysis like Joanna Russ's *How to Suppress Women's Writing* to understand where we'd been, and why. Learning our histories, or as we preferred to say, HERstories, took the latter part of my childhood and the first part of my adult life. Mother told me old stories and when she was able to listen, I told her everything new. Sarah was supposed to tell me. What have I learned? Maybe the limitations of fashion.

Sarah was born in 1965, two years after her brother John. I was lucky, able to decide not to have more children. Like Mom, I had wanted a daughter as well as a son. So now I was done. If men want sons to inherit the kingdom, women want daughters. But what a girl! She was never someone I could lead by the hand. Growing up, this child argued fiercely with my talk about women: generalizations about the patriarchy in the sixties, rants about male privilege in the seventies, obsession with female collaborations in the eighties, and women's memoir in the nineties. Her reading was never about women, never about gender relationships. She was a scientist, interested only in the natural world and the long histories of myth and science. This resistance seemed evidence to me of the astonishing variations women's brilliance might take. I knew she was supposed to help me understand the new generation of women. But Sarah had no interest in teaching me. She couldn't have cared less about women.

Of course, Sarah then didn't look like a son. Beautiful, smart, graceful, articulate, difficult, butch, at seventeen she left home for college on a full scholarship. Then she came home on visits, sometimes when her brother John was home. We all went out for lunch. We shopped together as usual, nothing different: pants, shirts, briefs, socks, boots—all from the men's department.

And then, after she had finished college and graduate school, one day on the telephone the voice was husky, deeper. Allergies? A cold? I didn't ask.

Then the telephone call promising a letter with big news. Right. Then the letter. Then Sarah, now Aaron, came home and stayed for a couple of weeks.

He'd made a plan, found a language. He was going to teach me his story.

Aaron and I both love stories. My favorite is the one about Demeter, goddess of harvests, and her loved daughter Persephone, who was kidnapped by Hades, the nasty CEO of hell. What did Demeter do? She went to hell to get back her daughter. I thought I would, too. But when it came right down to it, like Demeter, I had to compromise. The best Demeter could do was gain permission for Persephone to return six months each year. So we poor mortals got, in addition to the harvest, the seasons—leaf raking, ice-skating and hockey, skiing, and all those other good sports.

I've never felt like a goddess. But certainly I believed in my power to save my children from harm—by close watching and a lot of trips to the library. In the long run, I failed. Harm comes from the inner and outer

225

world, and no amount of knowledge protects us. My power to affect even the vagaries of fashion is severely limited. Mom, shopping is a waste of time. Clothes don't make the woman. Sarah is gone. Aaron is fully present, in his own life and in our family. I'm his mom without doubt, present at his birth, twice.

Instead of traveling to the underworld to bring back my daughter, I'm telling my story of one child's life in my care. As the editor of a venerable literary quarterly, a teacher in the academy, and a publishing writer, my work depends on careful reading and analysis as well as my belief in the writer's ability to transform experience into art, or its semblance. In fact, my intellectual authority depends on accurate perceptions and good judgment.

 In spite of my training, I'd missed the fact of my child's gender mismatch. Most people seem to think we have authority over the truth, what we see and think and know. I thought so, too. But someone in my care had suffered, in ways I couldn't name and barely perceived.

I'd given him a library card, braces, orthopedic shoes, glasses, but not what he needed, a sex change. While I felt bad, Aaron felt pretty good; he seemed to be fine, happy. Even after painful surgeries, he'd smile and laugh. He looked great. His friends and his partner Dawn, now Daire, still loved him and seemed not to notice much change.

In fact, his clothes and his shoes seemed the same, he talked the same way about the same things, only his voice was deeper. His shoulders were wider. And his shirt size was smaller. And the beard. He was very nice to me. He took my hand a lot. But now I felt useless in his life.

What was supposed to be his problem was in fact mine. I missed Sarah. In fact, I wasn't sure I wanted to be the mother of two sons, not even this one, so articulate, so handsome and fine. Occasionally I wanted to resign from this story, return to my editing and teaching, deny the impact of our experience. We in the family all got tired of trying to be brave, cheerful, smart about theories of constructed and performed gender. At least I did.

Throughout this time, Aaron was as he had always been, a gendered male self. He certainly listened to me as I struggled. Only I noticed that he was beginning to stand up straight. People smiled at him on our way to the gym. People rarely smiled at Sarah, who often scowled. I'd thought she was intellectual, not miserable.

When Aaron and John were little we used to tell family stories. Aaron heard this one often. Once upon a time, when my mother was alive and I was still a daughter in my teens, very tall, awkward, skinny, I worried about fashion. My own small and stylish mom Dolly always told me I looked fine. Forget about fashion, she said. Remember style. Choose, when you have a choice, what becomes you. Hey, Aaron, I suppose she's right with us now. And I think she'd approve of what you wear.

At the end of the Sumerian story of Gilgamesh and Enkidu, as a result of brave actions by the living king Gilgamesh, the two loving companions are reunited in the underworld.

Gilgamesh embraces his friend, who is now "a man all made of moss and weeds, of roots and the trailing vines of arbutus with its pale, sweet-scented, waxy flowers."

They talk and even as they talk, Enkidu's "body drops away like an old garment, and is filled with dust."

Gilgamesh, always the curious scientist, asks his dead friend questions about the underworld. He has decisions to make. Should he return to his kingdom to marry and have sons?

He asks Enkidu about a man who has died, who had eight sons. "Have you seen him?" he asks.

Enkidu answers, "I have seen him; his name is blazoned upon standards of red and gold; his house is of stone, his image graven on it; daily he receives gifts and tributes."

Then Gilgamesh asks about the man who had no son.

Enkidu says, "I have seen him; he lies unburied at the foot of the wall and castoff crusts of bread are his portion."

Aaron tells me that the original tablets end here. We don't know whether Gilgamesh returns to his mother, takes a wife, and engenders sons to remember and honor him. According to Bryson he doesn't but embraces Enkidu and turns to dust.

Both versions of this story mean a lot to me. In one Gilgamesh returns to life, to "conformity" as his mother suggests. For her sake and the sake of the community, the kingdom, the family, he renounces love for his twin,

227

his companion, his other self. He leaves Enkidu as he must, in the underworld. He goes on, back to his life, knowing he will never lie unburied at the foot of the wall of his city.

In the other version, the one Sarah and I read month after month, her warm head resting on my shoulder, Gilgamesh, knowing what he knows, leaves.

But then he turns back. "He turned and walked toward his friend. He bowed; he fell into the dust among the weeds and bracken and the trailing vines of arbutus . . . and the earth reached up and seized him."

Here I would stop reading and blow my nose.

And then we would continue, "But even so, his life was not as an empty wind, for he made an everlasting name for himself. When people heard the name and asked, 'Who was this Gilgamesh?' they were answered, . . . 'The most eminent of men, / And Enkidu was his companion!'"

I'm glad Aaron has not renounced his wild and true companion, himself. And I am glad, too, that he is alive now in the world we share as family.

Being a mother is fun, as pale Ninsun knew. She was right there for Gilgamesh, giving him maps to the underworld and blessings. In the end, I didn't need to be the mother of mothers. All I had to be was what I am, what most people are, a person who learns. All children grow up. They are not ours to hold, to give away. Some of them choose tactfully to teach their parents new lessons. A lot of us aren't mothers at all. And some, like me, are the mothers of sons.

Fact/Fiction

*As we descended through the clean air we saw, passing us
from time to time, new flocks of words coming from the people
in the streets who, not content with the weight of their lives,
continually turned the heaviest of things into the lightest of
properties.* | JEANETTE WINTERSON, *Sexing the Cherry*

The heavy stuff of this book is my experience of Aaron's identity. The
lightest of properties is the person himself, who is pure delight: brilliant,
articulate, charming, kind. His story is a quest. Mine is something else.
He is not the victim but the master of a story he has learned to tell. And
I have a story, too.

Sarah was thirty years old when she wrote to say she'd been using male
hormones for a year and would have surgery to change her body. She had
changed her name in court. She was Aaron now, not a child. He asked me,
should we continue together as a family? I had a question, too, and mine
was as tough to ask.

Sarah was born to her father Fred and me in the old, high-ceilinged
Saint Elizabeth's Hospital in Lincoln, Nebraska, the city where we both
worked at the university. We were very glad to meet our second child. Our
first child, John Franklin, named after my father, had been born two years
earlier at Richardson House, the fancy wing of Boston Lying-In Hospital
in Massachusetts where we were students at Boston University. Fred was
a teaching fellow in the PhD program in English, I was his undergraduate student. We'd met in his honors freshman English class one September. He asked me to marry him in February. We married in June in the
backyard of my mother's house in Rochester, New York, shortly after my
father's death. Fred was twenty-six years old and I was eighteen. Our family has divided since, the children gone into their adult lives, their parents
the same, but the surprise of our children's births has never left me. Twice
my body grew large to accommodate our child. Twice my body opened,

and I gave birth. Twice my body provided nourishment for another human life.

I grew up knowing myself primarily as my body, from infancy through puberty into adult life. I thought myself lucky, usually delighted by the accommodations my body could and did make. As a parent, I knew these changes in my children as they grew. Sarah grew from an infant into a little girl, then into a woman, or so I thought, just as John became a little boy, then a man. Now John is the father of Anna and Eva. He is bearing similar witness to astonishing events, one story of the human body. But my second child's body has been altered both gradually and suddenly by surgical and hormonal intervention, a dramatic change. I've told myself that change marks us all. Often it comes suddenly and without warning. Aaron's are surprising and elaborate, for sure. I tell myself that change brings opportunity as well as shock, joy, and grief, the Cesarean section and the heart bypass, the first blood of menstruation and sexual initiation. I know well John's scar from his heart surgery at five. Change means life for some. Certainly it has for us.

I wonder how best to tell my story, to blend it with Aaron's, which is not only the story of his body. I, too, have come to understand that I am not only my body. What I have to tell is located in the relationship between a parent and her child. It is true to the best of my knowledge. But nonfiction uses some of the techniques of fiction. Readers will and should assume our stories are true. But part of the truth is that for thirty years what seemed an irrefutable fact—I was present and saw myself giving birth to a daughter—turns out to be fiction.

What hard facts can I provide? Details of surgeries called metoidoplasty and chest reconstruction, and their cost to the patient, which our records show as $14,408, about the same as dental bills for braces. And some other costs. I have to mention the as yet unknown consequences of long-term testosterone use for transsexual men, as Aaron has told of the consequences of the lack of long-term testosterone use. And then I wonder how we know what we know.

Aaron reminds me that many cultures assign value to questions without answers.

Virginia Woolf, in "Sketch of the Past," says that the source of the power of biography is scene making, "making lives vivid through scenes and moments." What Woolf describes as the moment life floods into a written account is, for me, memory flashback, or sometimes post-traumatic stress. I didn't accept the news easily. As did the mythic Demeter mourning her lost daughter Persephone, I made a big fuss.

I tell you here and now that Sarah was real. Here she is—as I remember her and as I wrote about her in my journals:

Sarah at ten years old kneels on the living-room floor hovering over her drawing pad, at work on animal figures, hybrids, in charcoal. She is absorbed, truly at work.

I interrupt her to ask, "Are these figures different from the pictures in your books?"

"They're from other planets," she says.

Here's Sarah at sixteen with a palm-sized phoenix tail in blues and golds, enamel over etched copper, in her hands. She puts down the tail in the middle of the old teak table in the kitchen and leaves the room. She knows I will find it when I start dinner. She knows that I will figure out that she has learned the ways to apply enamel on copper, to engrave the metal she has cut with a jeweler's saw.

Two weeks later here's Sarah with the finished bird. The clay body is gouged deeply with stripes. She has set an old magnifying glass, bought or found, in a copper bezel in the middle of its chest. Under the magnifying glass in the bezel she has put a seed, which she exchanges for a leaf or any one of a dozen objects/emblems in the next weeks. To make the exchange, she carefully lifts the copper hinge and empties and refills the hollow chamber where the bird's heart would be. The wings are made of copper and enamel, feathers cut out and etched on the reverse side of each piece, the cloisonné perfectly set on top. And protruding from the lower belly, dried bird's feet, with tendons and skin and claws attached to the metal.

In the doorways of our house hang intricate fabrications made of brass and thread, feather and wire, copper and enamel suspended from copper wire. They are all Sarah's constructions, made over the seventeen years she lived with us before she left for college. We've rescued them from the welter of her room, from windowsills, bookshelves, drawers. Exquisite and powerful, tiny, detailed, precise, these figures still move in the air currents.

For years Sarah made complex figures, made them first of fabric and glue, wood, then wire, paperclips, metal sheet, clay. She called them her monsters. She kept them always close—in her pockets, under her pillow, wound around her arms and wrists. They reclined on her nightstand, slept on her desk, traveled in her lunch box.

She and her friend Jennifer began to make stuffed animals from brightly colored fur during our long summer visits to Fort Pond, a small lake near Boston. We couldn't find patterns to suit Sarah's ideas. So she made patterns on grocery bags, cut and stitched saurian monsters in purple batik with black furry stomachs, green coils with red satin tongues.

Sarah looked at insects during the rest of the year, in books, in backyards, on the sidewalks as she walked to school. Animals and plants seemed of interest to her along with her monsters. All fascinating. All to be replicated, duplicated, invented. And their power.

Then Sarah began working with poured metal. Now she made monsters with crooked backs, beaked faces, taloned fingers, dressed them in bright silver slivers of metallic fabric, rippling cloaks. They had spells in their pockets, tiny, hard squares of powerful protectors. When she traveled she wrapped the figures in rags and leather against harm, put them in her pockets.

Here is my account of Sarah as a small child, reading backward in my journals. I often wrote every day, sometimes as the children played, so their conversation and comments would stay alive.

Sarah is two years old now. We're living in London and I'm sitting in the lounge watching the children play. Sarah wraps her older brother John's popgun in a towel and says to herself, "I'm pretending this gun is me and I'm putting its clothes on." She's reasonable, can be convinced by talking if we're kind, patient, and the action we want her to do involves choice or, as a last resort, begging—PLEASE, Sarah! She's very courteous. She thanks us for everything—appropriately, too. Right now she is afraid of "wiggle-wormies" (bugs) that might be on the sidewalk. On bad days she refuses to walk there, preferring the grass, or better, to be carried. If we carry her, she thanks us. I'm astonished by her expanding vocabulary. She says to her daddy, "Let me in your clutches!" (He hugs her between his ankles.) "Now I'm trapped," and she falls over in a limp heap. He asks, "Are you sleeping?" She says, "I'm dead." She pops up, bumps him, and says seriously to his left foot, "Excuse me, Mr. Foot." Next morning I'm lying in bed. Sarah crawls over and proudly hits me on the breast, says, "That's MY mommy. That's John's mommy," punching again.

She calls out to John, "Bad news!" John says, "What's the bad news, Sarah?" Sarah says, "My wheels came off." John, sadly, "Your wheels came off, Sar? Well, you should have told me before." John is the fixer. He's two years older than Sarah. I'm twenty-seven.

Here's Sarah now, at twenty-three months,

learning at a rapid rate. She can count to twenty-five. Her fascination with words continues. She chants, "S A R A H spells Saarah." "Saarah Lint" is her current response to questions about her name. Or, "Saarah Mommy," for a joke.

4 January: Sarah is twenty-two months, talks fluently, though mostly single words, has some sentences, "Hi, Daddy." "Mommy, change me." She says, "Tank tu" (thank you) appropriately to many things each day. Tonight her father fixed her vaporizer and put it back into her room (she has flu) and he heard a "tank tu" from the corner of her bed. She calls herself SA-SA and so do we. She loves music and asks constantly for "retart" (record). She's one of the most beautiful children I've seen and she charms almost everyone. A friend came by on an errand today and he squatted down to say hello. She raced down the hall and flung herself into his arms. He said later, "I was overcome. She's exquisite!" She knows her ABCs and is learning to count, all this her own idea. About three to four months ago she began pointing to individual letters on a page we were reading and was interested in little else. We read aloud a lot.

15 November: Sarah is almost nineteen months old. She recognizes that a collection of letters arranged in a certain way is a word, and shocked the hell out of me by saying as she flipped the light switch,

"O-F-F, off." She reads the letters on everything and her father, who didn't believe my story, then taught her to read S-A-R-A-H, J-O-H-N, and B-A-T-M-A-N one evening. John calls her "Sis." She counts more than one object and gets very excited yelling "TWO, free, four, five." She loves to read, "Mommy, rea ABC boot" (read/book). She, like John, is stubborn and profits from an explanation. If convinced, she will cooperate, saying, "Otay, Mom." She understands much of what's said to her, knows many words, although she's more concerned with learning *about* things than names of things.

And again, reading backward in time (the journals I wrote in stenographer pads over the years of their childhood):

March 3: Sarah at twelve months is beautiful: sitting, still and grave face, huge eyes and funny hair, so unlike John at the same age that I am amazed and delighted to have produced them both. Their constant growth and change is unlike any adult experience I've known. What am I watching? I loved pregnancy, constant change, burgeoning, birth, nursing, the self split into two—nothing familiar in these ecstatic experiences, only mystery and no little fear.

2 November: It's one of those midwestern fall days, the air filled with leaves blowing down from our tall poplar trees. John, Sarey, and I are lying on the grass by the carport. Under us in addition to green grass is a crinkling mass of poplar leaves. It's seventy-five degrees in the sunshine. The sky is a blue watercolor wash. November in Nebraska. Sarey is beginning to crawl at eight months. She loves John's wooden toys, especially his milk cart, and sits for fifteen minutes at a time, taking out the milk bottles one by one. She's still nursing and I expect we'll keep on for another few months. She grows more beautiful, so much so that people (the gas meter man, mailman, clerks in stores, etc.) make comments. But she's still an infant.

The attitudes these journals document, my attitudes, are clearly gender based. Research on gender suggests mothers of transsexual female-to-male sons perceive their infants as unattractive, unfeminine. Not so here.

Sarah was a maker as she grew up, transforming materials into art.

What has Sarah made now she is Aaron? I wonder, remembering pink colloid scars. His hair is exactly as it had been, short with beads tied into a thin braid. At his throat the same thong of African cowry shells. Same clothes, same swagger. What he wears becomes him. Nothing is changed now with Sarah, except everything.

Soon after Aaron's recovery from surgery, a headline and accompanying article in the newspaper caught my eye:

COURT: WOMAN OK AS MALE HEIR Cairo, Egypt (AP)—Under Islamic law, a male heir inherits twice the amount that a female does. So what happens if one of the heirs has had a sex-change operation?

The son of a deceased millionaire recently asked the Alexandria personal statute court to limit his brother to a half share of his father's estate on grounds the brother had undergone an operation to become a woman, Al-Akhbar newspapers reported Sunday . . . the court ruled that the brother was entitled to a full share since he didn't have the operation until after his father's death.

Jordan Times, 12 November 1995

Furious and confused, I write in my journal, "Do we conclude that surgery CHANGED the man into a woman, in fact (according to law), but only AFTER the will was activated?" The point in time of this gender change seemed important to me. When did Sarah become Aaron?

At dinner with a close friend, I behave badly when she asserts with Judith Butler that we all reside on a spectrum of gender: always have, always will.

"Now he looks so much like you," she says across the table.

She means, I suppose, my short hair, my lack of makeup, my power suit. And she means, I think, that he is not like his father, whom perhaps he would prefer to resemble. My friend means to soothe me. I am not soothed. My daughter has chosen to repair her female body, to reinvent her identity. She has chosen to bolt. My daughter Sarah is missing.

Aaron hasn't gone to so much trouble in order to remain on a "spectrum of gender." He is a man. Which means "not like his mother." All this rational talk is painful as well as difficult. As a poet I prefer to let the bound mind free. Bound feet, bound—rational and theoretical—mind. But my frenzy is not helpful.

"Women want daughters like water," I mutter to Aaron.

"Why?" he asks.

I don't have an answer yet. He asks why women love other women better than men, why they choose each other as friends, intimate companions. He says he can't see how I'll ever love him as I loved Sarah. I don't love men as I love women.

"But Aaron," I say, "I love your brother John like water." Why am I so sad? My journals are silent.

Certainly I like being a woman. I enjoy the uses of my body, the pleasure. I assumed my child would enjoy her female body, even perhaps have daughters. Now I am sterile. Any chance to continue the matriarchal line is over. John and his wife Maria are expecting a daughter who will be named Anna. Maria's middle name is Ottilie, the name of her mother. Anna's middle name will be Maria, the name of *her* mother. In the naming, these women are linked.

Once my mother bought me a gray tweed suit with a tomato-red suede peplum and a hat to match. She bought me black leather high heels and white gloves to wear. We went to the mother and daughter luncheon. I gave a speech, thanked her for being my mother. Underneath the straight tweed skirt I wore my first girdle. Under her straight tweed skirt she wore a more lavish version of the same girdle. On her feet were high heels and in her purse the same white gloves as mine. Mother bought me my first bra, size 32 AA, the training style. When I came home from school, Mom's luncheon group was sitting in the living room. Mom asked me to pull up my T-shirt to show off my new bra. I did. They all applauded. Sarah refused to wear a bra. She refused to wear skirts, tights, stockings. In London, on the tube when she was two years old, she pulled off her coat, removed her tights and her black and blue corduroy dress with lily flowers, and refused to put them back on. Ever.

My younger child comes home in December. He is wearing jeans and a sweater, boots and cotton socks, same as always. We bake bread together, as always. We walk at sunrise and sunset. We talk and read aloud to each other, listen to opera, go shopping. We meditate in the mornings, one on each side of a candle. We eat out and talk about relationships, literature, art, ritual, family, ancestors.

He is smart, articulate, passionate. And day after day he is happy. He puts a clementine outside the kitchen widow. The orange fruit with its spiky green stem sits in the perfect center of a flat clay saucer, outside in the December snow. We watch, day after day sitting at the window, drinking coffee. Later, as we walk, we watch the crows and find the bushes filled with English sparrows.

Aaron says, "You can hear the bird bushes before you can see them." And so we listen in the cold.

Aaron and I, bound by temperament and love, are free to explore the closed corridor of our long experience. His body is changed. My body also is changed, one breast and no uterus or ovaries. Aaron and Hilda walk beside the reservoir, hand in hand. Let others tend to the future.

"Love the questions," advises the German poet Rilke. And I do.

The Letter

Not long after Sarah's thirtieth birthday, she called long-distance to say, Get ready for news. A letter was on the way. I pressed for a hint. I pestered. No go. To my questions—are you going back to school? Coming home with Dawn? Shaving your head? Getting a Doberman?—she laughed, no. When I asked, as I had several times in the preceding five years, Are you transgendered? she laughed, no, wait for the letter. Mailed this morning.

My friend Barbara, a lesbian scholar, helped me speculate on the news. We'd agreed that the letter sounded as if Sarah were coming out. But everyone knew she'd been with Dawn for years, was butch like several of my lesbian friends, and called herself gay instead of lesbian for the sake of gender politics I dimly understood. What then?

The letter arrived as promised, six days after the telephone call. I opened the envelope. Seventeen spiral notebook sheets feathered together at the top, each line printed clearly, for ease in reading.

I carried the letter outside, to sit in sun and read slowly. My stomach was feathery, scared. Sarah and I had been close for many years, then separated by flaming disputes over points of view, odd since I considered myself ardently interested in women's rights, feminist theory, and literature written by women. My husband Dale had suggested months before that maybe we couldn't settle into our favorite routines, our more usual amiable companionship, without these fierce, tearful arguments. His point of view helped me back off when she stiffened her language. But the fact remained that my cherished daughter and I disagreed, often violently, on gender issues.

I read slowly that Sarah was now Aaron (legal name change), in the twelfth month of testosterone therapy, and ready for surgery in three months. She hoped I would rejoice with him. He understood my possible rejection, but hoped we could talk through any and all of my questions when he came home. His ticket already in hand, he expected to arrive very soon, in five days. Would I pick him up at the airport? He looked forward to seeing me.

When Sarah was born, our branch librarian was distributing books at the hospital. She's known us for many years. Yesterday, as usual, after I read the letter, I went to the library, where we exchanged a few words. Wasn't Sarah beautiful right after she was born? she remembered. Well, yes. We speak softly, in the same register we use to talk about Naomi's funeral, a loved mutual friend who died unexpectedly at the New Year. We have to keep our voices down in the library.

I read the letter often over the next few days, called long-distance and talked to Aaron, to Dawn, to John and his fiancée Maria. Then I called Barbara. What had I supposed the news could be? Who knows. My adrenaline levels were so high I couldn't sleep. When Aaron arrived, five days later, Dale came with me to the airport. I was shaking. Aaron loped off the plane and into my arms, lay his heavy head on my shoulder, hugged me hard. We stood together, rocking slightly. Then he moved back, shook Dale's hand, hugged him hard, and we went home.

How does he look? Pretty much the same, but with a beard.

He looks like Sarah and not: same thin beaded braid from the back of a cropped head, same leather jacket, jeans, boots, same Israeli army surplus backpack. He's slender, but bulky in the shoulders. His skin is thicker, tanned. He has a sprinkle of acne (Sarah's fair skin was flawless and burned in the sun), a dark beard around his jaw. His breasts are hidden, as always, and the airline attendant at the checkout desk calls him sir. I'm relieved.

Dale seems unfazed. Aaron is radiant, happy in spite of his airplane queasies. The depressed cast of Sarah's face after travel is gone, absent. Happy Kid. My Happy Kid, home for a holiday.

I get ready to work hard.

In bed, I let my mind clear until the icy blank space promised to remain. Tabula rasa. A new slate. A clean page. All I can do. Aaron has been hugged goodnight in Sarah's bedroom. Whatever comes next for him from me will be a blessing of choice, fury, rejection, reconciliation, acceptance. I remember my favorite quote from Thomas Mann, "Enemies are evidence of a robust life." I can turn away.

Aaron turns over in his childhood bed. I hear him, as always.

Scars

You'd never know one of my breasts is a silicone sac. And the two top scars, from the biopsy and the mastectomy, are pale and thin. The hysterectomy left a low smile on my flat belly hipbone to hipbone. While Aaron is home he asks to see my scars; his eyes take them in. Is he wondering why I bothered with reconstruction? But no. He wants a reconstructed chest, flat as my right side was before reconstruction, but shaped like his brother's. For years he has been weightlifting, developing the pectorals we all have, his unscarred. He tells me his coming surgery is called chest surgery, chest reconstruction, not double mastectomy. I try to teach him about scars during his visit home.

I remind him that his brother's heart surgery scar is raised, a colloid scar, but mine aren't. No reason his will be.

At this time in his life I had expected to show him something else, maybe how to fold contour sheets or keep the linen closet neat. Instead I'll show his brother how to fold contour sheets. They both know how to do a bibliography.

Aaron and I tromp out to feed the ducks at Holmes Lake each freezing morning, his long visit to teach me about his coming surgery. He is teaching me his new name, too. Later we bake bread as we always do, together. We both know how to test the dough, braid the long snakes we roll out together with floured palms. I tell him again the story of his birth as we weave the braids into loaves. I remind him that the model for his body after surgery may be his namesake, my grandfather. For the first time I tell him about my only vision.

When I was a young woman waiting to meet her second child, in love with her first child, I knew I carried a boy. He would be named Aaron, after my papa, my mother's father who lived with us until he died when I was eight. Reading to John, my first child, one night, I had a clear palpable vision. I was sitting between my small sons, the younger one in Doctor Dentons, the older in his fireman flannel pajamas, reading out loud. Aaron leans his head on my forearm, to be closer to the book. John is under my other arm, his head on my shoulder. I am the Roman matron from my high school Latin textbook, Cornelia, mother of sons. I have never since had a vision, nor had I had one before. But in the delivery room at his birth, I raised up to meet my son and met instead Sarah.

"What's wrong with him?" I asked the doctor.

"Nothing's wrong," he said. "You have a daughter." And I wept with joy and relief.

Today as we walk, knead, and talk, I ask the same questions, express the same fear he meets patiently every day. Why can't I understand what he is teaching me? I can't teach him what he'll need to know—what I know about surgery—because I can't seem to learn what he wants me to know. I can't teach him about men. Each night I tuck him into my Sarah's bed, perch on the side of the mattress, and let my palm find his rosy cheek, hold it as I kiss Aaron hello, Sarah good-bye. Each morning I put on my snow boots and walk out to meet my child in our kitchen, drink our coffee, set out to find the ducks again. Our boots mark the new snow side by side, never again in the same tracks.

Surgery

I went to the apartment in a taxi. I climbed the steep, open stairs past the container garden—hibiscus stems new green under bronze leaves—and knocked on the door. Dawn's voice called, "Come in." I found my child slumped in his partner's arms, her head bent to his head, her calm voice saying, "Breathe, breathe." His lips and fingernails were blue. We called 911.

At the hospital we discover that Aaron's lung has collapsed. The thick bandages on his chest disappear, and then his torso is naked. The incisions with their black stitches seem familiar after a while, not shocking; the nipple grafts covered with circles of salve-impregnated gauze are sewn into his skin.

The 911 ambulance attendants came quickly in response to Dawn's call. They seemed unsurprised, unafraid of his heavily bandaged chest, his difficulty breathing. They lifted him onto the stretcher, strapped him in, checked his condition.

"Transsexual surgery," Aaron said immediately.

I watched, ready to intervene, to protect him, but they were as cool as he was. He was still unable to breathe freely but calmer. They negotiated the steep steps down. I followed, holding his hand.

"Come with me," he said, and I did, ten minutes later in a taxi. Dawn jumped into the back of the ambulance with the patient, only one person allowed, the right thing. Dawn is Aaron's immediate family.

The hospital was high over the city, the narrow ascent road scary, though the taxi driver easily managed the two-way traffic. As we went up I flashed onto another hospital ride, in California, driving Sarah home after her dangerous blood clots, after her ten-hour surgery. She'd told me on the telephone, long-distance, that she had a sprained leg, was really fine. As we talked I packed a suitcase, and after a few hours we were in the same room. I called my cousin, a surgeon in the area, and then we were going to a different hospital, where doctors saved her life. After her long hospital stay, I drove her home in her small car on the California freeways, squinting through a flashing migraine. Sarah might have died then and never become Aaron. "Mom," frowns Aaron two years later, walking through the zoo in Lincoln, Nebraska, "I'm the same person!"

In the emergency room after his lung collapsed, Aaron is lying on an elevated table watched over by nurses—all women—no one there seeming to be surprised by his newly unbandaged incisions or the discs of gauze sewn to his chest. Dawn is holding his hand. They are calm. The surgeon arrives in good time, orders tests and a lung expander, a breathing device I am dispatched to pick up from the hospital pharmacy a couple of buildings away. I run. The pharmacy anteroom is packed. Outside on the warm pavement several derelicts sleep or sit and rest; each seems profoundly debilitated but also each seems perfectly at home. No one disturbs them. A thin boy in frayed dirty jeans and a chrome-yellow T-shirt torn at the neck droops against the brick wall of the building. I enter the packed waiting room, stand in line. The woman behind the counter is patient with the fat boy and his mama, the woman with a bundled infant, and me, who has a prescription for something the hospital seems not to have. Someone looks up supply companies in the phone book, makes inquiries, and sends me away with an address. I run back to the emergency room to find Aaron pale and hungry. I order food he can't eat.

Everyone in this jammed place is civil, apparently concerned for everyone else in the midst of big-city hospital snafus. Lucky.

We stayed a few hours until the doctor said we could take him home, and then we did, in a taxi.

After a couple of days he felt better. To walk, he scuttled like a crab, his knees bent, legs as far apart as he could manage, leaning back for balance. His face shone. He was beautiful, like a Greek statue, but for the black stitches, the rounds of gauze. He wore a silk soccer shirt, open, barely grazing his wide tanned shoulders. (The new shirt was in my suitcase, silk to comfort his skin. He put it on every day with the new pair of gray gym shorts. They fit very well, too big at the crotch, close at the waist as I'd hoped. My mother always said that if you can manage wardrobe, you can manage life.) I looked and looked at my child, changed. What did I expect?

243

When Aaron needs help he asks, unembarrassed. Help to sit down, help with the bathroom, help with food, a drink, pain meds. He hurts--chest, genitals--but he never cries out, rarely complains. We read aloud his old books and new ones we bring in each day—all natural history. Darwin is a favorite. We read *The Voyage of the Beagle*, Darwin seasick, lying on deck, watching Patagonian natives run to the shore to watch Darwin lying on deck. He could have gone home, we marvel.

His friends arrive, sit cross-legged on the floor where we dye eggs to celebrate spring. I make tea, cakes, dinner.

One morning I discovered a gift store near the guesthouse where I slept at night. I chose candlesticks the owner had put by for herself. She heard our story--my son is post surgical, not why. The owner wrapped the box as a gift for him.

Some days later the surgeon comes to the apartment with his assistant to remove the stitches. Aaron is very weak after the lung trouble. His assistant, a young Vietnamese doctor, is *learning the ropes*, they say. They drive up in a red convertible Mitsubishi Eclipse, top down. The apartment is clean and tidy, except for the cage full of mice in the corner, food for the pet snake they've had for years. By now I don't care. The two doctors flank Aaron on the couch, remove stitches, gauze and all. Everyone seems pleased with the results. I make tea. They ask us for the name of a good Japanese restaurant in the neighborhood, for lunch.

After they leave Aaron laughs, tells us about his complaints to the surgeon and two other male doctors on one of his pre-op appointments. "I'm way too short!" he'd wailed.

Later, on the bus home, he realized he'd been the tallest person in the room.

While Aaron's breasts were being removed and his chest reshaped, his genitals changed in a three-and-a-half-hour surgery, I was attending academic meetings in Atlanta, sitting on a panel about female collaborations. After my part in the program, I flew directly to him from a city awash in scaffolding in preparation for the Olympics.

"Like childbirth," I've said on the telephone making plans for his recovery that I hoped would include me. For a while we didn't know if I should come. Aaron wasn't sure he wanted me. "If you were truly Sarah and had chosen pregnancy, I'd be coming to attend you in childbirth: sore bottom, incision and stitches, episiotomy and sore nipples from nursing," I've said to him on the telephone. This analogy helped us both, but I cried. What can I do for him now?

As I write this account, in San Francisco for another meeting, sitting at a wrought-iron table in the warming air from the bay, a man passes by on a bike with a little girl on the handlebars. She sits on the crossbar between his arms. She is wearing a small helmet, her curls springing around her face. In sun, both the man and the child, safe in her plastic bucket seat, remind me of my big brother Jimmy and me, riding along on his bike. I am small, balanced directly on the handlebars, terrified but steady between his arms. He was so steady. He's been gone for years. Aaron will never know him.

"You've been with your body since Day One. You should be the Boss. Access HMO Division of Blue Cross," says the billboard across the street from the café. An infant, eyes closed, with a pacifier, illustrates the picture that rides high at the corner of Columbus and Broadway, next to Big Al's Adult Bookstore Natural sex as seen on TV, Interactive CD Room, Adult Videos.

Whose body? I wonder. Why do I feel so bad? My every assumption, even to the subject of female circumcision, depends on a sense of owning our bodies: I may have lovers, husbands, enjoy the waters of Fort Pond with my naked and hugely pregnant friend, drop my miserable self, naked, into the icy Atlantic Ocean waves off the rocks in Maine shortly after sunrise. It's my body to suffer insect bites, too weak after surgery to track down the tiny gnats through the torn window screen, or mosquitoes, or worse, maybe fleas but glad to find my cat napping nearby on the bed after marauding outside all summer long. Maybe she's grown a planet full? I can no more give her a flea bath after my own surgery than I can walk the distance from bed to the kitchen to get repellent, or think up a way to change anything.

During that illness I lost my breast to cancer. My ovaries and uterus, too, another illness nine months before cancer.

The body Sarah changed was her own, is Aaron's body now. Not mine. Not my body, even though it grew in my center like the very air. Not from the start. Never.

. . .

And then she opened wide and swallowed a wave of sleep.

The night before my first major surgery, many years before, my friend Vera, who had come from Boston to help, walked me around and around the park near our house. I remember reading Harry Crews's novel *Car*, in which a desperate, angry man decides to eat a car and does, piece by piece. That's what I was trying to do, retching and gagging all the way. I couldn't get my mind to accept the fact of my body being opened by a knife. She stuck with me, using the tricks of her therapy practice, using her compassion, her empathy, finding us a bench, sitting us down, taking my head in her lap. The shock on her face at my fear and anger.

As a child I felt the same way about bleeding. Fourth grade. Morning recess. Irene told me. No, never. My reaction was scorn expressed in the hostile tone of voice used when someone says something I don't want to hear.

"I'll ask my mother," I said. Appeal to authority to set her straight. I stole her fraudulent news and raced home. Who did I think I was?

I raced home the mile over the bridge, around Smith Way to Harvard Street, up past the barking Dobermans, to 723 and my mother—who looked—what?—somber? amused by my stance, my shrill high voice reporting the absurdity of Irene's story? Women bleed from between their legs each and every month.

"Well," says Mom, taking off her apron, "It's true." And while I ate the peanut butter and jelly sandwich and the warm tomato soup she'd prepared, and drank my icy glass of milk, she sat down and told me how it is with us.

The night before my second surgery, nine months later, Vera come back from Boston. I went to bed early but got up in the middle of the night, left the house alone—oh, dangerous alone—walked to the park at the head of our street, only the loud sound of my feet hitting the sidewalk, *I'm here, I'm here, I'm here*, to bind me to earth, the deserted streets forbidden and dangerous.

To the playground where I slid down the high slide that scared me so much when my kids were little. Sometimes I didn't let them go down.

I slide down now. For their sake, for the times they couldn't, then

wouldn't go down. Over and over, the terror of more surgery and cancer making tiny my fear of the slide. Why not? And now, knowing other
mortal dangers in the dark, I stood at the foot of the slide and caught my
ghost children in my arms.

I made my trip to the park as if I believed that one terror might over-
take another for balance, for relief. So in the same way I remember traveling to Maine in order to swim in the icy ocean during the time of a
terrible separation, the pain apparently intolerable, the paid-up sense of
having lost everything clear in my mind so I might as well broach the icy
waves. Why not?

And the sweep of emptiness after the initial shock.

Stock

The universe is made of stories, not atoms. | MURIEL
RUKEYSER

The phone rings.

I've just come through the door, tired from an eight-hour remedial driving class called STOP, an option for speeders like me. Fifty-dollar fine, no points deducted, no ticket, and only a full day of writing lost. It's rush hour so I've walked to and from the class. The hot sidewalks have softened the rubber soles of my running shoes. The telephone receiver feels heavy as I pick up.

My husband Dale says in his soft voice, Get ready for a road trip, he's on his way home. Vernon, his dad, is in the hospital. I pack jeans and T-shirts for two, fill the cooler with sandwiches and cold grapes. We throw stuff in the car, set off, and as we turn onto the highway, the dashboard thermometer reads one hundred degrees—the hottest summer on record. Then we drive like hell. In three hours we're with the rest of the family in a second-floor hospital waiting room—three sons, daughters-in-law, their children, grandchildren, and a baby great-great in his papa's arms. What's wrong with Vernon? Does he have meningitis? His neck is stiff, he has fever. Or a stroke? Who knows? We go see. Vernon is sleeping, mouth open, without his teeth. He shakes, his fever rises. Nurse Babs jars his shoulder, asks him a question. He opens his eyes, answers her. She looks at us. Correct, she asks? Correct, we say. All three sons in the room. Babs asks Vernon how he feels. Tired, he says. Then he falls asleep for several days.

Vernon's doctor arrives. He went to school with Dale, who is the oldest son. The doctor walks on his toes like a tall bird. In his polyester slacks, sports shirt, and stethoscope, he looks decades older than Dale in his jeans. In the waiting room Dale looks different too, more solid. He returns to his father's room with the doctor, walks straight to Vernon's bedside, no hesitation at the door. He touches his dad's arms, forehead, then sits

248

down in the green vinyl chair for the duration. The doctor doesn't know anything yet.

All day and into the night Dale bends over the bed, moistens his father's open, empty mouth with green sponges on a stick. He wipes away brown spit with a tissue. All these transactions take place in silence, the family way. For the next days he takes turns, with his brothers, in the green chair next to the bed, to hold their father's hands through his growing agitation, scenarios, visions. Vernon was a jeweler in his working life. Now he spills tiny diamonds on the linoleum floor, reaches high into the air to sweep them up. Then he's in jail. The boys, grown men, cooperate easily with each other to help their father as they can. They sleep fitfully each night in recliners. The daughters-in-law leave at night with the kids. But everyone stays close. We're family. We have come far to be here. Finally Vernon awakens, improves, and the family visits nursing homes.

But before, in the middle of the third night of Vernon's crisis, in a motel bathroom, I fall desperately ill and am hospitalized the next day, two doors down from Vernon.

Nine entries to the body, seven matte bruises, seven IV sites, for support, seven veils of shiny mirage weaving their yellow leaves, paper pages I'm sorting, each swirl an event in the living world. The stories shift sleep to sleep, but always the dreamer is sorting pages, each a frame. Multitasking is a habit of mind, she figures, even as her body sleeps in its web of fluids. Pared down to the rinsed self, focus is perception: tears, wax, snot, vomit, urine, shit.

. . .

> *The thing that one gradually comes to find out is that one has no identity that is when one is in the act of doing anything. . . . I am I because my little dog knows me but, creatively speaking the little dog knowing that you are you and your recognizing that he knows, that is what destroys creation.* | GERTRUDE STEIN, What Are Masterpieces

In creation, self is supposed to go. No one knows me. Am I creating here? No, I am gone, but sick, narrowed to a point of consciousness, blink on blink off. The porches of my ears pulse hot in their tunnels. Who wants to know me? Not me. Am I afraid? No. Nothing abstract fears. Window light. This question I've been trying to answer, why is my daughter now my son, flickers dimly, even here. A voice says, *He doesn't want to be your daughter.* To be self-conscious is to exist, not create. Here I am not conscious of a self. My son is my son. Also he is himself. Where is Vernon? Where are his sons? Dale sits beside the bed. I tell him it's okay to go home. His eyes tear. Home is far away.

A loosely tethered identity has pleasures. When I was a child in elementary school, my mother brushed and plaited my hair each morning. I sat at my desk and chewed on the ends of my braids, in a kind of trace. A child chewing her braids has only the habit of working her jaws—which must be soothing in the context of the crisp resistance of hair. In the hospital that sense of self, that tether, attenuates still farther in a hot sugar taffy called fever. I have no gender here. I am not a mother, not a wife, not a writer. To have gender is to be self-conscious, not creative. Here is a continuing zuzz in the head, a kind of being present. Uninterrupted doorbell, sotto voce, of the monitors. A present, being here. But I am not. Being is sick.

Are you thirsty? No. To invoke thirst, someone says to cut the IV rate. Does it work? I don't remember. No. Intake is out. Sisters-in-law visit and watch.

Somewhere in my nighttime hospital room, a woman in her seventh decade, her waist as small as a girl's, floats and touches. When I moan she takes my head in her hands, promises in a whisper, "Sometimes in our lives we all need help." I need help. She helps me. My thank you note to her is burned work on iced linen. I am a big mess. She cleans me, holds my shoulder against her belly. I lean.

The untethered self is poisoned. Virus or disease. Untethered. Impossible, says Janus/Aaron, my son who lived in my body. You have a virus. Look both ways before crossing.

. . .

Photography taught me that to be able to capture transience, by being ready to click the shuttle at the crucial moment, was the greatest need I had. | EUDORA WELTY

What I do in writing of any character is try to enter into the
mind, heart, and skin of a human being who is not myself.
| EUDORA WELTY in 1980, who dies while I am in the
hospital

How does a mother enter the heart and skin of a human being not herself,
a boy/girl she "grew in her center like the very air"? Can she? The writer
untethered is working again.

Excuse me. What's wrong with the self? Answer: she's poison, which
she knows when someone she loves falls ill, or she does. What she is: dangerous to herself and to others. A Polish Holocaust survivor told me that
when she was safe at last, but still a child, she believed she smelled foul to
others. The sound of her urine pouring into the bowl was offensive and
distinctive, not like American urine falling without sound, not like Gentile
urine. Now I am tethered to tubes, a lucky girl in an American hospital,
who stinks. Did I pass on the sense of stink?

. . .

[W]hat is common to all transsexuals and what distinguishes
them from other sexual minorities is an aversion toward or
awkwardness with one's genitals and a desire for sex-assign-
ment surgery. | DEAN KOTULA, The Phallus Palace

To make everything worse, now metaphors abound. The stock market
is uncertain. The price of each certificate shifts as the market roils. Each
one represents a shifting piece of the family assets. The whole time I'm
sick, our assets fall.

Aaron calls me on the telephone each and every day. He reminds me,
for our book, when I am feeling better, not to write about him, only about
myself. This summer of my sickness I am supposed to be working on
our book, *What Becomes You*. Clever. My mother said this phrase about
clothes: Wear only what becomes you. What became my daughter Sarah
was becoming my son, Aaron. Who cares about clothes. His body is different from what it was. "Something extraordinary happened to me, and
it happened in the body," he says. And his surgery was difficult. Hospi-

tals, hospitals. Where is Vernon now? Down the hospital hall in his own room.

Why can't I write about Sarah? Because "the politics of identity . . . admonished the writer to 'tell her own story'; telling anyone else's risked eroticizing, objectifying" that story (Jan Clausen, *Apples and Oranges*). Clausen's explanation is as good as anyone's. Aaron is writing his own story. I don't want to eroticize or objectify my adult child. But my story, part of our story, rests directly in all its heavy weight on my daughter Sarah, who wasn't Aaron until she was thirty years old. Doesn't my life as mother and my daughter belong to me? For his part, Aaron has absorbed Sarah. Not me. I still hold precious seventeen years' worth of primary contact with Sarah, fourteen additional years of seasonal contact. Myself having disappeared because of the imperatives of illness and creation, what is left of my story, which includes a daughter? Of course, she can't use the telephone anymore. It's Aaron's deep voice that says, "Hello, Mom?"

. . .

> *That famous precept "the personal is political," once interpret-*
> *ed as encouragement to analyze women's emotional and sexual*
> *experiences for clues to gendered power dynamics, was now [in*
> *the middle seventies] increasingly seen as an admonition to*
> *mend the world by reforming not only one's personal choices,*
> *but the very fabric of one's subjectivity. To use the telling phrase*
> *with which Adrienne Rich concludes "Split at the Root: An Es-*
> *say on Jewish Identity," the good feminist's primary task was to*
> *"clean up her act."* | CLAUSEN, Apples and Oranges

To clean up my act, I say my children are half Jewish. I made this decision, without apparent thought, in order to save them from Red Cross refugee boxes after a holocaust in which I imagined I am killed, perhaps by fundamentalists like my father-in-law Vernon and his family, which includes my husband Dale, or Germans like my daughter-in-law, the wife of my older son John, and her parents and brother and his family. Labels.

When I was in second grade, all students folded and packed Red Cross white boxes smaller than a child's new shoe box. One toothbrush, one small tube of toothpaste, one white washcloth, two small bars of soap. We added shampoo, Band-Aids. The white boxes were assembled on long tables, then creased at the arrows, the lids folded and tucked in. Although no one spoke of the Holocaust, we knew. Our rabbi was a chaplain for the armed forces, and he knew. The boxes were sent to England, not Germany or Poland. But who knew geography then? My house, my street, my neighborhood, my city, my county, my state, my country. In that order. An education to find out where I lived.

The father of our two sons was raised in the Episcopal Church in Arkansas. My daughter-in-law is Catholic, raised in Bavaria on a farm. My own Jewish father was raised on the upstate New York farms of his uncles. He learned to ride a horse before he walked. The sound my urine makes in the bowl is very like the sounds made by my family down the hall in this small-town hospital. When I checked into the hospital, a nice lady asked my religion. I told her. The nice lady blinked hard. Imagine what she would have done if she'd asked my gender and I'd said male. Of course, I look female. My son looks like a man.

. . .

> *To his surprise, [Fernando] Nottebohm noticed that certain parts of the brains in the songbirds were as much as four times larger in males than in females. He also found that if you give testosterone to a female canary its song nuclei will double in size, and it will sing more like a male. "That was a real shock, because we had all been taught that an adult brain was supposed to stay the same size, with the same cells, forever," Nottebohm said. "It was one of the few uncontested facts about the brain. So how could it get bigger? That contradicted everything I had ever learned."* | New Yorker, 23 July 2001

At this point in time, I'm a very thin woman wearing a large white nightgown, thinking about a book manuscript on a computer. The computer and printer belong to me. My son does not. Is his brain growing? His story is not my story. What story is mine as I recover my identity? It includes regular news of Vernon, now in a nursing home recovering his strength.

We each have a room, a couch, a chair, a magazine, a pot, ice. He has coins in his pockets. In my purse, coins. Lying on the couch at home, for weeks I am afraid of being unable to care for myself. Vernon has nurses, if he will call them. Tending is women's work. In the hospital his sons attended to their father by staying close. The nurses did the mopping up. In the nursing home Vernon wants to get away. His sons have returned to their jobs. Their children have gone home. No wonder. I'd like to get away, too. No matter how loose the tether to my body, I can't leave it. How lucky I am. We worry that Vernon will die soon.

Getting better is difficult. I tend myself with care. Talk on the telephone to Vernon. Wash out the nightgown. Walk out before the high heat. Eat careful meals, peaches, melon, banana, fresh local corn and tomatoes, a little fish. Who tends the fruit in their fields, the vegetables? Aaron reminds me of the answers. I rest and read. Put on clean clothes dried in the sunshine on the clothesline, another exercise I do deliberately, slowly. I wash and dry only my own clothes. Stay home. Bend over the garden weeds for five minutes at a time. Avoid the poison ivy, another task for another day. Today is Friday. It is 10:21 a.m. and the temperature is ninety-two degrees in the fields. Vernon has moved to assisted living. Aaron calls from across the country.

Friends help us. Inge will be eighty on her next birthday. She and her husband have returned from a long holiday in Europe. She totes my cordless telephone to the store and installs a new battery so I will have a way to call out for help. She buys me a new ribbon for the fax machine so if work comes, I'll get it. Laura is sixty-eight with emphysema and other severe health problems. This morning she is having dye injected into her spine to discover the extent of deterioration in her hip. The socket is necrotic. She arrives with groceries and flowers, roses she piles on the counter and tears into shape, arranges in my largest vase. Neither of us can lift it with the flowers and water. She comes directly from Pilates class, from Take Off Pounds Sensibly class (she's lost sixteen pounds since May), from Rehab class at the nearby hospital. Her Lycra exercise shorts flash in purple, silver, turquoise as she bends. Her dangly earrings are gold, beaded, silver. They flash, too. Dorothy, with severe asthma and recovering from a broken spine, lives around the corner. Her eight-year-old triplet grandchildren and their mother have come for a long visit from Paris. She joins me for a glass of sherry. In Paris, in a rented room, she waited to recover from her spinal fracture, the result of lifting a big suitcase. Every day her daughter came to visit, bringing fresh fruit and vegetables. I am getting older, and these close friends are older than I am. If they have husbands, the husbands are far away from this room. My sons John and Aaron call often, sometimes daily, but they will forget to do this as I recover. They are far away.

Women my friends' age hunt and gather food during several daily trips to various supermarkets and health food stores. They lug paper sacks filled with flax seed oil and organic yogurt in and out of their kitchens, and mine. They want daily news of my progress, offer wise comments. What they don't know is, I'm in a rage. Why? I wonder. Is it death? Can I know that soon Vernon will die? Twelve months later his demented wife will die? A healthy friend who retired early has built a new house, established a new career as a translator and writer. She calls to inquire, Was I afraid of dying? My young nephew died last winter of a mysterious virus. I tell her no, I never thought of his death. I wanted to die. In the hospital I knew I couldn't endure chemotherapy if my cancer had returned. Who would tend me? Tending is women's work.

My husband is my primary contact with another human being. Our life together is ritual, boring and soothing at once, holy. But he is a bad cook. And a worse nurse. Meanwhile we are both afraid of having gone too far into illness and death. We do favors for each other. But our reconciliation is imperfect and he leaves each morning before I rise, I go to bed before he thinks of putting down his magazine. We are animals in adjacent cages. And this primary separation continues for weeks, until we are called back to Vernon's bedside. He is dying again. This time I stay home.

The peace and silence of our house is balm. Certainly my husband does his part for our lives, but he doesn't worry or tend. Have we paid our taxes yet?

But the news of Vernon is bad. The family gathers without me, but then Vernon rallies and returns to the assisted care unit.

The recovering and healthy parts of me ask (they are wearing my running shorts), What's the deal about being responsible? Why are you such a grown-up? You have no one to take care of, no bills to pay that you can't pay. Why be a grown-up? Because I have been, have met my responsibilities in the past, and now someone else should take over. But of course there is no one else to take over. What does taking over mean? Fresh food. I think about food, feed myself with the care of a parent responsible for a young child. What does Dale eat? What I fix, as always. But Aaron thinks about the fields where fresh food grows, the nurture of the fields and of the workers in fields. He is close to these issues. Vernon walks down two halls leaning against the oak railings. He sits down in the dining room at a table of eight, eats a little ham with gravy, canned pineapple, mashed potatoes. He laughs and coughs.

Now I am stronger, enough to work a few hours each day. I think that Aaron's and my story may be interesting to others not because Aaron was born Sarah, not because he's queer and I'm straight, not because he's a genius and I'm a professional woman, not because he's a scientist and I'm a poet, not because his male point of view is so often at odds with my female one, not because we are mother and child. Maybe what's interesting is my folly of grief, the willful projection of a gendered identity onto an inappropriate subject, my kid. And my deep concern with gender identity and roles. In his old age, Vernon is handsome and frail. His caretakers are deferential and charming. The entire world is turning into high summer, bearing. Vernon's sons begin to prepare for a new season.

We drive into the country, to Beaver Crossing, for Sunday breakfast with friends. The hour's drive through a hot Nebraska countryside is lucent, the verges green and lush, and I'm alive and outside again. Where does Sarah live in this resurrection?

> Find someone like yourself. Find others.
> Agree you will never desert each other.
> Understand that any rift among you
> means power to those who want to do you in.

ADRIENNE RICH, "Yom Kippur 1984"

Sarah was born to Hilda, who was born to Devorah, called Dolly, who was born to the first Hilda, her mother.

Sarah was like me, someone who says in the silence over the newly lit candles, make with us celebrations of joy or of mourning, rites of passages for one another, the kneading of bread, the leavening of wounds, flesh healing between stitches, the slow unlearning of silence, the slow recession of nausea, weakness, the intolerable flesh cut off by the friendly surgeon engaged with the help of the other. We will never leave you, never turn our eyes from each other, never shake off the fingers entwined with our own, never refuse presence at births or deaths, you are my child. I am your mother. Who is flesh of my flesh.

For a while I am better and then entirely well. At Aaron's suggestion, I try to remember my childhood.

Greg Johnson, in his biography of Joyce Carol Oates, *Invisible Writer*, notes that "she patiently endured the ritual familiar to most students of the 1950s: 'emergency' drills in case of an atomic bomb attack." Oates said that the 1950s were "a period of extremes, of myths and false impressions. But there was this other world—dark, exciting and turbulent—that was inhabited by kids who were really tough."

Oates and I are nearly the same age; both women; both grew up in upper New York state; an important detail, though she was Catholic; we're both lapsed; both were regularly exposed to liturgy. We were tough.

Who was really tough was my grandmother. Greg Johnson writes that car ownership in the fifties was reserved for boys. Yet it was Victoria Raz, my paternal grandmother, who was the first woman in New York state to drive a car, in the twenties. Yesterday at the shopping mall I thought for a minute I saw my mother, a small old lady nicely turned out, and instantly felt afraid. Because she's been dead for thirty years? Maybe not. Was she a good caretaker, a good woman, or helpless, tough, violent? Who knows? I often prefer not to remember her in life.

At Syracuse University, Oates found racism on campus "enormously disturbing," especially because in the late fifties it "went unacknowledged, unspoken." She remembers a sorority alum explaining to the girls the "sorority's exclusion of Jews and blacks: 'You see, we have conferences at the Lake Placid Club, and wouldn't it be a shame if *all* our members couldn't attend. . . . Why, it would be embarrassing for them, wouldn't it?'" As an undergraduate student at Boston University, I don't remember racism expressed directly, except at the dinner table of the famous and rich family of a student of my first husband. Why didn't I leave the table? I did, but later. Vernon and his wife Kathryn have been married for sixty-four years.

Greg Johnson's contention that "few women were encouraged to pursue graduate study in the 1950s" is dead-on for me. How could I have done so? My teacher, a graduate student, was the best I could have done, and I did it. (Our grandchild, three-year-old-Anna, shouts, "I did it, I did it," when she uses the potty. And she asserts on the telephone, her first comment each conversation, "I'm a gurrl, a very good gurrl." You bet, honey.) Vernon joined the navy in World War II. He volunteered for exacting work grinding lenses in the ship's optical lab, anchored in the Philippines. His skills were superb but his story ends, "it was the only air-conditioned space on the ship!" We find his entire uniform in a trunk, as small as Frank Sinatra's. Graduate study was not for him, not for his three sons nor his wife.

And then resurrection lilies rise around neighborhood mailboxes, dark is dawn, and evening walks in before dinner. What should we do with my life? Teach, says the self heading for the computer, building bibliography for class. The measure and purpose of the line, a new book about a favorite writer, the backlit text on the computer screen lead me to myself. Aaron is far away although we speak on the telephone, often about weather or what he should do with his life.

We talk on the telephone to Dale's brothers, at first twice a week, then every night.

Dale gets into the car, and this time I am with him. We drive. And one day, after Vernon's three sons have gathered with their wives to sit next to his bed, hold his hand, whisper their love, after a luncheon spent together in a sunlit room, after the praise blessing, and the holding hands, just after his family has heard a good report from the hospice nurse who sits in for us on our vigil, just as we've raised our voices around his bed, laughing in good friendship, in fellowship, just as Dale takes his hand, at that minute, hearing us, Vernon is dead.

And suddenly the gates close.

Bias

Aaron has come home for two weeks before his job begins. He arrives hours after my return from a meeting where I gave a paper and a reading from my new book. He will leave the day after I leave on a professional three-week trip.

Last night, after a day at work, a sprint to the grocery store, after cooking and serving a birthday dinner at our house for friends, after they leave, and I do the dishes, and Dale goes to bed, Aaron and I get into it. The talk we've been avoiding.

I hear myself say to him that men have a better deal in life, men make more money, men can leave their children to be raised by Mom, can shrug off the responsibility of even knowing that their kids need—never mind get—shoes, braces, orthopedic consultations, shirts, books. And men can satisfy themselves as responsible parents by paying half the price of a plane ticket, in cash, without even understanding the kid can't pass along the money to his mom, because she can't take cash from him he's so poor.

Aaron sits quietly, listening to me rant. His face stays calm, open. He flinches from time to time.

I modify my statements. Not all men. Only people of my generation. My class.

He is patient and interrupts me to point out that my rant is about "men" and so either he's a man and I blame him, or else I exclude him from the category and don't believe he's a man. What's he supposed to do? he asks.

I say I want him to respect me and thank me for being a good mom, for taking the responsibility both to know and to get because I didn't have a choice.

He says everyone has a choice.

Not slaves, I say. Not prisoners. Not in a concentration camp. What I don't say is, not women.

259

He says he read about a woman who lived seven years in a cave to avoid being a slave. Everyone has choices, he says, or we can't live.

No, I say. We don't all live. Who survives does so by accident. I am remembering my mother and my brother, both suicides. My long nights sitting on the kitchen floor, writing the work that eventually led to a professorship, tenure, promotions. Wanting to die. A woman afraid, with two kids asleep, making lists.

As we talk I take off my silver earrings shaped like rose petals, then my gold watch.

I recover myself enough to point out that I am talking about myself, not all women. My complaint, I say, is about men who earn a lot more each year doing the same work I do at the same institution.

Aaron's face contorts. He says that he has never earned even half of what I make, except when he as Sarah won an education worth $150,000. He says to me, See, you hate men.

I say I don't.

We have had this talk before, walking together through every green place in the city where he grew up and in the city where he now lives. On the phone, e-mail, and in the office of a psychologist.

He says that he has heard man-hating talk since he was a small child and we mistakenly thought he was a girl. Then and now he is hurt as a man. What should he do? He says he is sorry for all the pain men have caused me and the women of my generation, class, and race. He says what should he do, resign from life with a note saying he's sorry? Should he pay reparations to all the women on earth for all the pain men have caused us?

As he talks I slip off the beads he has made, over my head.

We calm down.

He says he is no more male than Michelangelo's portrait of God in the ceiling of the Sistine is God.

I listen and interject. But Aaron, I say to this man who so strikingly resembles someone in my family. But Aaron. I am so tired of trying to be reasonable, trying not to be furious when he returns from another visit to his father and he sounds and looks and carries himself like that father, the one who left the children to me, who never noticed that Aaron, this visit, badly needs shoes, shoes I buy him once again, money I give him in small dribs to help out as I can. The father who was for years chair of an academic department when I worked for an hourly wage, not a professor's salary as I do now. A man who never noticed that his children needed braces and special shoes.

Stop, Mom, Aaron says. We didn't need braces and special shoes. And I don't need shoes now, or money for vet's bills to pay for our cat, who is dying. We need food, clothing, shelter, love. Everything else is want. Making wants into needs is an idea of the rich, not the poor. I am poor.

I am really angry now. I take off my amber bracelet with the rose leaf clasp, from the set Aaron has made me.

Who is this visitor on the old couch? I don't have to listen to this tripe. I've figured out how to pay for braces, plane tickets, mortgages, clothes, shoes, food. I've raised this guy who was my daughter, who chose against me, who chose to be a man. I've learned the lessons necessary to make my way as a woman, representative of a minority class in higher education, to help my sons and my grandchildren. I've learned to be a successful woman.

Also I take off his bracelet made of silver links, the red and blue beads turning on their wires. I don't touch my wedding ring or my mother's diamond on my right hand.

Aaron, I say, who wouldn't want to be a man? I reach inside my T-shirt, hook my thumb under the Velcro, unzip the shoulder pads and throw them on the table. What time is it?

When we part for bed, the moon through the window is waning. The pile of jewelry on the coffee table leans against our empty cups. The kitchen clock says 3:15.

Aaron has explained, patiently, once again, that he didn't choose to be a man, he is a man. We get up from the couch. In socks, without his new shoes, for once he is shorter than I am in my dress pumps. We hug each other. He must feel my resistance. He is hairy, balding, coarse skinned. He has said things he will have to explain, not my responsibility now.

I want only to sleep, to leave my own skin for a while. My arms as I undress look like the arms of Babar's grandfather in the children's books I'll buy next week in Paris for baby Anna, my first grandchild, Aaron's niece.

As I crawl under the down duvet next to my warm and sleeping husband, our feral kitten leaps onto my chest with a cry, circles and settles down, purrs. Who wants this life?

261

Pity and Laughter

One month later I'm in Washington DC sitting at a long restaurant table with six women very important in the writing business; I'm the seventh, who has just told her friends about Aaron's sex-reassignment surgery. We drink a good cabernet, maybe the house wine in this fine restaurant one of us, the parent of a restaurateur, has chosen. I can't understand why I am talking so much, coming out.

After a while we begin to laugh, a new response after hours of serious questions, thoughtful comment. Hilarity rises, they laugh in unison, crack jokes on any subject, tell stories, anything silly to make us giggle, anything to blow off steam, oh, I should have expected this hilarity, of course we laugh, the world is so silly and we have eaten well—halibut, cactus buds laid out in a circle on a huge white plate, garlic mashed potatoes under squid, braised lettuce.

Now I remember something important, something to say, but too late, the serious mood has broken, we're off on waves of laughter, all except me, I think I want to say something important. What was it?

After this dinner, or another—all weekend long as I drink wine, talk, and eat—salmon, mu shu pork, the plum sauce too salty—I try to think what to say to these groups of people so interested in the subject of reassigning gender, at this conference of writers, agents, publishers, friends, and colleagues.

I don't say that loving my child is loving someone for years knowing for certain the configuration of face, triangular cheek bones, the loveliness of triangular eyes slightly dipped at the corner, brown eyes ringed with black around the iris, black brows to smooth with a damp thumb. I wake up to enter her room, lift her up out of her crib, and find in her place a stranger, lovely too but unwelcome, not fitted out for life in this household, where did *this one* come from, do I feed him? And where is my loved one? Where have I misplaced her?

Nor do I tell this dream on a sleepless night I wake vomiting large globules and small ones and the plumbing is broken so where am I? My child's residue is next to mine, large globules and small ones in the same vessel.

And here is something else I don't say. My family is a family of learners. I want to learn the mystery at the heart of our experience. This is not a constructed mystery, not a constructed history, a made-up story of gender, not now.

I imagine a library of books to explain *transsexual*. Somehow I have made a bibliography, but each book is written in a language unfamiliar to me, or anyone I know, or know how to reach. Translation is out of the question, no one will translate this library. But I can learn the language, with patience can learn to read these texts.

"A landscape looks different when you know the names of things—and conversely, can look exceedingly inhospitable and alien when it seems nameless. But there is a point where, when a place looks very strange, it is not an indication of its remoteness but simply a mark of your ignorance," promises the travel writer Paul Theroux in *Dark Star Safari*.

My task will take a long time, until breath leaves my body. The deciphering of *transsexual* is as urgent as any research on Sappho, the Holocaust, the reasons for Abraham's betrayal of his child, learning Greek. I must learn because now I am a stranger in Aaron's life. Theroux wrote, "being a stranger can be analogous to experiencing a form of madness—those same intimations of the unreal and the irrational, when everything that has been familiar is stripped away." I feel mad. The wise ones tell us the reason for learning is learning itself, always and always. The act of study. I want to see the pattern in our lives.

Child, when I enter your room to pick you up from your crib, you are changed utterly. But you are my child. Changed, you are to be picked up. I am to bend down, place my hands under your arms, and lift you to me. And oh, I am tired. You are heavy, I lift you, you look into my face, touch my triangular cheekbones, smooth my left eyebrow with a damp thumb. You are familiar to me but not welcome here, where is my child?

After the hospital, after your bandages came off, I entered your room. I saw your wide chest, your narrow waist, your small nipples sewn on with gauze and black thread, your swagger, your soft cotton shorts over mayhem, and son, you were familiar, someone I'd known before, someone I had never seen or met before, a stranger. But familiar. Familiar.

Pity and laughter.

Girls Just Want to Have Fun

What does a woman want? asked Sigmund Freud. Aaron asked me the same question, maybe for diversion. Cyndi Lauper gave one answer in 1983 when she released the recording "Girls Just Want to Have Fun." Twelve years later, testosterone and surgery reconfigured the body of my younger child; the courts certified the name change. Not fun.

Ironic distance from her materials should be a habit of mind for a writer. I try. But the contract made in the delivery room requires that I do for my children, to the best of my ability, anything at all; they are my family. So I started to answer Aaron's question as best I can.

My story is familiar. Aaron's story is unusual, although the statistics from his surgeon, one of the best, document a growing number of gender reassignments: four operations each week, plus or minus a few, year after year. Most of his patients are thirty years old, as Aaron was, or older. Ninety percent of his patients' families disown them.

We didn't disown Aaron. He is still mine as I am his; and the others in the family did not disown him. To turn my attention from him is difficult. In fact, it's not easy for me to think of myself away from a family where I am the mother.

At eighteen, when my teacher and I married, we made a decision that marked our lives—of course. I made it deliberately, knowing it would mark our children's lives as well. We have two sons, and Aaron wears my ill-gotten gains, a suburban midwestern childhood, under his monster cloak.

A while ago our older son John and his wife Maria sent photos of their baby Anna Maria, my first grandchild. They live in New York City, where they settled during their PhD programs. The most remarkable photos document not the delighted parents nor the wide-eyed baby but rather the single room where they work and cook, sleep and bathe Anna in the tiny, leaky kitchen sink. They have lived in this room for ten years. To deliver Anna they walked to Beth Israel hospital, stopping every few blocks for Maria's contractions, John supporting her, then walking on in the early morning light. In one photo, a multicolored bouquet of ribbons tied to a nail is Anna's mobile, souvenir of a baby shower in Nebraska. Anna is now the focus of these pictures, surrounded by toys in her nest of the baby carrier where she sleeps during the day. At night she sleeps in the parental bed, under one window. Maria's computer faces the other. Both windows are barred. John's computer is on the kitchen table. On the fire escape, reached by climbing out a window, Maria sets out bulbs in winter, tomatoes and herbs, beans and potatoes in spring and summer. Their nearest neighbors, in an identical room, a young couple and their two small children. Across the street is the local headquarters of the Hell's Angels. This is the now-fashionable East Village. When Maria moved here and John followed, this area was slum. Now rents soar, renovations surround them, and Maria and John will have to move. With the help of a city program, they have bought and begun to renovate a house in Hamilton Heights in Harlem, two blocks from Sugar Hill. My older son and his family hope to become a part of the community. In Nebraska, the Roto-Rooter man Andre tells me that he'd grown up two blocks from their new house, in a place "worse than hell. I saw more before I was four than most people see in their lives, and I shouldn't have. No kid should," he says. "Nebraska is paradise. My mom saw my older brother in a lot of trouble and grabbed the rest of us, sold everything, and moved out of New York, here, to my uncle's place. We've done well since." Aaron's older brother John is half of an urban couple—highly educated parents settling in one of the world's great cities in a historic and changing neighborhood. I'm both proud and worried about John and Maria, but both of my kids have courage like Andre, the Roto-Rooter man, as well as the kinds of privilege most American children of professional parents have these days.

I'm not forgetting my promise to Aaron, who is the younger son here.

In mythic stories, it is the younger son who goes into the world to seek his fortune. I also was the younger child, and I went into the world to seek and find my fortune—although in fact, for the past thirty years, I've lived in the same ranch house, built in 1953, across the street from the convent of the Catholic Order of the Pink Nuns. Fortune is no longer something I seek. The quest, however, was fun.

In spite of my reluctance to answer his questions, Aaron asked me one day why my closest friendships and apparently most intimate connections were with women. He wondered why, in spite of intense loyalties and affections for women, I chose to live in a family of men for so many years, through three marriages.

My husband Dale and I have been married now for twenty-five years, during which time the children have thrived and graduated from high school, college, and graduate school.

For years I believed that my early first marriage, to Aaron and John's father, was a bad substitute for finishing the degree that might have allowed me to join the community of academics. Marriage, children, a divorce, another marriage, and another divorce were distractions from my calling as a writer, or so I thought. In fact, my first marriage was pretty good. The children have been and are one of my life's continuing pleasures. And I became a tenured professor of English anyway, at a good university.

But to tell the truth, except for stories about war, the worst stories I knew were about women alone with small children. Most of my decisions were made to avoid becoming the hero of one of these stories. To my generation of middle-class, educated women raised in the fifties, men provided protection for mothers and children, food, shelter, support. When the judge on the bench asked why I was divorcing my children's father, I said that he'd refused to buy the children snowsuits. I was kidding. What else could I say? Our divorce was granted. Apparently everyone thought that buying snowsuits was what husbands were for.

With a husband I lived in spacious apartments, first in Boston, then in the capital of a midwestern city where he had a good job. Both my first and second husbands were stars of their respective PhD programs. I don't remember any women, lesbian or straight, who were allowed to join the community of tenured professors at Boston University, where we studied, or many women professors at the land-grant university where my husbands were offered full membership in the academic community.

My lesbian friends were often brilliant, single, and surviving on scholarships. They became business managers, secretaries, or went on to graduate school where, if they had children, they took tenured (male) faculty members as lovers for the duration. A few met and set up house with older, wealthy women, often divorced women with children, who helped to support their blended families. Some created their own communities, living in shared households for decades.

Other women I knew chose to stay with men, as I did. One strong friend told a long narrative of abuse from her graduate school professors. She prevailed, received her degree, and taught for thirty years, but not in her field. She and her husband remained childless, which seemed to me at the time to be another aspect of being alone. Two other women I knew, with husbands as well as PhD degrees, worked for several years as nontenured teachers at low pay and without benefits. Another became a university librarian by earning a third graduate degree, which allowed her to care for the textual evidence of a dialogue from which women, except as token authors or scholars, had been excluded. Most of these women's husbands were tenured professors. Many faculty wives I knew hadn't finished their degrees. After a while many left their marriages, or were replaced as wives by talented graduate students, and gained the independence and poverty of the seventies, with their children. Even the shelter of men proved illusory, temporary. Some took women lovers and finished their degrees and raised their kids, found and kept good jobs. One died at forty, of breast cancer, leaving her three children to the care of others.

Although I'd finished my BA at Boston University and worked as the assistant director of a social agency serving women and their children in Boston until the day John was born, from then on, until my first marriage ended, I was a housewife. I cooked for and often entertained my husband's friends and their wives. I wore nice clothes my mother bought for me. She bought clothes for the whole family, except for my husbands, who could buy their own. Compared to my daughter-in-law Maria in New York City, I was a woman of leisure. Later, when I was pregnant for the second time, my mother gave me the down payment for the house where Aaron was born.

When the children were small, women friends spent a lot of time talking to each other—on the telephone, at the park, at the zoo or the museum, in the supermarket. When we weren't cleaning, cooking, child tending, grocery shopping, we talked about the feelings and ideas of lively women with tedious and exhausting work--and the books we read in our few off hours. We tried together as women with young children to make our own shelter. We knew how to do it; girls like me had grown up in communities, families of girlfriends. We trusted each other, and, in high school, the boys we took as boyfriends.

My husbands—first one, then another—had few questions to ask when they came home for dinner. They turned on the music and were silent or spoke of their own, separate lives. They both graded papers in their separate studies, worked in the yard, bought and used electric saws, routers, grinders in their basement workrooms. They had hobbies they paid for with their salaries. I wondered if their wives and children were hobbies, too. My own hobbies were reading library books, writing poetry and prose in my journal, and practicing independence by taking off and putting on my wedding rings. I had a small amount of my own money, a gift from my brother Jim, the firstborn son who had been given all rights of inheritance by our father's will. Mother paid for plane tickets, toys, and a lot else from her large widow's legacy. Both my husbands disdained her, as I did, as representative of a generation of pampered and supposedly adored women who were left undereducated, depressed, and well off on the deaths of their husbands. I was so naive that I didn't know the term heterosexual privilege. As a wife, I and my children had enough food to eat, a warm place to live, a peaceful neighborhood, good public schools, and, if the public transportation system was unreliable, we still had the fare in our pockets and even a car to use in the garage. We had health insurance and could take the children to a pediatrician when they were sick. When John at five needed heart surgery, we were able to provide it for him through his father's health insurance. Without the surgery, he would have died before he reached his twentieth birthday.

What I thought I knew in those days was that you couldn't trust men who had authority over you, only those who were your peers. And no adult man was really your peer because men were a superior force—the boys you loved swollen with authority into husbands, bosses, professors. Sex was the closest thing you could get to an alliance. The men whose erotic life included only other men must be uninterested in alliance. I felt invisible to them; women had nothing of value that they wanted or could use.

To complicate things further, I was writing again, while the children took naps and late at night. The canonical nineteenth-century writer Nathaniel Hawthorne had written to his friend James Fields, "All women, as authors, are feeble and tiresome. I wish they were forbidden to write, on pain of having their faces deeply scarified with an oyster shell." I understood that his threat was to a woman's beauty, apparently her true and only source of power. I was ready to give up my writing, but not at the threat to beauty. I kept on. Writing was not power but it was fun.

When I was a small child in the forties, all important news on the radio in the living room was war news. My parents and uncles and aunts whispered in the kitchen news that came from overseas, in letters, reports that we later came to understand as the Holocaust. The language of an unequal conflict was part of our daily lives. My mother had been born in England, her parents refugees, her mother from Russia where she had fled from home, a shtetl that was burned by the Cossacks. So I had another legacy of separation from the larger community in which we lived, and of powerlessness, for both men and women. We were strangers in America; in Europe our identity brought us death.

My mother's name was Dolly. She used to tell me a story about her mother, after whom I and many cousins are named. Dolly was her mother's favored child, the third of six children. At my mother's birth, in England, the doctor brought the infant, a third daughter in three years, for inspection. Her mother turned her face to the wall. That story. My grandmother must have given birth, leaned on her elbow, risen up to meet her first son, only to find another daughter. In exchange for the rejection, Mother had a lifetime of devotion, which she returned in kind, and amply. The story of this long affectionate companionship between a mother and her daughter, and its genesis, lives on in the framed photo on my desk: two women walking arm in arm, each step matched by step, each identical small foot in its leather shoe. Each turned-out ankle. Both women wear fur collars on their cloth coats. In my mother's fine face, little trace of the Russian peasant who walks beside her. Both women are smiling.

Another story my mother told me: Dolly, a young wife living in the next town away from her parents. For some reason—maybe a fight with her husband, the something always unspecified—she left her home, put her infant son, my brother Jim, in the car, and drove the several miles to her mother's house. As my mother walked up the long path to her mother, the baby in her arms, she heard the front door slam shut. "Go home to your husband," her mother called through the door, refusing to answer the bell. And so, with no place else to go, my mother went.

Aaron, for a safe place I took shelter with men. And for fun I wrote and worked my way into what was—in those days—a man's profession, in my spare time.

In looking for ways to articulate a changing connection to Aaron and to answer his questions, I read an astonishing essay by the founder of queer theory, Eve Kosofsky Sedgwick. In her essay "White Glasses," she uses her own enameled glasses frames as a mask and an emblem for her friendship with Michael Lynch, who also wore white glasses. She reveals and explains her deep sense of herself, "my identity, along with Michael, as a gay man." She also is writing his eulogy. Later she says, "If what is at work here is an identification that falls across gender, it falls no less across sexualities, across perversions. And across the ontological crack between the living and the dead."

Last weekend some friends and I saw director Bill Condon's *Gods and Monsters*, a movie about the final weeks in the life of director James Whale, father of the horror movie classics *Frankenstein* and *Bride of Frankenstein* that Sarah loved so much as a child. The movie suggests that the image of the monster in Whale's work came from his experience as an officer in the trenches in World War I. His lover was shot and killed just outside their trench. The decaying body, wearing a gas mask, tangled in barbed wire under constant fire, impossible to rescue, swelled daily in Whale's line of vision. The body of his dead lover, changing and swelling, became, through Whale's art, the monster—part other, part self. As I left the movie theatre, the monster mask seemed to me now to be transformative and protective, but useless as an agent of change. Whale's monster, like his openly gay creator, was lonely, apparently dangerous in a closeted society, huge in his spasms of moving, finally eloquent. Joyous and powerless.

And so I began to understand something important about Aaron's need and ability to make art and monsters and science in the years before his transition, before he put to use the lessons of his art. To me then it seemed no accident that Aaron's art had turned to making stage masks that could be put on and taken off about the time of his decision to take the hormones and have the surgery that transformed him. I'd been engaged in similar transformations of grief into poems in my books *Divine Honors*, about breast cancer, and later *Trans*. And I'd put on and taken off the several masks I'd thought were available to women.

Jorge Luis Borges wrote a poem "of the ancient food of heroes: humiliation, unhappiness, discord. These things are given to us to transform, so that we may make from the miserable circumstances of our lives things that are eternal, or aspire to be so" ("Blindness").

For months, even years, I grieved hard for the loss of my daughter. Like Demeter, I searched Hades looking for her. But she was not there. Instead I found the challenge that Sedgwick identifies, to find and name the ways in which Aaron and I are members of the same family, heroes, more like each other than different. Now, looking back, I'm amazed that the one thing I wanted—more than anything else—was a daughter to carry on the next generation of my life as a woman. Women just want to have fun. I wanted brilliant Sarah to enlarge and expand my understanding of women and what we can be in the world, the best kind of fun for me. Instead I am learning from Aaron new uses for our story of power taken, earned, and transferred from generation to generation

And what of Aaron? He had his own agenda. Aaron, whose first job as Sarah after graduate school was a scientific specimen preparator in a museum, flensing the flesh from dead animals in order to find and cherish their bones.

Reading Garber

I've been reading Marjorie Garber's book *Vested Interests*. She helps me remember something I've known for a long time. She quotes Joan Nestle, a writer who lived in New York City in the fifties when I was growing up. "Lesbians have always opposed the patriarchy; in the past, perhaps most when we looked like men."

Nestle helps me to reconcile two points of view. I tend to think of *lesbian* as both a commitment to broad and various identifications of women and a passionate connection to all identifications with women. *Female-to-male transsexual* is a passionate disconnection from any identification with women. I never thought that my daughter Sarah was transsexual. I'd always understood Sarah's identification with men as butch. His behavior seemed familiar in that way, both from my reading and my life.

In the fifties we all knew about bohemians, artists in revolt against a society they understood as confining. I, too, was called bohemian by my more conservative friends. I was interested, as they were not, in an older friend's political activism and her new assertive manner, her knowledge, her swagger, and her fondness for men's clothes. I wore men's clothes, too. We girls all wore our fathers' shirts, so when I borrowed sweaters from my father and bought pants in the men's department, the stretch wasn't far. Our school shoes were oxfords, white bucks, and saddle shoes, just like our brothers'. In fact, I didn't want to look like a girl. Women, in my experience, were powerless. Change was impossible for them. My own school crowd of girlfriends was pretty conventional. But their passionate devotion to each other made another kind of community in my life. We hung out together, tried and did solve problems, and generally talked to each other to figure out ways to extend or conserve our power as we grew up. We also swam, bowled, biked, and played cards. Somehow we began to know that in the wider world of adults our strongest trump card was sexual—and heterosexual. I was drawn to my summer camp's senior girls' counselor, a law student who read children's books out loud to us and wore men's-style shorts, T-shirts, and open sandals. In winter when we met downtown, she wore plain sweaters, jeans, and boots. On her recommendation, I read for the first time Radclyffe Hall's novel *The Well of Loneliness*, then called a lesbian novel, now sometimes a transgendered text (perhaps because the author, who was John among her friends, named her autobiographical protagonist Stephen). I cut my long hair and began to wear it short, then shorter. On weekends I dressed up, put on high heels and dresses, began to date boys. My more traditional girlfriends and later our boyfriends formed a circle of mutual support. When we had to ensure our freedom from parental strictures and learn details of female/male sexuality and behavior, we lied for each other, traded information, transportation, and protection. We helped to make life better for each other. When they made plans to attend college near home, to become engaged and marry, I made plans to apply to Antioch College, where an older female friend was a student.

At the last minute I decided to go to Boston University. Boston wasn't too far away from New York. I wanted to live in a city and be a student at an urban university where I'd learn to know more people, maybe some like me. My friend was at Antioch, in a tiny midwestern town, and our weakening friendship wasn't enough to substitute for the prospect of an adventurous life on my own in a big city. At BU the freshmen dorm for women was Charlesgate East, a huge Victorian mansion converted to suites. The electrical system in the building was still direct current and some of us burned out our alternating current stereos by plugging them directly into the outlets. Many young women in my dorm were conventional in dress and manner but some of us, at least in our suite, were clearly feisty, rebellious—butch. We refused to wear the skirts and twin sets we'd brought from home. Jeans and sweaters, boots and pea jackets from the navy surplus were our daily costume. And we were tagged "intellectuals, hippies." In my freshman year my best friend's roommate was a tough dyke from Roxbury, out from age twelve. We girls loved each other with the same passion we loved our classes and our new unsupervised lives. And we loved Honors English class and our teacher. He was brilliant and handsome and when he transferred me out of the class, then asked me for a date, I said yes. In February he asked me to marry him. Like Molly

Bloom in James Joyce's novel *Ulysses*, which we'd been reading, I said yes, again.

For most of second semester we were engaged and I spent less and less time in the dorm. When he and I married in June, my best friend from the dorm, Libby, was my attendant and she came to live with us in our first apartment. My husband and I talked less and less so I left him and went away with her, hoping our friendship could provide us both some stability and calm, an alternative family of women. When it didn't, I returned to the marriage alone. She and I had been connected by a friendship that felt like love in the community of the women's dormitory, but we were both eighteen and in fact we had no other community. Certainly I remembered the story my mother told me about leaving my father, traveling to her mother for support, and finding the door closed.

My husband and I were deeply connected by sex and marriage. He was older, more settled; we wanted to have children together, and later we did. The three-way knot dissolved but I certainly took my place on a gender spectrum, not of sex but of identity, a spectrum that feminists in the sixties called lesbian—a deep and primary allegiance to women and a sturdy resistance to male-defined and -centered culture. If I lived with men, I strengthened my knowledge of women's culture. I began to read the work of Gertrude Stein, Audre Lorde, Adrienne Rich, Leslie Feinberg, Gloria Steinem, and others as I continued to write poetry with Robert Lowell as my teacher. I was a member of the generation of Lowell's students after Sylvia Plath and Anne Sexton, whose passionate friendship with Maxine Kumin provided a model for life collaboration for women writers. My rebellion against behavior I considered conventional and patriarchal continued throughout my life as a parent.

As a young girl I'd read the poetry of Walt Whitman with serious interest. His compassionate and passionate connection to all continuing life I'd read as sure evidence of my connection to future generations. Maybe my true parents were vegetative rather than human, but surely I would continue as the mother of mothers—and didn't he mention also the father of fathers?

This week in my office at the university I've been reading an interesting manuscript. Ostensibly the subject is the writer's friendship with a lesbian colleague and the complications that ensue when both women become parents. But I think the nexus of this essay is motherhood/passion/rebellion. I want the writer to break the silence in which she locates herself, the silence of heterosexual women about homosexual love.

Aaron's and my recent silence seems to be about the labels *gay* and *lesbian*. I know that the term *transsexual* has to do with gender, not sexuality. But we're not saying important things to each other. I hate this silence, feel miserable about an unusual breakdown in our communication, our friendship.

Today is the last Monday before my classes begin, the end of summer: cool, overcast weather. I stay home. Dale and I spend afternoons in the garden, weeding, planting blackberry lilies, and transplanting ground cover. Aaron is at home far away. I worry about whether I can understand his life now. He has told me to stop trying to understand his life.

"Understand your own life," he growls on the telephone.

For distraction I have been reading mysteries, Laurie King's feminist gloss on Sherlock Holmes, the detective Sarah and I both loved. When she was little, she'd lie on the fireplace hearth for hours reading through long winter days. I walk a lot and work on introductions to two books in progress. I try to be mindful of each moment as I can, as I learned from Thich Nhat Hanh when I had cancer. My students have crises, my young colleagues, too, and I try to help; a friend is in intensive care at the hospital with brain trauma. And I continue to read Marjorie Garber and am enlightened and myself helped: "If transvestitism offers a critique of binary sex and gender distinctions it is . . . because it denaturalizes, destabilizes, and defamiliarizes sex and gender signs."

I sit here in cargo shorts, T-shirt, and running shoes, my hair cropped shorter than my sons'.

To further break the silence between us, Aaron and I have been talking by e-mail about the signifiers "masculine" and "lesbian." He says that I have never talked to him about my early life. Now he asks me directly to answer more questions, specific questions.

I write back, "Okay."

His next message is very long. "What did you think about . . . ?"

. . . What did I think about my "daughter's" jockey shorts, her refusal to wear any "female-coded" articles—cosmetics, dresses, skirts, hose, bras, women's shoes (he remembers we had a hell of a time getting men's-style shoes in Sarah's size), glasses (same thing, before small frames were in), jewelry, socks, hairstyles, her insisting on buying all her clothes in the men's department, her highly "male-coded" articles—the black leather jacket, traditional-styled cowboy boots, waffle-stompers, her buzz cut, single earring?

. . . What did I think about my "daughter's" interest in male images or her disinterest in female images in film, television, etc., Sarah's continuous use of birth control pills, her vocal disinterest in marriage, family, children, her regular put-downs of women?

. . . What did I think of all this, given my "daughter's" celibacy, her lack of deeply personal relationships with women (other than me), her forceful rejection of the idea she might be a lesbian?

Of course Aaron's e-mail message omits any female pronouns and never mentions the name Sarah. Well, I'm glad we're talking but why is Aaron asking me these questions? Was I supposed to know something he didn't? Maybe I'm the one who thinks so.

The time compression in the list shocks me, as if all these things happened at once. All the clues laid out by Sherlock Holmes's friend Dr. Watson for our examination. But during the children's growing up, my time was spent mostly feeding our family, which included then four children, two adults, and felines. The rest I spent climbing the academic/literary ladder, negotiating two divorces, and moving house twice. In fact, when I had time to think, to consider Sarah's behavior, it always seemed to make perfect sense. I thought she was growing up butch. To be butch meant to be rebellious, unconventional, independent. Before adolescence, she seemed to be a tomboy with three brothers—two stepbrothers and John. After adolescence, she seemed to be butch, and maybe lesbian. For years I'd understood that to be a woman active in a male-centered society meant performing aspects of male gender, just as I'd done growing up. Feminist action required a rebellious spirit, an unquiet mind, difficult reassessments of almost everything central to a woman's life. I'd wanted to assume power over my own life. I assumed Sarah was the same. I had been and was still passionate in my ongoing rebellion against patriarchy, that old-fashioned term. I knew Sarah was passionate, like me. Only I didn't quite understand the nature of her rebellion. "What patriarchy?" she said over and over. Boy, was I wrong!

I've said that Aaron has worn men's clothes since he was a child. He came home from college wearing men's briefs. During his entire life, we shopped for his clothes in the boys' department, then the men's. He settled on Birkenstocks for shoes, then Doc Martens, the same styles for men and women, ostensibly because of his knees and feet, the legacy of orthopedic shoes. Choosing glasses frames was tough, but I agreed that the men's styles he favored looked good on him, and on me, and on John and Dale, too. Our family tended to wear similar clothes. For years we all wore the same men's corduroy pants in the same size, the same button-front jeans. Certainly now I know that Aaron was responding to wardrobe choices as a boy, then a man.

At the time, if he'd been a boy wearing girls' clothes, I might have begun to understand the precise nature of his predicament. When boys wear girls' clothes, parents notice.

I wouldn't have forbidden Aaron men's clothes. I was wearing men's clothes, and still do. I wouldn't have made him wear makeup. He used theatrical makeup with the same passion that some young women use cosmetics. His reticence about things of the body I understood as my offspring's natural reaction to my maybe overly flamboyant delight in pregnant women, movies about human and animal birth, and female sexuality. I believed then and still believe that an artist's primary engagement with the world is through the body. I assumed that Aaron's rejection of everything female, including his body, had more to do with rejecting women's behavior and roles than with being a man. I couldn't and didn't believe he hated his own body. How could he? He was making art.

What did I think about Aaron's being celibate during adolescence, at a time of life when I'd been sexually active? He may have been celibate but his friendships were passionate, and with girls as well as boys until he left home at seventeen. Even then he'd mention Nicki, or another woman or two. He was not a solitary child. Nor was he silent on the subjects of his rebellions, or his disagreements with me. Our arguments were highly vocal, loud, and passionate. Sarah as a youngster seemed to me to be independent of female sexuality which, God knows, had gotten me into a mess of trouble. I thought celibacy was just fine. Clearly he was passionate about life, and healthy.

He wanted a leather jacket and we found one, bought it with his approval. The leather was much better in the jackets from the men's department than anything for women. And it looked better on him. He wears it still. He wanted only one earring. Some women friends wear one earring.

Each behavior on Aaron's list seemed perfectly natural to me. Even his decision to take birth control pills without a break I understood as the right of a woman to control her own body. Athletes often took the birth control pill without a break. And my research showed that the break for an artificial cycle was intended as "psychological comfort" for women who didn't want to lose their periods. I rarely wore sheer stockings or high heels. Why should my kid? As Sarah grew older I respected all decisions about style. If I'd understood she was a man, I would have said so. As is, when I asked him whether he was transgendered, the minute I learned the term from writer Minnie Bruce Pratt, he said no. Apparently he thought transgendered was a word for exactly what I'd thought Sarah was, a lesbian resisting patriarchy, or a woman pretending to be a man. He wasn't pretending anything.

Even if I'd known that my younger child was transsexual, what could we have done? Not so long ago doctors and psychologists would have been bewildered by our questions and I couldn't have controlled their diagnoses or their treatments. Now I'd get on the Web for bibliography and to learn about gender research and other kids like mine and to find guidelines for what we could have done, which now have changed, thanks to transsexual psychologists.

Sarah was fine. I loved her and felt lucky to have such an interesting kid. We had a good time together. Only she was Aaron and I didn't know it. I can't think of anything more important that I've failed to notice.

John was as smart as Sarah. When he came to the upheavals of adolescence, he seemed to find relief by making friends with bad influences. He wasn't home much. But one day he came into my study and said, "Mom, we have to talk." He pulled me onto the patio, brought me a cup of coffee, and said, "Something's really wrong with Sarah. You've got to do something. She can't go to the high school in our neighborhood, it's filled with cliques and drugs, and the kids will eat her alive. Make her go to the alternative school where I am. And she's acting strange. I think she needs some kind of help." That's all he could—or would—say.

At thirteen, like many boys, John had moved emotionally far away from his family—and that included his little sister. He was present at meals and that was about it. Dale got him an after-school and weekend job, watched out for him, and I smiled, hugged him when I could, and pushed books through his door. We didn't become close again until an auto accident put him into intensive care when he was twenty, the autumn of his fourth year at the university. He came home to recover, stayed for the rest of his undergraduate years. Back in our house, first in bed then during the time he was learning to walk again, we talked for hours. I brought him the books he wanted, and he began to read again in earnest and to write music, his profession now. But when Sarah was trying to grow up, John was largely absent. By the time John came back home, Sarah was gone.

Looking back, what I found most compelling in my "daughter" was her passionate engagement with life. She fought everything she found confining and wrong. With characteristic fierce spirit, she had stamina enough to discover and make provision for herself, to change name, begin hormone therapy, arrange for and have surgery, and profoundly to change appearance for the sake of congruence, inside and out. Sarah, then Aaron displayed remarkable energy, resourcefulness, and courage during the difficult time of his transformation and the decades before. He was generous and understanding with his family and incredibly patient with his mother, when he might have been bitter and isolated.

Aaron's growing love for and connection to his longtime community of friends seems impressive, even as I begin to withdraw from community in favor of the more solitary pleasures of middle age after major family responsibilities are done. I like to see him at the center of a large family of friends, parents, stepparents, brothers, nieces and nephews, and cousins. I like the pleasure he takes now in his strong and beautiful body, to know that he thinks about and enjoys love and connection, everything that binds us to each other even during this long and difficult period working on this book together. But I'm ready to stop, to let time take over, to replace recollections of my life as Sarah's mom with participation in

Aaron's life. So many of my recollections were based on mistaken assumptions, my own assumptions.

Aaron used to say, "That same old bullshit, the story of your guilt and grieving for Sarah." I understand what he meant.

For Aaron, he's the same person he's always been. It's taken me a long time to understand that Sarah was my hopeful projection into a future generation more generous to women. Maybe I was a thoughtful and diligent parent trying to excel at yet another role with my usual resolve to figure out everything at once.

If Aaron and I are not connected by gender, ever more firmly we are connected by temperament. We are both questers, sometimes disruptive in our efforts to break, remake, and understand all varieties of experience. His connection to the world as a man is not different from my attachment to the world as a woman. We are together in our effort to understand human behavior and our commitment to each other.

If we have tried to write the world with our bodies, as Aaron has done with his transformation and I have tried to do in my work, we assert our belief in the power of art and nature as good partners. Aaron and I have been collaborators: parent and child, strong adversaries, compassionate allies—as well as writers together and editors of each other's work. He is as he has always been, my friend and companion, my true and cherished attachment to future generations of passionate rebels.

Aaron's life as a man retains direct connection to mine; he has witnessed and identified my struggle to assume power as an aspect of his own struggle. In this way he understands his experience as like mine. My stories about the women in our family are quite properly his. He, too, is a transmitter of family and other stories, and a person with an identity that we share. And in turn, I am glad to transform my early assumptions about men and women and to enact our affection for each other, to experience our power together and separately, and to know and appreciate what we are to each other.

Surely my mother would be astonished that what becomes me also becomes my son.

Looking at Aaron

Midnight, and Aaron is sitting behind the wheel of our rented car. "So what's this book we're writing?" he asks. His voice is uninflected. We're both exhausted from the day's heat. The night sky is flat black. The car is parked in front of the guesthouse where I'm staying with my laptop computer, working on our collaborative book.

"I don't know," I say.

He shifts impatiently. As far as I can tell, his part of the book is done. I hope to finish my part now, the mother's part, years after his surgery.

Aaron says he hates everything he's written. His voice is speeding up. He articulates very clearly. "Who cares about this kind of book?" he asks me. "You don't read books about breast cancer, right, Mom?" He's talking fast now. He knows I've been well for twelve years.

"Transformation happens in all lives. We'll tell about ours," I say in a soothing voice.

"Okay," he says. His shoulders relax a little as he leans back in the driver's seat.

I lean forward in the passenger seat. "Okay," I say. "But don't expect me to provide any analysis of our experience. Analysis is beyond me."

"You must want to analyze, since the negative always implies the positive," he says.

I reach underneath the seat, grab and open a fresh bottle of water. We could go into the cool guesthouse where I'm staying, rest on the beds underneath the ceiling fan, switch it on high. I could say we're both tired, let's talk tomorrow when we're fresh. Instead I say, "Let's begin with the garage sale today. You liked my story about the clothes."

"Okay," says Aaron.

Aaron and I look through the newspaper over breakfast and find neighborhood garage sales. It's going to be a very hot day. The first house has fabulous stuff in the backyard. Aaron opens a bag and collects Swarovski crystal beads in amber and black, a broken necklace of dyed onyx beads with Mexican silver charms, and a designer skirt from the seventies in chrome-blue Thai silk. The belt loops on the skirt are made of metallic crimson thread. Seven dollars for the lot. He'll tear the silk on the bias, string it with vintage beads and charms to sell as treasure necklaces. Gorgeous. I find a dusty rack of clothes on the cracked, hot driveway. An Anne Klein bomber jacket in silk embroidery lined with candlelight chiffon, a browned-butter cashmere jacket with a diagonal placket, an amethyst satin underskirt from the fifties.

"Hooh boy!" I say, "look at this slip."

"Why is it a slip, not a skirt?" asks Aaron, who comes over to see.

I show him the elastic waistband stitched to the satin and the pliable hoop attached at the hem ruffle. Exquisite.

"How did you wear it?" he asks, turning up the hem to see the fine stitches. He wants me to tell him a story about my clothes. He knows I'll write down what we say.

I tell him about a pink lace overdress with scallops cut out to show the yellow satin knife pleats, the gray tweed skirt with a tomato suede blouson jacket, the matching cloche hat in suede and tweed. Some favorite clothes in the sixties.

Today Aaron and I are both wearing green shorts and white T-shirts. He has on canvas basketball shoes, one red, one blue, and I'm wearing tattered sandals. We're about the same height, but his shoulders and torso are muscular, his chest flat, his waist slender, his hips flat . . . he's very handsome. The guy with the cash box has been looking and looking. As usual, Aaron is oblivious. The driveway is very hot.

"How did you get these clothes?" he asks. "How did you feel wearing them?" Suddenly I know he's working hard and in subversive ways. He wants my attention off him. He thinks the book will be better if I write about myself. I want to write about him, his extraordinary story. Still, such beautiful clothes. I try to answer.

I tell him that when I was a teenager, these clothes helped cover the space I felt inside. I'd learned that I was a girl and should plan to marry a man of substance and have his children. I could help by dressing well. Like Aaron I was handsome, and I earned the clothes by runway modeling. I wore the samples to appear negotiable, of value and substance. My generous parents bought at discount. And so I wore the *peau de soie* two-piece in navy with my big hair balanced above a thin neck where the key-hole closure fastened at the throat with a soft bow. The skirt was molded high above the waist and fastened with a tiny zipper, thin and long like a scar. Who was I? Who knew? Such beautiful clothes. And the shoes! Black velvet dance slippers with rhinestone clasps at the instep. Kid flats in gold and another pair in silver gilt for dates with short boys. The small heels in layered wood attached to soft leather in camel, the crisp spectator pumps in navy and white. Delissos. Capezios.

"That's enough," I tell Aaron. He shrugs, pays for his purchases. I leave the clothes behind.

Next day we move, a vacation from our work on the book. We go to the beach.

It's a cool and rainy evening after a day with Aaron driving, negotiating the scenic but winding back roads. Daire, Aaron's friend, sleeps on the back seat. She's carsick. Last year they celebrated ten years of friendship at the Sylvia Beach Hotel at Nye Beach on the Pacific. This year they've reserved rooms for us all. When we arrive, we unpack, eat dinner, and talk. Then Aaron and I put on our parkas, take a walk near the ocean. It's dark and chilly but the sand feels warm. Two boys are running around pushing sparklers into the sand. Then they light them all at once. One jumps into the sparkly circle and the other takes his picture, a tiny flash.

"Hey, nice fire," Aaron calls out to a group sitting around flames in a circle of stones. They call back for us to join them—two youngsters, one a teenager, and their parents from Arizona. The dad says, "These kids just up and moved out here two months ago!" The folks have traveled from Arizona to Oregon with a trailer to bring them their stuff. Aaron talks to the kids. I fall into place beside Ed, the dad. I can hear Aaron saying, "If you've got insomnia because of the cloudy weather, try a light box." They're telling the stories about leaving home, new places, adjustments. Aaron says, "We moved to LA, lived there for three years, and then I was done. We moved here."

Over the sound of their voices, Ed tells me that he collects cash registers and he's a school counselor back home. He asks, "How could our kids just up and go?" Alcohol on his breath. I shrug my shoulders. They just do. The mom smiles at me across the fire. We've discovered that we both have little granddaughters, another generation. Then Aaron and I get up, walk away into the mist, call back good-bye, good-bye. At the hotel, we hug each other hard. I rub my cheek against his rough beard and then we return to our chilly, damp, and salty rooms.

Daire and Aaron are sitting at breakfast as I join them in the communal dining room. They hold hands, rub each other's necks, look into each other's eyes. Aaron will leave soon to go back to school, in California. Daire will stay behind in their apartment. What shall we do today?

We walk the estuary with a tour group and our affable guide of retirement age. Aaron, a biologist, adds information, answers questions. I take photos of him picking up all available wildlife, naming each, standing in the middle of a crowd of interested kids. He's wearing a black baseball cap. We leave the group, drive to the bay, eat lunch—Aaron's first Dungeness crab, which he orders in black bean sauce and enjoys a lot. Then we shop—jewelry, glass floats, wood sculptures. So much to buy, and we don't. We all eat ice cream. Later, dinner. Daire goes off to bed.

Aaron and I walk again, this time through the small town. I'm quiet, so glad to listen. We haven't been together for six months. His conversation is fluent, elegant. I know that he's leaving his job as director of a program in art and theatre for homeless kids. He's decided to study physical theatre. After two years of trying, he's been admitted to a famous school, with a scholarship. A big risk. He talks nonstop about his plans for a theatre/dance company when he finishes his studying. One project, in choreography, will use the vocabulary of movement from Parkinson's—his father's disease—and muscular dystrophy patients. Another is to make a safe place where multicultural homeless youth will meet with macho gym guys, he calls them gangsta guys, to develop performance projects for urban theatres, community centers, and college campuses. He hopes to attract national talent for a board of directors; he has good contacts. His voice is low and steady. He walks fast with his hands in his jacket pockets. Right now he doesn't know what else he wants. He's worried about leaving Daire. They both get migraines, stomachaches, need expensive medicine from the drugstore. Maybe their separation will be good.

Then Aaron remembers a secret story from his childhood, something that involved me, something he's never told me he knows. He's going to tell this story no matter what I do. I zip up my jacket. The streets are damp and empty, few lights anywhere, and everywhere the sound of the ocean.

Aaron remembers when our family was on the way to visit my old college roommate, Libby. Aaron was still Sarah, and she's probably twelve. The tension among the adults in the car is so great that Sarah is going to refuse to get out of the car until someone tells her what's going on. When we reach a big house in the woods on a pond, the adults and the other kids jump out, race around. Sarah waits in the back seat. After a while Libby comes out of her house, opens the back door of the car, and suggests Sarah come with her for a walk through the woods. They walk on fallen pine needles, a soft path over gravel. Then Libby takes Sarah's hand and tells her if things had been different, Libby would have been Sarah's father.

I am astonished, breathless. I wonder if this dialogue is exactly right. The story is so crazy. Aaron and I, walking on the sandy tarmac of the parking lot next to the Pacific Ocean, are walking faster now, through wind. I ask Aaron what he said. Aaron said, "You wouldn't have been my father because I wouldn't have been born."

What do I think? I think that this little person Sarah was my young daughter. What could she have thought? She sounded angry. Certainly she knew that two women don't give birth to a child. Not then. Apparently Sarah also knew that Libby was drunk. Sure enough, she falls in a hole and twists her ankle. She has to lean on Sarah as she limps from the woods. Sarah decides to come into the house since she knows the secret.

I ask Aaron why he hadn't told me this story before. Silence. We walk on, come to the hotel, hug, and separate for the night. I've concealed my distress but later I have flaming dreams. Why didn't I know this story? Where was I? In the house, tending the others. I didn't worry about Sarah. She was so much a tomboy we thought she might be lesbian, like Libby. We were wrong. She was a boy.

The summer after my freshman year of college, shortly after Aaron's father and I married, Libby drove to Newport, Rhode Island, with her sisters to wait tables at a grand hotel. We followed, slept on the floor of her room or on the beach, wore swimsuits all summer, walked and drove the winding road along the ocean to see the grand houses of the very rich. Libby, very tall, very thin, very blond, beautiful and brilliant. My best friend, who had been maid of honor at our wedding. Frilly dresses of embroidered organdy. Who came to live with us after the honeymoon. She and I both eighteen. Best friends.

I wake after a fitful night, finish eating breakfast alone, and wander into the library at the top of the hotel. This place is an old beach house where pictures of authors and copies of their books are backdrop for guests reading and writing, drinking hot tea or coffee. The ocean whispers outside the windows. Aaron has gone off to chase a dream. He wants to rent a horse to ride the beach. When he was a child we sent him to horse camp where neighbor kids went each summer. Aaron hated camp. He came home, refused to go back. But he was Sarah then. Now he wants to ride the beach. Daire and Aaron both seemed in good spirits as we started our day, but they left breakfast early as I was talking about Aaron's brother, a composer of new music. The guests were talking about the Ernest Bloch festival this weekend, apparently a showcase for new music. Bloch had a summer home here.

Later in the day, the distance between Aaron and me is palpable, then permeable, then dissolves. We sit in adjacent deckchairs on the high, narrow balcony that opens from the library over the beach. High tide. Midnight. Daire has gone to bed. The ocean is loud, the air saturated with salt water. Below us fires flare on the sand, shine on faces. We watch. Aaron is wrapped in a blanket from the library couch. I hold my hands tightly in my sleeves in order not to pat his hair, rub his shoulders, touch his cheek, reach for his hand.

I have no idea what to do. Analysis out of the question. But my grown son Aaron, who was my daughter Sarah, has control of his own life now. His resolve is strong and his powers of analysis are keen. He says that he will try to live in a way that anticipates and avoids future regret. He will treat Daire and his friends with love and respect and try to avoid bitterness and accusation. He'll use lessons from his work with homeless kids, who have learned to live in their extra-large sweatshirts they call hoodies, their only reliable homes.

By now, many hours later, in the top-floor library, people still read or doze in easy chairs in front of an ocean at low tide. The room is damp and salty, quiet. The lights are low and flicker. On the balcony with Aaron, I drink coffee with cream, listen, speak. We leave the Sylvia Beach Hotel in the morning. When we get back to the city I have only a few more days before flying home. Already the distance between Aaron's life and my life is increasing. For nine months I will not see him as I write. I feel my limits even as I push to extend them to this young man beside me, my son.

And then we all eat breakfast. Before we pack we walk Nye Beach one last time, to explore crevices in the rock we've seen filling and emptying from the balconies outside our windows. Anemones in tide pools are both green and beige, their tentacles drift among the snails. Daire gives everything we see a name. We laugh and run. In the car we decide to take the scenic road back, make side excursions to Cape Meares to climb to the lighthouse tower, explore more tide pools. We take pictures, eat, talk, tell jokes. Then we stop at Siletz Bay, where Aaron goes missing.

For an hour and a half, Daire and I look for him in the water where the seals sleep on the rocks and on the sidewalks around the bay. The ocean pounds. Last night in the hotel library I'd met a woman writing a book. She'd survived the attack of a serial murderer to testify at his trial. An editor, I was careful to pay attention to her book proposal, not her life—but of course I was scared by the danger she'd survived and the madness of the serial murderer, who had been a professional pilot with a wife and kids; he'd traveled so that his crimes were impossible for the police to connect. And now Aaron is missing, who for his entire life, since he began walking at eighteen months, has disappeared at regular intervals—at playgrounds, shopping centers, in airports and bus stations and train stations. He always reappears in short order. But now I'm thinking that a transsexual man can attract violence anywhere. Even here, at an Oregon Coast National Wildlife Refuge, where someone wearing a chrome-yellow kayak is paddling so close to the seals that they slither away in a group, faster than you imagine huge mammals can move. Foolish man. Aaron is wildlife, like the seals. He is not safe from a crazy man wearing a yellow kayak.

An hour and a half later Daire shouts, "There's Aaron," and sure enough, the little tough guy, as his kids call him, is walking toward us, sopping jeans rolled to the knees, carrying his sneakers and socks, grinning. His face is deeply tanned. His high forehead is shining.

"I've had an adventure," he shouts.

At the dock where you can rent kayaks, Aaron had met a man with a small child, returning a boat. "You've got a free twenty minutes left," said the man, handing Aaron a paddle, pushing him off into the water. Aaron had paddled to the seal island expecting to see us scanning the horizon. He didn't see us, but we and the seals saw him in the borrowed chrome-yellow kayak.

I walk away, buy an ice cream, sit in the sun to eat and calm down. I have been so afraid. I mean my silence to be a gift to him. He has been so happy. I think about insane maternal privilege that has kept me secure in a world that holds our children safe so long as we practice rituals: wear warm clothes in cold weather; tell me where you are at all times; don't cross streets alone or without looking; never talk to strangers and refuse all rides; be home by dark and sleep in your own clean bed wearing your superhero pajamas. In this fabricated world, kids always have enough to eat, drink clean water, their bodies are covered with clothes that become them and announce their identity. They will never lie down to sleep in their extra-large hoodies on the streets of cities.

Aaron is in the third decade of a life I grew inside my body. I sit on the sand, look out to sea, watch the steady huge gray rocks on the island in the bay. The largest rock on the island raises its head, turns into a bull elephant seal before my eyes. Aaron has seen this transformation from the yellow kayak. He is waiting to tell me the story. I walk back to the car and get ready to listen.

Watching Aaron Teach

Many of us are teachers in our family. Aaron is teaching homeless students. They are at high risk for AIDS, hepatitis, STDs, drug abuse, and death, and they're all between seventeen and twenty-four years old. My students are enrolled in a graduate program for writers. I'm a professor teaching in a university actively recruiting more female faculty. The majority of direct service workers in the agency where Aaron teaches are female. Aaron's advanced degrees are in science. I'm a poet. We both find that teaching is scary. I learn from my students and I learn from my son, sometimes more than I want to know. Sometimes I learn about my life as a teacher, sometimes about my life as a woman, a construction that excludes Aaron.

I've wanted to watch Aaron in his classroom. Maybe I hope to learn something new. This week he has made arrangements for me to visit. His classes meet in the new building of the agency where he works—his students designed and built the entrance mosaic—as well as an old building where he has his office. I'd hoped to visit his men's group but I'm not invited. I know the guys in his men's group are tough. Aaron is a man among men there. But I am a woman and I am not invited. At my university, no class is separated by gender so explicitly. My poetry seminar is usually fifty-fifty.

Aaron comes to meet me at the airport. He looks healthy and handsome. Now he has closely cropped hair, a short dark beard, and he wears small gray metal rectangular glasses. His familiar hazel eyes are crinkled in the corners. He's wearing a sky-blue shirt with a pattern of small feathers. His shorts are checked the color of the feathers and he's wearing high-top sneakers, one red, one sky blue. He's smiling hard. We hug and he rests his heavy head on my shoulder. No trace of the girl he was, who much later visits me in a dream at the bed-and-breakfast where I stay at his recommendation. Aaron carries up my bag and we sit in the chintz armchairs under a slow ceiling fan and talk for hours as night becomes morning. His news is good and bad at once.

Aaron lives at risk. His students are street kids who have been physically, emotionally, and sexually abused throughout their lives; some have felony rap sheets. They're always at risk for death, whether as perpetrator or victim. One of his students, "much loved," he says, died this week from a flesh-eating bacteria, *necrotizing fasciatus*, the same rampant infection that killed my nephew Jonathan, a professor of biostatistics. In Aaron's photos the young man is smiling, someone who got the infection from a needle or, since he was a skateboarder, a bruise or scrape. As Aaron talks, I try to understand his stories, which include the rape of a young trans man. Is the class under suspicion because it is Aaron's class and they are discussing gender? As his mother I hear myself ask, are you afraid of rape? He says, "Hypervigilance is the rule here. We all spend the day watching out for things that don't happen." I've just come from the state where Brandon Teena, who was young, female, and lived as a man, the protagonist of the movie *Boys Don't Cry*, was raped and murdered. Aaron was born and raised there as Sarah. No more trace of Sarah than if she'd never been. Teachers here work under constraints: no touching, no friendships outside of class, no faculty interaction outside of the program.

Since Aaron has told me the number of the bus to take to the city center, we meet there after work. He is flushed and pleased. His class overfilled by seven. Only ten students are allowed in each class, with participants chosen by lottery. Because his class is theatre, Aaron asked them to finish with an action. They chose to form a circle and sing a four-part round together. The factions in Aaron's group are clearly defined, loud, messy, and potentially violent. Aaron must seem a model of conservatism, since he rarely drinks alcohol and uses needles only for testosterone injections. All his students are drug and alcohol savvy. I remind myself that he needs his injections as much as they need theirs, for identity and survival. And that they chose to form a circle and sing in harmony.

Next day I ride to work with Aaron on the bus. Before he goes off to his classroom, he introduces me to his supervisor, who asks me into her office. She tells me about my son, her "miracle gift," and she describes his presence in the program, his compassion, and what she calls his double-sided brilliance that's bridged by his ability to write. One side of him is cerebral and talky, the other theatrical, quiet. He's a teacher who knows and deeply cares for each student, in the moment, fully present for each as they are for him. He knows them—not for their potential or their damage, but for their presence as individuals in a world that, for them, is always difficult and dangerous. To him they're not difficult, or intractable, or inferior. He learns from them and they know it. And he can teach them, too.

I'm glad to be with someone who knows and respects Aaron as he is embodied now. As Sarah he was a scholar, a display preparator in a natural history museum, a biologist, a maker of masks and stories, an intellectual working in the context of academia. Here he is doing his work of teaching in an entirely different way. His supervisor sees him now.

After his class is over Aaron comes to the main office to pick me up. He's all flash and dazzle, energy and enthusiasm. Seems that I am invited now to join "Voices," his studio art class. We walk down the street to the porch of an old house, where a volunteer artist waits for Aaron to unlock the door. Her studio is around the corner and she came to help the kids make a show called *Art from the Streets by People Who Have Experienced Homelessness*. Now she has joined them on a sculpture project—Aaron calls it the torso project—so she has brought materials she scavenges for her own work. Later I learn that she's chair of the art department at the local university.

Aaron sits cross-legged in the center of a group of kids. He jokes around, mixes up paste with water for Jessica, who has cast her torso in papier-mâché. She smoothes the bumpy surface with squares of peach paper shot with gold. David, with blue hair and baggy clothes, is filing arms he'll paint black, part of a sculpture called *Identity is about the soul, not the body*. The arms are beautiful, delicate at wrist and muscular at once, life-sized, the fingers cupped as if to hold flame. Aaron asks Jessica questions about being a mother. Was she changed by the experience?

"No," she says, although labor was long and delivery hard. "But maybe my not changing was the problem."

Aaron tells me later that child protective services took away her baby. She was a child with a child and couldn't grow up fast enough. He's learning from Jessica how it must feel to be the father of a teenaged girl, to be a parent to them all.

"Where's the little bald guy?" Jessica called to Aaron as she stomped in the door for class. She's young, blond, big, cute, and in control. Several times during the class she refers to the cast from her body.

"My boobs," she says. "Don't touch my boobs," she says, "they're mine."

Aaron selects papers for her to choose, tears small pieces he gives as she needs them to work with; he banters with the group, provides directions as needed. As we talk about mothers and children, Mary, a young African American woman, says, "When I have children, their names will be tattooed on my body."

"What if they change their names?" asks David, also known as Alice, as s/he files apart the fingers of the right hand.

"I'll have the new name tattooed next to the old name," says Mary. "Lovers come and go, their fathers may not be my husbands, but the children will be mine forever."

Seven years ago, before sex change surgery, Sarah made casts of her torso. After his recovery, Aaron made casts of his torso. He's teaching here the lessons he learned from making these double sculptures.

Is teaching like everything else, all experience and technique, guts and blunder? My class of PhD student poets is both like and unlike Aaron's class of homeless student artists. Maybe teaching itself is like art, on the streets or in the classroom. Teaching involves and invokes risk, a necessary condition. I am afraid of Aaron's choices, but to watch him teach encourages me to watch myself. One consequence of close attention is appropriate fear. A few of my students have died. Two were suicides. Two survived suicide attempts. Most of them become teachers. What will become of Aaron's students when this day ends?

A few weeks later, during an art show, Jessica's body cast was purchased to hang behind the reception desk in the new building. Then it was taken down because too many people spoke disparagingly, reaching out to touch the female papier-mâché torso.

Six months later Aaron left his job to return to school to learn physical theatre.

Three-Minute Autobiography

Every kind for itself and its own, for me mine male and
*   female,*
For me those that have been boys and that love women,
For me the man that is proud and feels how it stings to
*   be slighted,*
For me the sweet-heart and the old maid, for me mothers
*   and the mothers of mothers,*
For me lips that have smiled, eyes that have shed tears,
For me children and the begetters of children.

WALT WHITMAN, "Leaves of Grass"

When I looked at it, I saw my better self
in the makeshift kingdom of a vase. In
cutting it, I cut myself from the swollen field,
out of what I was in, becoming alien.
Thus separation was the power I could wield.

MOLLY PEACOCK, "Cut Flower"

Aaron and I have been talking—first in the community garden as he waters corn, zucchini, greens, raspberries, nasturtiums, marigolds, the rad-
ishes, the tall sunflowers, and the rest of the plot he works with Daire.

"Why are you writing? For whom?" he asks me as he shifts the spraying
hose from right hand to left hand. His voice is harsh.

I know this territory. I am supposed to write about my own life,
not his. No good will come from this talk. The garden is lush, the light
translucent.

"I'm here to find out about your life and write about it," I tell him.
"Your life is part of my life." I feel brave.

293

He is impatient. The hose is coiled on the ground. He is beginning to pace.

Sarah was so smart. Aaron is smart and wise. Why can't he understand my desire to write about him?

I hold onto his shoulders, look into his eyes.

I say carefully, "You are mine. You grew in my body. I delivered you to the world, cared for you, nursed you from my body. You slept in my arms, woke in my body's cradle. Understand me, Aaron, you grew in my eyes as my daughter. To me you were always Sarah. So your transformation to Aaron was mine, too. Your life is part of my life. My stories will always be your stories."

By now my voice is loud. "Aaron," I say, "for you I divided again and again, I budded, I *podded*."

We both laugh. We sit down on the garden bench in what's left of the sunshine.

"Hey," he says, "I was just asking."

The sun is going down again. We start to pick raspberries from the bushes behind the bench.

"Oh, Aaron," I worry. "Who will even care?" We're both eating the raspberries.

"Everyone," explodes Aaron. "Everyone wants double lives. We all want wings and fins and hands and feet. Look at the stories: the oracle at Delphi, Tiresias both male and female, and the shape-shifting gods in their fleece tents. Tlinglit masks. Science fiction. Myth."

"Myth," I say, "my foot. Our life happened."

He takes my small basket of berries, empties it into his own.

"Okay," he says. "Do you want to see my three-minute auto-biography?"

The new social services building where Aaron teaches theatre and art is locked down for the night. He bends to the speaker at the locked gate, then uses his several keys and we enter, unlock other doors, descend to the basement. We go into a long room with tables and chairs.

At his direction, we break down the collapsible tables, stack the chairs. Then we carry a clothes tree, an aluminum easel, a poster from the movie *Frankenstein* like the one from Sarah's room at home, when she was fascinated by monsters, into the room. He brings in a box, a goldfish in a bowl, and furniture.

Then Aaron says quietly, "The performance will begin when I reenter the room." He leaves.

I sit quietly in a yellow chair painted with black squiggles, and wait. The room is chilly. I am wearing Aaron's orchid-printed Hawaiian shirt, his warm familiar smell, and he has taken away my black T-shirt.

The door opens a crack. A small figure, wrapped in a short white sheet, throws open the door, enters the room with a crash. It has a high bald dome—an ancient crone, an infant? My child. I recognize my child.

"That is no country for old men," he chants.

The figure grows, straightens, takes off the bald dome mask, hangs it on the coatrack. And the sheet slips. Soft-pink conical breasts, huge and naked, suddenly appear. A comic and horrified look down, a take to the audience, a hasty adjustment of the sheet to cover. He turns to the autopsy table. A pile of animal bones is waiting to be reconstructed. He draws a fox pelt from the box, cradles it in his arms, hangs it on the coatrack. He pauses, then hangs up the sheet. I see that the breasts are held on by straps. A spasm and a fierce struggle to slip them off. He wins. Now his chest is a Superman breastplate, deep sky blue, smooth and sculptural, a Greek torso. But where the S should be is the universal symbol for biohazard, exquisitely painted in gold and rust. He hides the breasts on the autopsy table, bows low before the Frankenstein poster on the easel. His face contorts. He hurls the poster to the floor and crouches, weeping. Then he straightens and begins his struggle to wrestle free of the Superman breastplate. Again he wins. He is coming to the end of the poem. Aaron moves center front, faces the audience in his black tights and my black T-shirt and says in his own quiet voice,

> Once out of nature I shall never take
> My bodily form from any natural thing,
> But such a form as Grecian goldsmiths make
> Of hammered gold and gold enamelling
> To keep a drowsy Emperor awake;
> Or set upon a golden bough to sing
> To lords and ladies of Byzantium
> Of what is past, or passing, or to come.

At the end he is whispering. Quiet. The end. Three minutes.

I sit still in the dark, waiting. I am filling with something like water, my lungs and heart filling up. This playwright is my child, author of his own life. He is in transition again, leaving his loved but taxing job, his partner, his friends. Soon he will be gone from here, taking along his fierce strength and patience—and the part of me that is his own, continuing self.

It was he who set his strength against the bone and muscle of the living world. Even its huge population of the dead. His voice grows taut when he's angry, his diction more clipped—pain behind his eyes, which are the variegated color of turf, part green, part brown. The lines around his eyes deepened, from laughter. One eyelash is white.

Homage to Aaron. I want to make a permanent tattoo on the blank screen of my computer, sitting open on a gold-painted table where the eternal mother who holds our stories writes in front of lace window curtains to the sounds of guests arriving for the bridal suite.

In the dark, waiting to leave the building, the foam breasts on the autopsy table seem to be mine. The webbing straps around my shoulders hold a child in place against my breast, my memories of Sarah. My eyes are dead open as I watch my son, a man, Aaron, open the heavy door and reenter.

UNIVERSITY OF NEBRASKA PRESS

Also of Interest in the American Lives series:

Falling Room

By Eli Hastings

Eli Hastings recounts how a privileged, white, fiercely leftist American male tries to make sense of himself in relation to the contrary people and situations he finds in books and his travels to Cuba and Central America.

ISBN: 0-8032-7364-9; 978-0-8032-7364-1 (paper)

The Fortune Teller's Kiss

By Brenda Serotte

Shortly before her eighth birthday, in the fall of 1954, Brenda Serotte came down with polio—painfully singled out in a world already marked by differences. Her bout with the dreaded disease is at the heart of this poignant and heartbreakingly hilarious memoir of growing up a Sephardic Jew among Ashkenazi neighbors in the Bronx.

ISBN: 0-8032-4326-X; 978-0-8032-4326-2 (cloth)

Bigger than Life: A Murder, a Memoir

By Dinah Lenney

Bigger than Life is a compellingly edgy memoir describing how Dinah Lenney navigated her life amid the complex feelings that surfaced after she learned her father had been murdered by three teenagers during a botched kidnapping and robbery.

ISBN: 0-8032-2976-3; 978-0-8032-2976-1 (cloth)

Order online at www.nebraskapress.unl.edu or call 1-800-755-1105. Mention the code "BOFOX" to receive a 20% discount.